Of Giants and Windmills

An Autobiography

MOOSA RAZA

PAPER MISSILE

NIYOGI BOOKS

Published by
NIYOGI BOOKS
Block D, Building No. 77,
Okhla Industrial Area, Phase-I,
New Delhi-110 020, INDIA
Tel: 91-11-26816301, 26818960
Email: niyogibooks@gmail.com
Website: www.niyogibooksindia.com

Design: Shashi Bhushan Prasad

ISBN: 978-93-91125-32-5
Publication: 2022

Printed at: Niyogi Offset Pvt. Ltd., New Delhi, India

CONTENTS

PROLOGUE

My entry into the world was rather reluctant. In fact, I had to be pulled out with forceps. The hospital in Tindivanam, where I was born, had no facilities for managing difficult births. The medical facilities in suburban India in the last century were still primitive, and child mortality was high. It was a miracle I survived!

After the delivery, my maternal grandfather, Jafar Hussain Shakir, who called himself a 'landlord', took me and my mother to Minambur, his native village, where I spent the first few years of my life.

Minambur had to wait for more than two decades before seeing a light bulb, more than four decades for a water pipeline, and most houses in the village don't have a flush system in their toilets even today. Minambur was populated by a Muslim clan called Navayatas. They were, and still are, known for their excellent biryani and Navayata sweets like *ande ki mitthai* (egg sweet), *kaddu ki mitthai* (squash confectionary) and *amritphal* (milk sweet). They are equally notorious for their misplaced pride in their genealogy and bloodline. They claim, with some historic evidence, that they are the descendants of the Arabs who were exiled from Basra in Iraq for rebelling, not once but thrice, against a very despotic governor, Hajjaj, in the eighth century. Hajjaj gave them a Hobson's choice—exile to any territory outside the Islamic empire, extending at that time from Algeria to what is today Pakistan, or enslavement. They wisely chose exile and came to settle on the west coast of India. The Navayatas, apart from their biryani and sweets, are also known for their short temper and constant bickering amongst themselves. They are ever ready to argue on any or all subjects, whether the outcome affects them or not. If you agree with a Navayata readily, he is disappointed for being deprived of a vigorous argument. There was one old man, who was ready to argue that a sinner was better liked by God, since He gets an opportunity to exercise his quality of mercy. Long before the expression 'argumentative Indian' was made popular by Amartya Sen, that old man was called Hujjat-al-Kekdi—quibbling crab—in Minambur. Navayata women usually wear the pants in the house, and within a short span of their marital life, manage to reduce the men of the household to menial drones (the honeycomb variety, not the American), mere hewers of wood and drawers of water. So it was in my grandfather's household. Though he called himself 'landlord', it was my grandmother who lorded over all the territory she could see with her failing eyesight. She issued her staccato diktats from the swing on which she spent both her waking hours and her nights.

Both my aunts came from the same stock, viz., Navayatas of the pure pristine bloodline, as did my uncles. My elder aunt had already reduced her husband to a household pet, though sometimes he tried to break the chains, ineffectively. My grandfather, grandmother, a blind great-grandmother and a large retinue of servants made up for the absence of my parents.

My grandfather somehow persuaded my parents, who lived in Madras (now Chennai), to leave me in the village when they returned to the city after my traumatic birth. Since he had no son of his own, he wanted an heir to inherit the mantle of his landlordship, and to write 'Landlord, Esq.' after my name, eventually. I was left behind to be brought up in the village household, pampered and spoiled, by a host of raucous relatives and grovelling servants. My every misplaced whim was satisfied, every ill-tempered tantrum tolerated, and every unreasonable desire fulfilled. In the abundance of his love for me, my grandfather often antagonised me.

I was admitted, against my wishes, in the village school, at the age of four years, four months and four days, an age at which every Muslim child has to undergo the ceremony of *bismillah khwani*, marking their initiation into the reading of the Holy Quran. In village parlance, it was known as *maktab*, and celebrated with great fanfare. All the relatives and friends in the village were invited to a grand feast. The initiate was dressed in special brocade garments, sat on a *masnad* (cushioned mattress with bolsters) while two very large laddoos, each weighing three kilos, adorned a low table. This laddoo, made of *boondis* (fried lentil droplets), dry fruits, etc., was broken up and distributed among the attendees after the ceremony.

In the village, most Muslim boys and girls were made to learn the Quran by rote. Sitting cross-legged on mats, they swayed to-and-fro as they recited the sacred verses, without understanding a single word. Their ignorance lasted a lifetime, a blessing in disguise. Had they understood, many of the verses would have kept them sleepless.

The village primary school to which I was admitted was a primitive thatch-roofed structure, with unplastered brick walls, no water-closet and no toilet. Needless to say, my experience of the very first day of school was traumatic. Besides, there was no blackboard, no chairs, no tables. Students sat on low planks on the sand-strewn floor, and wrote on the smoothened sand with their index fingers. My cousin, Bawajan, older by two years, had stolen a march over me and was far advanced in the learning experience. To me, he appeared a veritable Socrates. It was my cousin, the Socrates, who taught me a simple way to master writing the figure 'eight'—two circles, one above the other, touching each other.

Apparently, my difficulty with the figure eight persisted well into my youth. When I joined the National Academy of Administration after passing the civil services examinations, my riding master was Subedar

Nawal Singh, deputed by the cavalry regiment of the Indian Army. Once I reached the parade ground late, and I ended up with a particularly unruly stallion under my saddle, a veritable unbroken Bucephalus. It was given to taking the bit in its teeth and refusing to obey any commands. They say the horse senses the inexperience of its rider and knows how to deal with him—with contempt. On that cold morning, it took the iron bit between its strong teeth and took off at a gallop. Nawal Singh had ordered me to execute a figure of eight on that vast riding field, but I had to contend with maintaining my unstable seat in the slippery saddle on the back of an unruly horse galloping at breakneck speed towards our mutual destruction. I don't know whether the horse was equally ignorant of the figure eight. Suddenly, he decided to take a wrong turn at the corner. Since I was preoccupied with my existential crisis, I did not notice the turn the horse took. Even if I had the prescience to notice, I could not have done much to make the horse change its mind. Nawal Singh charged at me on his horse shouting 'Halt, halt!' at the top of his stentorian voice, well-suited to an army parade ground. I pulled the reins with great difficulty, dislodging the bit from the horse's clenched teeth and halting the horse within a hundred yards of the first Nawal Singh bellow.

Nawal Singh drew up neck to neck with me, and with a sarcastic lilt to his tone said, 'Pray, what were you doing, sir?' 'I was making a figure of eight,' I said, with as much dignity as I could muster, whilst my withers wrung with the Herculean effort to control my prancing mount.

'Ah! So that was a figure of eight you were making?' This time the sarcasm was not a mere lilt. It was a gong. 'It seems your primary school education is incomplete!'

But this happened years later, long after I had outgrown my village sojourn.

Back in the village, we lived in a village house with no electricity, no running water and no door. Since the village was assumed to be inhabited by honest Navayatas, there was no need for doors or locks. The toilet was located at the far end of the large backyard. One had to cross the entire weed-infested expanse by a path that meandered through overgrown shrubs and vegetable patches. Occasionally one met a prowling wild cat on a hunt or a large monitor lizard basking in the sun. A variety of bugs and beetles hummed and buzzed, while toads, mongooses and bandicoots abounded. The toilet was a mere hole in the ground, surrounded by crumbling brick walls. It had no door or roof. A roof would have rendered the toilet unhygienic in the absence of running water and a flush. One had to carry an umbrella if it was raining, and a stick to ward off the occasional snake, which, unaware of the squatter, made a foray into the premises in pursuit of a frog or a field rat. A visit to the toilet at night, even in compelling emergency, was a most scary experience. Even with a lantern in one hand and a stick in the other, one was not very confident of returning home safely. And, of course, one heard all sorts of banshee noises and saw all the jinns of Koh-e-Qaf flying overhead.

By the time I reached the fourth standard in the primary school in Minambur, the land in the 'landlord' had been sequestrated by the recently installed socialist Congress government under the 'land to the tiller' policy. My grandfather, who was no hewer of wood or drawer of water, was left with no legacy to bequeath to me. The tilling had been left to his tenants, who had now become the owners. Having sorrowfully realised that he could not bestow a jagir on me, he started to explore alternatives, finally deciding that I should be a collector instead. As a village munsif, he had to make occasional *bandobast* whenever the English sub-collector visited the taluka headquarters in Gingee. He also had to present the annual revenue accounts at the *jamabandi* (audit) when all village munsifs gathered at the taluka office, where the sub-collector conducted the annual audit for the revenue division. The sub-collector, generally a young English officer belonging to the elite service of the British Empire—the Indian Civil Service—was the one in charge. My grandfather often used to carry biryani and the specially made Navayata sweets to feed the *tehsildar* and the English sub-collector. Most of the other village munsifs, too, brought their special viands. The poor sub-collector must have suffered stomach cramps for days after the *jamabandi*. My grandfather had a vague idea that there was a boss bigger than the sub-collector who reigned in far-off Cuddalore, in a world unapproachable by the likes of village munsifs. For him, the collector meant the sub-collector who was held in so much awe by the landlords, village munsifs, *tehsildar*s, police officials and the general public. He, therefore, could not wait to see me in the sub-collector's 'uniform', which consisted of a white linen suit and patent leather shoes that he wore when he sat for his evening drink in the verandah of the guest house or the khaki shirt and shorts that he wore on field visits. To save himself from sunstroke, the sub-collector often wore a pith hat, a topee, which became the hallmark of a British civilian. My grandfather would get me dressed up in khaki shorts with a pith hat on my head and take me to the camp to be introduced as a future collector. His friends in the village would snicker behind his back. Such overweening ambition on the part of a mere village munsif was just a ludicrous utopian dream.

When I was eight, my father, who worked in the city, returned to the village to retrieve me from the clutches of what he considered to be inadequate rural education. By this time, my grandfather, who was a scholar in Urdu, Persian and Tamil, had inculcated in me a basic knowledge of the first two languages. It is my misfortune that I did not take to Tamil with the same zest and enthusiasm as I did Urdu and Persian, though not for any want of effort on my grandfather's part. By the time my father came to collect me, I was well into Urdu classics like *Dastan-e-Amir Hamza* (an epic of a legendary Arab hero who went around the world fighting against ogres and rescuing damsels in distress a la Galahad), *Qissa-e-Hatim Tai* (the tales of the Arab Hercules who solved seven difficult labours), *Char Dervesh*, *Gul-e-Bakavali* and *Qisas-al-Anbiya*. Most of these writings have stuck in my memory.

The city of Madras, to which I was exiled, was a shocking contrast to Minambur. Gone was the large house with a haunted backyard and many fruit trees, the retinue of servants who could be lorded over, and the daily morning walks with friends through the rice paddies to the village water tank for a vigorous swim and bath. Our much smaller city house was located in a congested locality of Madras, in the old part of the city.

The household consisted of my father, mother, my younger sister and my toddler brother. My father was a taciturn man who had no pastime save reclining on an easy chair, reading the newspaper on returning from work. He rarely went out, and had no friends outside the closed family circle.

Much later I learnt the reasons for his detachment. Before marrying my mother, he used to live in Bangalore with a wife and four children. His whole family—except for a daughter who was away at Madras—were wiped out by an epidemic of cholera in just a week. The trauma of having to bury four members of his family, his wife and three children, in one go, made him look at all relationships from a different perspective. Though he cared for all of us, he had no deep attachment.

My mother was made of entirely different stuff. She made up for my father's taciturnity by being voluble and effusive in her personal relationships. It was she who had to entertain even my father's relatives; he having made himself scarce within moments of a visitor's arrival. My mother had only a young live-in housemaid, Zaitoon, to help her with the household chores, in contrast to the feudal retinue I remembered back at the village. The house had no backyard, no fruit trees, no running water, no electricity, not even an open privy to house the resident ghosts. Horror of horrors, the toilet was located right inside the house.

Not only had I to adapt to my changed physical surroundings but I had to give up all my tantrums, whims and wilful behaviour. They were already being fully monopolised by my resident siblings. My self-respect would not permit me to join these Johnny-come-latelies already well-ensconced in my parent's affections.

My class teacher in the fifth standard, at the neighbourhood government school which I first joined, was a moulvi, Abul Barkath. His son, Abul Fazal, who was my classmate, became a lifelong friend. I recall Moulvi Sahab for two impression-making characteristics: he wore a long white shirt that fell well below his knees, with a multicoloured lungi peeping shyly from under the hem of the shirt, and he always swayed to and fro, like a palm tree in the gentle breeze, even when he was standing.

I found that my classmates were far ahead of me in the knowledge of English, a language, whose existence was unknown to me in Minambur. I did not even know the alphabet. This gave me a terrible inferiority complex in their company. My mother engaged a cousin, who was in college, to come and give me English lessons in the evening. My inferiority complex drove me to burn the extra midnight oil, not only to achieve parity with them but to excel. Within a few months, I had advanced enough to read children's books in English.

A year later, I joined the government school Madrasa-e-Azam, on Mount Road, in the first form. The school had been modelled on English public schools with 'forms' instead of 'classes'. It was located on the vast grounds on the banks of the Cooum River, with cricket pitches, hockey and football fields, tennis and badminton courts and even a boxing ring.

Looking back on my school days in Madrasa-e-Azam, I feel a deep sense of nostalgia. Somebody said, it is good to visit the past but not to live in it. That is what I am doing now, visiting Madrasa-e-Azam, my alma mater, as it was more than sixty years ago.

Perhaps some of my old friends, reading this, may find my memory at fault. Memory is a strange faculty. It has the knack of falsifying images retrospectively. You tend to forget the unpleasant things and recall only those that make you happy.

I joined the Madrasa in 1947, the year of India's independence. My relative, Rasheed Ahmed Sayeed, took me for admission to the school in his old but serviceable Austin. Of course, I learnt it was an Austin much later. In those days, we simply called it a 'touring' or just a 'motor'.

The first sight of Madrasa-e-Azam to my young eyes was breathtaking. The long avenue leading from the gate on Mount Road to the central building was bordered on both sides by a line of flowering trees mostly gulmohur, portia and the flame of the forest. As the car went crunching over the freshly laid river gravel, I saw on both sides, two large playing fields—international-sized football and hockey grounds. As the car stopped at the central wing of the school, an imposing edifice rose up before me. Later I learnt that it was actually a palace—Umdah Bagh—donated by the then Prince of Arcot for the school. It was named Madrasa but the founder had planned it on the lines of an English public school, with a strong emphasis on modern subjects and sports. The first headmasters of the school were all Scots and Englishmen. The walls of the large lobby in front of the headmaster's office were adorned with the portraits of Hunter, Papworth, Swinburne and others. In 1947, Madrasa-e-Azam was favoured even by the rich and well-to-do. I recall meeting tall young men, some of them wearing suits with colourful ties and others wearing well-pressed sherwanis, walking around purposefully in the campus. For long, I took them to be teachers and used to greet them with respect. It was much later that I was chagrined to learn they were only fifth and sixth form boys.

The recollection I have of the headmaster is of an imposing figure, a tall, fair-complexioned man with a rugged face, wearing a scout's uniform.

Mr Abdul Qadar, the then headmaster of Madrasa-e-Azam, was the first Indian to occupy that office. He had studied at Oxford, spoke with an English accent, wore shorts and a solar topee when walking around the campus, and was a proclaimed atheist at that stage of his life. I trembled in my old worn-out pair of chappals as I stood before him with my unkempt hair, my shirt tails hanging out, as my hands miserably tried to find some refuge in the pockets of my shorts.

I still remember the first day of my school. I was all of ten and reporting to first form—sixth standard to the modern generation. From the gate to the main building, my walk took me on the gravelled path through the two well-kept grassy grounds, fringed with well-mown borders. There were slogan-painted boards every hundred yards that read: 'Keep off the grass.' Abdul Qadar Sahab, the headmaster, used to stand in the open balcony of the school, his booted feet planted widely as a ship's captain on the deck, to ensure that his diktat was carried out in letter and in spirit. Once I remember straying off onto the grass to pluck a flower from the bed. Suddenly, I heard a stentorian voice booming at me from the far-off balcony, 'Keep off the grass, you fool. Can't you read?' I never dared to stray again. Winston Churchill wrote in his autobiography, 'Headmasters have powers at their disposal with which prime ministers have never yet been invested.' Abdul Qadar Sahab wanted the campus to be kept spotlessly clean. The headmaster also hated anyone disfiguring the walls with graffiti. In several corridors, he had put up sign boards saying: 'The wall is the paper of a fool.'

Everyone was expected to be in the central courtyard, under the mango trees, to attend the morning assembly. The headmaster stood on the platform under the tiled roof, facing the assembled pupils. All the teachers stood in a row behind him, with their backs to the wall. A group of younger students would initiate the beautiful school prayer and everyone would harmoniously join in. It was the famous child's prayer *'lab pe aatī hai duā'* written by Allama Iqbal.

After the headmaster had made important announcements, the student pupil leader would step forward smartly to initiate the school's rallying cry, 'Azam! Azam! Madrasa-e-Azam!'

Our first-form class teacher was a memorable figure—Janab Hamza Hussain Sahab. Students had nicknamed him 'Qutab Tara', the Pole Star. An old fracture in his left leg had restricted his movements. It was his immobility that had earned him the nickname. Hamza Hussain was a stern but fair-minded teacher. Short in stature, stocky in build and clean shaven, he was always neatly dressed in a cotton jacket with no tie. He had a peculiar system of rewarding scholarly merit and appreciating good performance. On the first day of class, all the students would be seated in alphabetical order of their names. After the first lesson, he would ask a question from the textbook starting with the first boy in the front row and go down the line until someone gave the correct answer. Then the boy who answered correctly would move up to the first position, in the front row. All others would move one seat to accommodate the promotee. Again, the process would be repeated. In the process there would be a lot of to-and-fro traffic in the class. I suspect, in retrospect, that since he himself could not move, Hamza Hussain Sahab enjoyed constant movement in the class. Once, one of his favourite students, Mumtaz, fell from grace. Whenvever he saw Mumtaz, the teacher would cry out in a heartbroken voice, '*Ajab kaam kismat ka gola hua, main pera tha khurma sandola hua* (A tragic result indeed has destiny shown, I sowed a date palm, and it came out a stone).'

Janab Abdul Ali Sahab took the primary classes for English and arithmetic. In 1947, he was in his late forties. A tall man, well-built, always wearing a dark sherwani and loose cotton trousers, with a stubble on his chin turning grey. He was rarely seen without his maroon *fez* cap (it was called '*turki topi*' in the school) when out in the open. He was the most influential person in my life after my mother, and I still remember him with great affection and reverence. He had been my father's classmate in school, and they had remained good friends since then, addressing each other with terms of familiarity. Abdul Ali Sahab lived in a large kind of house, divided into two sections. The front portion was the *mardana* (male quarters of the house), where he had his large library of English books, numbering more than two or three thousand, neatly arranged in bookshelves with glass doors. He also had his clinic, where he made his medicines and treated patients in his off-time, for he was a very popular Unani hakim (a Perso-Arabic traditional medicine practitioner).

'This boy has spent most of his life in the village. I am handing him over to you. He knows little English and even less arithmetic. Make a man of him,' said my father, handing me over to Abdul Ali Sahab.

'Leave him with me, *ka*,' said Abdul Ali.

He had a habit of ending almost every other sentence with 'ka', perhaps an abbreviation of *kya* (what).

'I will take care of him. You don't worry, *ka*.'

Then he turned to me, with a rather stern look.

'You come here daily, *ka*. No Fridays, no Sunday holidays. Every morning after prayers, I want you here, *ka*.'

It was Abdul Ali Sahab who made me what I am today. The very first book I ever read in English was R.L. Stevenson's *Treasure Island*, the original, unabridged version. I still cherish the pocket Oxford Dictionary he gifted me, with an inscription, 'To my beloved pupil, Moosa Raza - Abdul Ali, 1947.' It was he who introduced me to the world of classics in his wonderful library. By the time I finished schooling, I had read the works of Captain Marryat, Fenimore Cooper, G.A. Henty, Alexandre Dumas, Walter Scott, Baroness Orczy, Rafael Sabatini, Marie Corelli, C.S. Forester, progressing to Thomas Hardy, George Eliot, G.W.M. Reynolds, Cervantes, Dostoevsky, and Tolstoy. By the last year of my school, I had read all the plays of Shakespeare, his sonnets and long poems, Ibsen, Bernard Shaw and others. It was Abdul Ali who inspired me to prepare for the Indian Administrative Service (IAS).

I met many schoolmates from the madrasa in Abdul Ali Sahab's anteroom—Usman, the short; Ejaz and Iqbal, the hockey players; Nazam and Kazim, who, for many years, I thought were twins; Anser Ahmed of Amir Mahal; Fareed Ahmad (name changed to protect myself from any libel charge) with his maroon velvet cap, and many others. Fareed's cap was such a favourite that every time someone saw it perched precariously on his shaved head, they would snatch it and run, with Fareed in hot pursuit. The cap would then pass from hand to hand in a wild melee like the Afghan sheep's carcass in *buzkashi*, until it became a shapeless mass. Then somebody would pick it up, dust it and perch it back on Fareed's head, only for it to be snatched away again the next moment.

There were, of course, the juniors—Mahmood, who provoked me to write Urdu poetry and himself gave up after his first foray; and S.A. Rahim, whose sense of humour, I am told, has not been blunted even after fifty years (he is settled in Bangalore after retiring as principal of a government engineering college).

Some of these schoolmates I continued to meet from time to time. One of them, Ejaz, in fact, married my younger sister, Qamar. Abul Fazal claimed he was already an old man when he retired 25 years ago. Every time I came to Madras and asked after his health, he used to tell me that he was, 'sitting with his feet in the grave.' He is still sitting there. The grave must be quite bored, watching his dangling bare feet.

After Abdul Qadar Sahab's departure, the post of headmaster was occupied by Janab Ahmad Ali Sahab. He had a more popular nickname associated with a dry shriveled mango seed, and anyone who has studied under him, knows him only by that name. The mischievous students of the school had an uncanny knack of discovering the one characteristic of a teacher's personality or his appearance that distinguished him from others and then coining a suitable nickname to reflect that. Once the name was conferred, it went viral. So, we had teachers named after rotten fruits, decaying vegetables, papads, sugarcane sticks and various edible and inedible foodstuffs. Even classmates were not spared this munificence.

And how can I forget Abdul Sattar Sahab, our Arabic teacher. Sattar Sahab was a great teacher in the classical mould. He was born in Medina and had taught Arabic to the Arabs in a school there. Naturally, his grasp of the language was fantastic. It is because of the firm foundation that he laid and the way he taught us Arabic grammar that I am still able to read and understand classical Arabic.

We were taught mathematics by Abdul Ghafoor Sahab in the initial classes. What I remember most about him is his sense of humour and his earthy jokes. Once, to save repeated visits to the shop, I had brought a thick arithmetic notebook to school. Abdul Ghafoor Sahab found it difficult to handle and remarked, 'I asked you to bring a notebook, not a *naat-baak*.'

Thiru Kannan taught us or rather tried to teach us Tamil. And if none of us turned into a Tamil scholar, it was not for want of trying on his part. Thiru Kannan was a sorely disappointed man most of the time. One of his trials was that he had to teach us Tamil through the English medium. Unfortunately, neither his English pronunciation nor his vocabulary in that language was as good as his Tamil. His difficulty was compounded by the fact that most of the teachers in the common room spoke with each other in Urdu. For some odd reason, he believed that when the letter 's' occurred before the letter 't' initially, it was not to be pronounced. 'Tand up on the tool,' he would shout at a recalcitrant pupil whenever he found our failure unbearable. 'I have never come across such tupid tudents. You there, tand till. Don't move.' Ultimately, the train of having to traighten out our tupid minds and make us tudy tandard Tamil drove him to seek greener pastures elsewhere.

Our science teacher, Mohiuddin Sahab, was himself a scientist. He used to spend most of his time in the dark and dingy laboratory located in the eastern wing of the school. He was in the habit of pausing in the middle of his lecture, taking out a grey horn snuff box from the pocket of his jacket and snort a pinch up his nostrils—left and right alternatively. Thirty years later, when I was called upon to manage complex chemical and fertiliser plants, bits and pieces of what Mohiuddin Sahab taught me came in handy at opportune moments.

Our English teacher in the third form was a short-statured portly man, Mr David, who was kindness personified. Whenever I remembered him later, I thought of him as Mr Chips. I became his favourite after a strange encounter. Since the prescribed English textbooks appeared so puerile, insipid and inane, what better way to spend the hour than reading a classic, concealing the book below the overhang of the writing desk. While I was so engrossed, Mr David still talking, walked across the aisle, bent down and gently picked up the book. He glanced at the title. 'Meet me after the class,' he said and walked back to his table at the head. After the class, I stayed back in trepidation. As I stood before him, he opened the book at the flyleaf. It was Dumas's *Twenty Years After*. 'Have you read the earlier one?' he asked me. 'Yes, sir, *The Three Musketeers*,' I replied. 'There are four more books after this,' he said. 'What other authors have you read?' he asked. I told him. 'Any book of Thomas Hardy?' he asked. 'No, sir,' I replied. 'You will like him. His *Mayor of Casterbridge* and *Tess* is very good. But don't read *Jude The Obscure*, though. It is no good.' He then told me, 'I am glad you are reading such books in the original. Don't read the abridged versions or the comics based on them. But reading in the class is not good.' Needless to say, immediately after this, I made a beeline to the library to pick up *Jude The Obscure*. I found it to be a boring book. Perhaps Mr David did not want my young mind to be corrupted by reading about adultery. However, contrary to his own advice, it was Mr David who introduced me to the comics based on the classics.

Madrasa-e-Azam in those days used to celebrate every national and international event. I vividly recall the celebrations of the first Independence Day on August 15, 1947. I was just ten years old. We had only a vague idea of what independence meant. But we learnt we would get sweets that day. We all stood in a hollow square, in disciplined ranks, the British flag was hauled down and the tricolour was raised. Only when the flag was hauled down and the Indian flag was raised, was there an upsurge of patriotic emotions.

In 1950, when George Bernard Shaw died, our school declared a holiday. I recall Abul Fazal, Fareed and myself walking back home at 10 in the morning. Opposite Amir Mahal, on Pycrofts Road, we met Fareed's father, a doctor of indigenous medicine, rushing on some errand in the opposite direction. Perceiving us, he came to an abrupt halt and demanded to know what his son was doing dawdling on Pycrofts Road at such an hour instead of being in the classroom. 'Bernard Shaw has died, and the school has declared a holiday,' I said.

'What!' he exclaimed, shock and consternation writ large on his face. 'My God, My God, Woe is me, alas, alas!' saying which he beat his breast and forgot the errand on which he had set out, and returned home mournfully, weeping for Shaw. I wondered, even at the time, why the death of an English playwright in far-off England had so deeply affected a doctor of Indian medicine in an obscure corner of Madras. What was Hecuba to him and he to Hecuba, would have occurred to me! But I had not yet read *Hamlet*.

In sports, too, Madrasa-e-Azam was not far behind. It produced some of the best hockey and tennis players. For years, a Madrasa-e-Azam hockey player always found a place in the Olympics team. Jabbar, my classmate, had the distinction of representing India several times. Another player from the school is said to have reached the quarter-finals of Wimbledon.

I left Madrasa-e-Azam in 1953, seven decades ago. After a two-year stint in Government Arts College in the same campus, and a three-year stint in Presidency College, I joined the IAS and left Madras. Visits to my home city remained rather infrequent during the intervening decades. Many years later, when my son was keen to see my early alma mater, I took him to the school. The very appearance had changed drastically. Instead of the wide vista that used to greet our eyes from the entrance, I found high walls put up everywhere, taking away some land here for a ladies' college, some there for a commercial complex. Both wings of the school and the central balcony had collapsed, both due to deliberate neglect assisted by the ravages of heavy monsoons and commercial greed of the authorities for the prime land on which the palace stood. The roof had fallen, exposing the two-centuries old teakwood beams to the mercy of the sun, the rain and thieves. All the broken slats from the doors and windows had vanished. Many mango trees, under whose shade we used to stand and recite our prayers, had been cut down. Some half-clad workmen, perhaps refugees from the neighbouring slums, were playing cards under the trees. They glanced up resentfully, looking askance at us for intruding their peaceful pastime.

The wooden staircase at the back of the palatial edifice, whose banisters had been polished by the bums of countless generations of schoolboys, were missing. Rats and termites appeared to have had a field day and devastated many of the steps. When I tried to reach the riverbank, another high wall confronted us. A road had been laid on the other side of the wall.

We returned to the debris of the main staircase to find it overgrown with weeds and young peepal shoots here and there. The only thing left was the marble plaque commemorating the founding of Madrasa-e-Azam in the early years of the last century. Standing there forlorn, I recalled the verse of Ghalib:

> *Dagh-e-firaq-e-suhbat-e-shab ki jali hui*
> *Ek shama reh gayee thhee, so woh bhi khamosh hai*

> (Consumed by the heartburns of the parting night.
> A lonely lamp had survived and that too is silent.)

I looked at the ruins for a long while, recalling the happy days I had spent in these halls and corridors. '*Sic transit gloria mundi,*' I murmured, turning towards my young companion. 'What does that mean?' he asked me. 'Thus passeth the glory of this world,' I replied.

The storm and floods of 2015 have wiped out, I am told, what little had remained of the vestiges of that great institution, which has produced some brilliant minds and left such pleasant memories behind.

In those days, after the sixth form or the Secondary School Leaving Certificate (SSLC), one went for two years to college for an intermediate course, which was also called FA (Fellow of Arts). I took the first group, comprising of mathematics, physics and chemistry, and joined the Government Arts College located in the same campus as the school.

In the second year of intermediate, there was to be an English debate organised by the college union. The subject was 'World Government—its pros and cons'. A search in the college library produced very little literature on the subject. Since I had been chosen as one of the debaters, I was in a quandary. The morning papers had announced that Dr S. Radhakrishnan, then vice president of India (and later, president) was in Madras, and was staying in his house in Mylapore. Dr Radhakrishnan was a world-renowned philosopher and had several books to his credit. I had read some articles of Dr Radhakrishnan on the 'World Community' and his belief that without a federal government for the world, chaos stared us in the face. So, I suggested to my friend, Rahim, that we should call on Dr Radhakrishnan and pick his brain on the subject.

There was a lone sentry in uniform standing at the gate of 'Girija', the vice president's private residence on Edward Elliots Road (later named Dr Radhakrishnan Salai, to honour its most distinguished denizen). We said we had come to meet the vice president The purpose? To discuss 'World Government'. That was beyond the comprehension of the constable. We told him we had no visiting cards. He tore off a slip of paper from a bunch hanging on the gate. We wrote our names, and he took it in.

The bungalow had been built, I learnt later, in 1936, when Dr Radhakrishnan was a professor at Oxford. I had occasion to visit the bungalow recently, more than six decades later. Nothing has changed.

After a wait of a few minutes, we were ushered into the sitting room. It was barely furnished with a few rattan chairs and an ancient cane sofa. An old electric fan was groaning overhead. We had waited but for a few minutes when in walked the vice president.

Dr Radhakrishnan was in his mid-sixties and in his second term of vice-presidentship when we called on him. Clad in a white kurta and dhoti, he had a modest but imposing presence. He had doffed his pugree, the white turban he always wore, and we could see the wisps of sparse grey hair on his balding head fluttering in the gentle breeze of the fan. The way he treated two teenage boys who had the temerity of ignorance to approach the vice president of India still remains a lesson in kindness, courtesy, magnanimity and modesty.

The second episode relates to a paper I read in the physics department on Einstein's Theory of Relativity in the second year of intermediate. This was later published in the college magazine. For the Annual Day function, Shri Rajagopalachari, then chief minister (CM) of Madras and the former governor general of India who succeeded the viceroy, Lord Mountbatten, had been invited as the guest of honour. Student secretaries of the various associations went up on stage and read out reports of the activities conducted by their respective associations during the year. The secretary of the physics department announced that I had read a paper on the Theory of Relativity.

When his turn came to speak, Rajagopalchari talked of many things. Then, with tongue in cheek, he remarked: 'I have read somewhere that there are only four people in the world who have understood the Theory of Relativity. I am glad to learn that one of them happens to be in your college.' There was a round of laughter in the audience.

A year or so later, the famous historian Arnold Toynbee was to visit Madras and address an elite audience of academicians, writers, journalists and historians. The lecture was to be chaired by Sir C.P. Ramaswamy Iyer, in the University Senate Hall.

Sir C.P. was a very well-known figure in Madras circles in those days. During British rule, he had served as the Law Member in the Viceroy's Council and had been conferred several honours. Later he had served for more than ten years as the diwan of Travancore State (now a part of Kerala), succeeding Sir Habibullah Mehkari, a distant relative of mine. He had his admirers as well as numerous detractors.

Since I did not fall in any of the categories of academic, scholar, writer or journalist, I was not considered eligible to receive an invitation. Mere students did not qualify, however much they may be interested in Toynbee and however deeply they may have read his *Study of History*. So, on the day of the lecture, four of us gatecrashed into the Senate Hall, and since a gatecrasher should always avoid the first two or three rows, occupied the fourth row.

Sir C.P. in his welcome address paid some left-handed and condescending compliments to Toynbee, damning him with faint praise.

Then he proceeded to point out, page by page, all the errors—both typographical and factual—that Toynbee had allegedly committed in his magnum opus. He spoke for more than forty minutes, trying to prove that had he written the *Study of History*, he would not have committed any of the 'blunders' that the historian had committed.

Toynbee in his turn thanked Sir C.P. for his welcome and said, 'I hope to correct all the mistakes you have pointed out in the next edition.'

Then he proceeded to deliver his lecture without another glance at Sir C.P. Toynbee was the bigger man.

My meeting with Haldane had an interesting prequel. As a student, I was a regular visitor to the University Library of Madras. It was a real repository of the best books on every subject accumulated in the pre-Independence era. I had the pleasure of reading Plato, Aristotle, Euripides, Sophocles, Thucydides, Herodotus and Gibbon among the humanities, the Babylonian Talmud and the Mishna and Havelock Ellis, Haldane, and Davies among the unclassified, during this period. Haldane's *Possible Worlds* was one of the books that had shaken my faith in traditional religion. It took me a long time to regain it.

Haldane was known to be a pioneer in genetics, biology and physiology and a great opponent of imperialism. He gave up his British citizenship and his lucrative job to migrate to India in the wake of Britain's unprovoked attack on Egypt during the Suez Canal crisis of 1956. As a pioneer in the field of mathematical theory of population genetics, he was highly respected in Indian scientific circles. What made him popular in India was that he also took Indian citizenship.

So, having read all the greats, both living and dead, in the library, I was in love with that repository of knowledge. The flipside was that every time I came to the library at eight in the morning, I had to brave the presence of a Cerebrus in the guise of an old decrepit attendant who guarded the wicket gate that allowed entry into the Valhalla. He had an outsized register before him, and every visitor had to enter his name and time of entry there. Since the attendant could not read English, and all the visitors wrote in English, he never knew what anyone wrote. Since I was always irritated at the importunate insistence of the attendant to make the entry before he would let me in, I would write my name as William Shakespeare one day, James Jeans, the next day, Einstein, a third, and so on. Once I had exhausted all the greats, including Plato, Thiruvalluvar, Socrates, Ghalib, Charlie Chaplin and Kalidas, I would repeat them.

One day, as I was about to sign in as Haldane, I saw someone before me had already beaten me to it. Quite amused, I was curious to see who had stolen Haldane's identity before I could. I glanced around the vast reading room. And in the gloom, I saw an Englishman, clean shaven, but with a clipped grey moustache, almost invisible, clad in a kurta-pyjama, sitting at a reading station immersed in a book. I knew at once that that was indeed Haldane, in the flesh. Quietly, I sidled up to him and stood by his chair.

'Yes, what can I do for you?' he asked, in a low voice.

'I am a fan of yours. I have read your books,' I said breathlessly.

'Oh, have you?' he asked. He did not appear impressed 'But this is a reading room. We would be disturbing other readers, if we talk.'

'Can I offer you a cup of coffee, sir, at the library canteen?' I asked him.

He looked up with an amused smile. What an importunate boy, he must have thought. But still he got up and walked with me to the canteen. I had a delightful half an hour with him, and he paid for the coffee against my insistence. Even today, I recall his kind gesture to an importunate young student.

Another brief encounter I recall was with Sir C.V. Raman, the great physicist, the first Asian to win the Nobel Prize. He had, then, just been conferred the Bharat Ratna, the highest national civilian award. He was to be honoured, I recall, by the Presidency College, as an alumnus of the college. I was one of the student volunteers deputed to escort him to the college. He was staying somewhere in Mylapore. Not to be late, we reached the house a bit too early. We were asked to go up to the terrace. When we reached the terrace, we found him engaged in *surya namaskar*, the worship of the sun. After he finished his prayers, we escorted him to the car. On the way, I raised the issue of science and religion, reason and faith, and related questions that were engaging me. Though C.V. Raman's answers did not help me much, his patience in dealing with my questions and his equanimity at my youthful brashness are still fresh in my memory.

Omar Khayyam wrote:

> Myself when young did eagerly frequent
> Doctor and Saint and heard great Argument
> About it and about, but evermore
> Came out by the same Door wherein I went.

After passing the Intermediate examination with high marks in physics, I decided that I, too, would like to be a scientist. Who knows, I said to myself, I may chance upon some discovery and win the Nobel Prize. Did not Alexander Fleming discover penicillin accidentally and get a Nobel Prize for it? So, I applied for BA (Hons) in physics at the college that was nearest to my house, viz. Presidency College.

I was so confident of getting admission into Presidency College that I did not apply to any other college. But Burns had remarked, 'the best-laid schemes o' mice an' men Gang aft agley.' Since there were only 15 seats in the physics honours class, the principal, T.B. Nair, decided that there was a better chance of my getting a Nobel in literature than in science. So, he allotted me to the English language and literature honours.

I met the principal and remonstrated, but to no avail. He pointed out that since I had scored higher in English compared to that in physics and mathematics, I was better suited to study English. Mr Nair deprived the world of a great scientist but failed to provide a Nobel laureate in literature. The honours course in Presidency College ran for three years, and was equivalent to a postgraduate degree. We had three highly erudite professors to teach us the various subjects. By the time I joined college, I had already read most of the great classics—Shakespeare, Milton, Dryden, Pope, Swinburne, Browning and so on. I, therefore, thought that I had nothing more to learn in class.

My first professor, Mrs G. Parthasarathy, was a compact bundle of energy. GP, as she was known officially, was called 'Gun Powder' by the students behind her back. She was even called the 'White Terror' by some of the bolder students. She was a Parsi lady, formerly Subrukh Mugaseth, who was disowned by her parents for having married a Tamil Brahmin. All of five feet tall, fair-complexioned like most Parsis, she spoke in staccato sentences and taught us Shakespeare and linguistics.

I would study Shakespeare very diligently to challenge her. It is to her credit that she never asked me to shut up.

Professor Ramaswamy, in contrast to Mrs Parthasarathy, was a mild-mannered man with a subtle sense of sardonic humour. He was a twice-born South Indian Brahmin, who brought to the college his own frugal lunch and a bottle of water from home. He and Mrs Parthasarathy never got along well. Professor Ramaswamy would not pass an opportunity to make snide remarks about Mrs G.P., without specifically naming her. Mrs G.P., in turn, would never miss an occasion to needle Professor Ramaswamy.

Ramaswamy was a great teacher, affording full opportunity to his students for dissent and challenge. When he was teaching Milton, I used to have a running debate with him in class. He firmly held on to his conviction that Adam was the hero of *Paradise Lost*. I was equally strongly convinced that Satan was the real hero, not the namby-pamby character

Adam, who could not stand up to Satan's wiles. And while Adam meekly submitted to divine commands, Satan not only defied God but was also willing to enter into battle with Him.

In the half-yearly examination, one of the questions was: Who is the hero of *Paradise Lost*? Naturally, the whole class plumped for Adam, perhaps convinced by the professor's arguments. I alone stood by my conviction. Ramaswamy gave me the highest marks.

My three years in college were the best years of my life, or perhaps I am indulging in a bit of retrospective falsification. During my second year, I was appointed as one of the two secretaries of the Literature Honours Association along with Radha K.S. Nayar. Next year, we both became vice-presidents of the association. I was also chosen to be the editor of *The Presidencian*, the college magazine. I represented the college as a member of the debating team, quiz team and mock parliament. Most of my friends desired that I should contest for the presidentship of the college union. But G.P. told me that no college union president had ever got a first class. Since she was one of the examiners, I preferred discretion to valour and withdrew from the contest.

During college, I made some good friends: K.S. Subramaniam who retired from the Asian Development Bank, has translated many of the books of Kannadasan into excellent English and has helped me in getting my book on Ghalib's Persian poetry translated into Tamil and published at his own expense; Vadivelu, whose hostel room in the Victoria Hostel we treated as our own; K.R. Venugopal, who rose to become principal secretary to the prime minister (PM) of India; Radha Nayar, who married a banker and taught Afghans in Kabul and Creoles in some outlandish South Sea Micronesian islands, and many others.

The three premier colleges in Madras were rated very high. But the pedagogic style of the three differed. So, the students of the three were known as the 'Princes of Presidency', 'Lords of Christian' and 'Slaves of

Loyola'. There was a pact between Presidency and Christian College in those days. On Tuesdays, the final year students of Presidency would take the electric train and travel to Tambaram to hear a couple of lectures from the professors there. On Fridays, the students of Christian College would come up to Presidency. There was always a sense of competition and rivalry in those joint classes. Often, to justify their sobriquet, the 'Princes of Presidency' would arrive late for the class in Tambaram. The 'Lords of Christian' were always punctual. Once, Professor McPhail, the erudite professor of Christian College, made an acerbic comment: 'It appears that the distance between Presidency and Christian is much longer than the distance between Christian and Presidency.' We took the hint.

During my stay in Presidency, I competed for seven medals in various departments, a feat equalled only by Krishna Menon, who later became the defence minister of India. I never reached such heights. I have had several unfulfilled dreams. I named my collection of Urdu poems *Khwab-e-Natamam* (Unfulfilled Dreams).

Professor Martin, from Oxford University, was on a sabbatical and was the head of the board of English Studies of Madras University. He presided over the viva-voce held after the BA Honours finals. Since I happened to emerge as the winner of all the three university gold medals—for Literature, Shakespeare and Linguistics—there was an external examiner who perhaps believed that one student should not be awarded all three medals, as that was an unprecedented honour. He put me through a rigorous catechism, opening the dictionary at random and asking me the philology and semantics of various words. Even though I satisfied him, he persisted so that he could catch me in a failed attempt. It was Professor Martin and Professor Ramaswamy who held out for fairness and merit, and ensured that I got all three medals.

Another giant that ruled over the University of Madras with an iron hand and established its pre-eminence not only in India but in the international academic world was Sir Lakshmanaswamy Mudaliar. A doctor by profession, he remained vice chancellor of the university for 27 years, a record equalled by none.

Within a couple of months of my graduation, I received a letter from Dr Mudaliar, which I have treasured more than even my appointment letter to the IAS issued by the president of India. The letter goes as follows:

Dear Moosa Raza,
Congratulations on your having passed your honours with a first class first, winning all three gold medals.
I offer you the post of Assistant Lecturer in English in Presidency College, your alma mater. I hope you will accept it. You may collect the appointment letter from the Registrar at your convenience.

With warm regards,
Lakshmanaswamy Mudaliar.

My grandfather and my elementary school teacher had both wished for me to join the civil services. My mother had to sacrifice much to enable me to reach graduation. In those days, the preferred avenues of advancement in life were the civil service, medicine or engineering, in that order. Before appearing for the civil services examination, I found that my job as lecturer and social service left me hardly any time for preparation. However, my vast reading over the years and a good memory compensated for the lack of time. When I was called to Delhi for the interview by the Union Public Service Commission in the month of January, I found myself in a thin cotton suit, waiting with ten others in the anteroom of the UPSC. One of them was a fair-complexioned, tall Bihari gentleman. We got into a friendly conversation, which was interrupted when I was called in.

When I came out, the Bihari gentleman asked me how the interview went. I was not very happy, and I told him so. Just then he was called. As he got up to go in, he waved at me and said: 'See you in Mussoorie,' with an air of supreme assurance. I wondered how he could be so confident of his getting into the IAS. More than that how could he be sure of meeting me there.

That confident gentleman was Yashwant Sinha, who later resigned from the IAS, joined politics and rose to become the foreign minister and finance minister of India. We have remained lifelong friends.

Unlike him, however, I was happily surprised when I found out I had passed the examination in the very first attempt. I was among a large contingent of Madrasis, mainly from the three colleges—Presidency, Christian and Loyola.

The National Academy of Administration (later renamed Lal Bahdur Shastri National Academy of Administration) was located in an old colonial hotel called Charleville, in Mussoorie (now in Uttarakhand). I spent a year in training there, learning horse riding, driving, shooting, first-aid, and climbing hills and trekking. I also learnt how to tie a Windsor knot, eat properly with knives and forks, and wear black-and-white closed-collar suits on formal occasions. It took me some years to develop a taste for north Indian food. Deprivation often leads to dreams of near fulfilment. Many a night, I used to dream of sitting down with my mother at a sumptuous dinner.

We had to suffer lectures daily on law, economics, political science, history, public administration and other such arcane subjects, both from resident professors and guest lecturers. Except the keen-type probationers, most of us paid scant attention to these lectures. We preferred to sit as backbenchers.

Since we were bombarded by so much erudition and profundity daily, one of my predecessors, V. Ramamurthy, who had been my senior in Presidency College, had started a weekly handwritten bulletin to restore the balance. It was called 'The Edward Lear Bulletin for the Propagation of Pure Nonsense'. I made it into a daily bulletin. Dr A.N. Jha, ICS, director of the Academy, who was deeply interested in literature, used to read my contributions to the bulletin and enjoy the quips. Dr Jha weighed somewhere in the vicinity of 160 to 170 kg. One day, he regaled us with a lecture on 'Light Verse'. Next day, the Edward Lear Bulletin carried the headlines 'Light Verse from a Heavy Man'. Dr Jha quite enjoyed the headlines. He used to claim that he was exempted from the riding classes, since no horse could trot, canter and gallop sustaining his weight.

Two of the highlights of our training in the academy were an attachment to an army unit on active duty in Kashmir for a month and a tour of most of the important landmarks of India by train—the Bharat darshan. The real character of most of the probationers was highlighted during these two stressful events. The army treated the IAS probationers with barely concealed condescension, holding us up as namby-pamby civilians who could hardly hold their own in times of law and order emergencies. They put us through a tough schedule, waking us up at 4 am for an uphill cross-country run of five miles at a breathtaking pace, an obstacle course scaling smooth walls, climbing trees with the help of knotted ropes and crossing streams clinging with hands and feet to a rope strung across the cold rushing waters down below. When I completed all these fairy-tale tasks, the best compliment Colonel Lalla could give me was to say, 'Ah, Moosa, you have missed your calling, you should have been in the army.'

When I had applied to sit for the civil services examination in 1959, I had opted for the Bombay State cadre. In the middle of our training in Mussoorie, the old Bombay State was split into Gujarat and Maharashtra. Gujarat became a separate state in 1960, with Ahmedabad as its capital.

This time, the government gave us no choice. Since there were more than a dozen officers earmarked for the erstwhile Bombay State, the government allotted the first one on the list to Maharashtra, the second to Gujarat and so on. That is how I got allotted to Gujarat and was informed that I had been posted to Surat district in Gujarat for a year's district training. We were given a month's respite to visit our families. My mother was distraught that she had the pleasure of my company for only a few weeks.

Thus began my career in the IAS in Gujarat—a region in which I have nothing but pleasant memories. By and large, the political leadership and my seniors in the cadre treated me with fairness and affection. Above all, the people of Gujarat—the common folk, the Dalits, the Adivasis, the Rabaris and the fisherfolk—gave me an abundance of their love.

Writing this book is not only a jog down memory lane for me but a deep desire to highlight some of the personalities who impressed me. Perhaps it is also an opportunity for me to talk about some others who thought of themselves as giants but turned out to be only windmills, or rather windbags, on closer acquaintance.

There is a story that somebody approached Thomas Hardy with a manuscript and requested him to suggest a title. Hardy, who was bombarded with hundreds of manuscripts from all sorts of acquaintances and strangers, found little time to read and suggest titles for books. So, when the importunate budding author met and asked about the manuscript he had sent, Hardy asked him, 'Tell me, young man, are there any drums and trumpets in your book?'

'No, sir,' said the young man. 'It is not that kind of book.' 'Then call it "No Drums, No Trumpets".'

I thought that would make a good title for my book. But the internet told me somebody had already anticipated me.

OF CHIEF MINISTERS AND GOVERNORS

The collectorate of Surat was housed in the Surat castle or Old Fort in the sixties of the last century. The cost of maintaining this four-centuries-old edifice was beyond the budget of the public works department (PWD). Like the skin of a mangy dog, the old plaster on its outer walls was peeling off, exposing the old bricks. The fort had been built at the command of Sultan Mahmud III of Gujarat by Khudawand Khan, his governor in the sixteenth century. It was to protect the city from the rapacious Portuguese who had attacked, pillaged and burned Surat more than once. Since it was built as a military bastion, its interior was a maze of rooms, barracks and arsenals. The original military architect may have known the design. It took one a long sojourn to find one's way around in that labyrinth. I spent two years in a tin-roofed office on the wide rampart of the fort.

The first person I called upon, when I joined Surat district in Gujarat as the supernumerary assistant collector, was Mr Shrotriya. He was, then, the resident deputy collector, or RDC for short. The RDC was in charge of the entire administration of the district, leaving the collector free to tour the district and play a few rubbers of bridge at the Gymkhana whenever he feels the urge. The subordinates all knew where the centre of power lay. As a result of the onerous responsibility and power that he wielded, Mr Shrotriya preened himself constantly. Mr Shrotriya was in late middle age when I met him. He had grown bald in the service of the British Raj, as he had started his career as a clerk under the white man and rose up to the rank of a resident deputy collector—a great achievement for a dyed-in-the-wool, thrice-born Brahmin from Umreth. In his heart of hearts, Mr Shrotriya believed he was thrice-born but refrained from claiming it publicly, as that would rile Brahmins from other areas, who perhaps had not had the blessing of a third coming. There was an additional reason for preening, as he believed, sincerely enough, that he was surrounded by a bunch of inefficient, incompetent and corrupt officials. Mr Shrotriya, it must be said to his credit, was a scrupulously honest man. He would not even accept a lift at the bus stand when it was pouring cats and dogs. And since the collector's burden was considerably lightened with the diligent help of Mr Shrotriya, he was also acknowledged to be highly efficient. As a result of this deadly combination of honesty and efficiency, Mr Shrotriya was universally disliked as a highly self-righteous man—the 'self' predominated over the 'righteousness'. He reminded me of an Indian version of Malvolio from Shakespeare's *Twelfth Night*—he frowned upon every kind of official and diet that was not *sattvic* even beyond the Gita variety.

So, on my first day, after having made a brief call on the collector, Mr S.M. Dudani, I was directed to meet Mr Shrotriya to learn my training schedule for the next one year. Mr Shrotriya looked me up and down as an alien intruder from Madras and reluctantly offered me the favour of a seat. The offer was not verbal, merely visual.

'So, you are coming from Mussoorie?' Mr Shrotriya asked in a condescending tone. Condescending because he was older and an RDC, next only to the district magistrate (DM), and I was young and a mere supernumerary. In his view, all supernumerary assistant collectors were a redundancy that the collectorate could very well do without. Moreover, they were a burden, as they had to be provided both office and residential accommodation, stationery, office assistant, peons (called *pattawala*s because of the red sash they wore across their shoulders) and so on. Why should the district go to all that trouble when the supernumerary contributed nothing to the administration? Mr Shrotriya implied all this with his frowns whenever I asked for some help.

'No, I am coming from Madras,' I said. 'I had gone home for a month after completing my training at the National Academy in Mussoorie.'

'Of course, Mr Pai told me that you got a month's rest at home after the rigours of your stint in Mussoorie.' There was a hint of sarcasm again in Mr Shrotriya's comment, not verbalised.

I had met Mr Y.V. Pai, my predecessor, who was about to complete his district training before being given a regular charge as *prant* officer, i.e. assistant collector and subdivisional magistrate (SDM), in charge of a subdivision. (A *prant* is a carryover term from British colonial India, and denotes a revenue district.) Mr Pai had come to receive me at the Surat Railway Station. A short-statured handsome man with a receding hairline, Mr Pai tried to put me at ease when I mentioned my disquiet and discomfort at the sight of middle-aged lady porters, clad in red saris, carrying more than two or three heavy suitcases on their heads. 'This is normal in Gujarat,' he said. 'And more than normal in Surat. Men here believe that women are born to be beasts of burden and men are born to ride on their backs. Wait till you see the handcarts on the roads being pulled by the women, while their husbands recline on the carts smoking their bidis.' Sure enough, the first sight that met my eyes when I came out of the station was not one but several women waiting at their carts for customers, while their husbands were drinking tea reclining on the planks, with half-smoked bidis in their hands.

'So, you speak Madrasi?' asked Mr Shrotriya. 'Mr Pai also speaks Madrasi.'

'Yes, I speak Tamil. Mr Pai speaks Kannada. They are two different languages,' I explained patiently.

'They all sound the same to me,' he said, 'You know what? You put some large pebbles into a mud pot and roll them around—that is Madrasi for you.'

For Mr Shrotriya, the whole region of India south of the Vindhyas was Madras. For him, there was no distinction between a Tamilian, a Telugu, a Kannadiga and a Keralite. They were all Madrasis. Mr Shrotriya hailed from the town of Umreth in erstwhile Kaira district of Gujarat. And the Brahmins from Umreth counted themselves among the purest of the pure. Mr Shrotriya believed all others (including other Brahmins) belonged to a class that need not necessarily deserve any regard. Even Morarji Desai, who was a cabinet minister in Delhi, and Hitendra Desai, a minister in the Gujarat Cabinet, while being Anavil Brahmins, were merely to be obeyed but not at par with the Umreth Brahmins. 'We will not intermarry with the Anavils,' he asserted proudly.

'But they are also Brahmins,' I remonstrated many months later when Mr Shrotriya had developed a reluctant tolerance for me.

'Yes, but they are only honorary Brahmins,' said Mr Shrotriya with a sneering smile, 'Lord Rama had conferred Brahmin-hood on the Anavils for some service they had rendered him. They are not original Brahmins.'

For Muslims, Mr Shrotriya had nothing but contempt. 'You Muslims are a cowardly lot,' he remarked to me once. 'You only sacrifice goats and cows—poor innocent, harmless creatures—on your Bakra Eid. Why don't you sacrifice lions and tigers?'

'They are not available in the market,' I remarked in the same jocular tone. 'Why don't you persuade some enterprising Umreth Brahmins to open tiger shops?'

With a loud guffaw, he changed the subject, 'Why do you Muslims always do everything opposite of what we do?'

'Such as?' I asked.

'When we wash our hands, we pour water from the elbow down to the fingers. You take water in your hand and pour it down to the elbow. When we wash our face, we wash it down from the forehead to the chin. You do the opposite. We call the 'jaw' *jadba* in Gujarat, you call it *jabda*. We use *tapeli* for a saucepan, you call it *pateli*.'

While Mr Shrotriya had his strong reservations about Muslims, he reserved his real hatred for the Jains. He believed that the Jains were bent upon destroying Hinduism and converting all Hindus to Jainism by building beautiful marble temples, installing marble idols ('closely resembling our deities') in the sanctum sanctorum and tempting the gullible Hindus with money and blandishments to convert.

'We have a saying in Surat,' he told me one day, 'If a Hindu is pursued by a mad bull on the road and he sees a mosque and a Jain temple on opposite sides, he should take refuge in the mosque.' Knowing Mr Shrotriya's views about Muslims, especially their 'unclean' habit of eating eggs, fish and mutton, I was rather taken aback when I heard this.

'Wouldn't the Hindu face a greater danger of pollution in the mosque?' I asked.

'Yes. He may face a physical danger there. That pollution can be washed off with the help of cow's urine. But in the Jain temple, he would be facing spiritual danger. Seeing the beautifully carved marble idols, he would be tempted by the Jains to convert.'

'Let me assure you, Muslims are not interested in converting Brahmins and Jains. That will be counterproductive. If they all become non-vegetarians, we will be helping raise the price of chicken and meat,' I said.

Lower than the Muslims and Jains, in Mr Shrotriya's estimation, were the Harijans, Shudras and the Dalits, some of whom had risen to become deputy collectors, equal in status to Mr Shrotriya himself, the thrice-born. Though he did not voice it in so many words, he made disparaging remarks about the state policy of reservation.

'But that was initiated by Mahatma Gandhi,' I protested.

'Who was Gandhi? A Baniya!' Mr Shrotriya dismissed the Mahatma in two words.

Mr Valadre, the SDM of one of the subdivisions of the Surat district, was one such 'upstart'. Mr Shrotriya tolerated me, he even tolerated Mr Shah, the treasury officer who was a Jain. But when it came to Mr Valadre, his sufferance reached its limit. He merely endured Valadre's existence.

Once I had invited my colleagues for dinner at my house. They all accepted the invitation. They got wind of the fact that Mr Valadre, too, had been invited. The only person who turned up for dinner was Valadre. Valadre had warned me of that probability, but I had disregarded the warning. None of the others would even sit at the same table with Valadre. 'He should have had the courtesy to refuse. What is the *sanskar* (standards of ethical behaviour) of a Harijan, if he does not recognise his place?' Mr Shrotriya asked.

Mr Shrotriya assigned me a small office room on the wide rampart of the fort that had an embrasure originally meant as an archery window. Since I was a newcomer to the collectorate and a mere supernumerary to boot, I did not merit a proper room. The room had no roof, the PWD had put up a temporary tin roof. The gun embrasure that now stood for a window looked over the Tapti River, and during monsoons, the rain sprinkled me with cold showers. In summer, the tin heated up, and the room became an oven. But since I was always on tour and rarely sat there, Mr Shrotriya's tongue-in-cheek solicitous enquiry as to whether I was comfortable did not affect me.

After Mr Shrotriya gave me my training programme—three weeks with the *talati*, the village officer; one month with the taluka chief *mamlatdar*; two months with the Surat SDM Denis Bose; one month with the treasury officer; one month with the session judge and so on—he handed me over to one Gopalji. Gopalji was a handyman, a man for all seasons, a jack of all trades. He was a native of Surat and knew it like the back of his hand. He lodged me temporarily in the dilapidated old guest house of the district local board (DLB), situated on the bank of the Tapti, near the old Mecca *pul* (bridge), from where all pilgrims for hajj used to embark on ships sailing to Mecca during the days before the rise of Bombay (now Mumbai). It had crumbling walls and roof, and the paint peeling from the doors and windows. The bathroom had a tin bathtub and a thunder box (a portable tin lavatory seat, invented by the British in India, placed over a hole in the ground). That is all the accommodation one could afford on the pittance that a supernumerary was entitled to for the first-year training in the district.

Mr Sadhuram Dudani, the collector, I found, was a very affable man, when I met him on my next visit to his office, occasioned by a 'summons' from his PA.

'Have you settled down? Is the DLB bungalow okay?' he enquired solicitously.

Naturally, I could not tell him that the steel cot's ancient springs, having borne the burden of thousands of guests of the East India Company, had given up the unequal struggle to remain flexible. The bare steel springs were covered by a lumpy mattress stuffed with coconut fibre—stuffing of cotton being a luxury. It sagged so much that every time I turned in my sleep, the springs whined and groaned so piteously that half the night I remained awake in sympathy with them. Nor could I tell him that having been fed up with the monotonous fare that the antiquated cook, a discarded relic of the British Raj, doled out day after day, I had to take recourse to a Punjabi roadside dhaba to restore my jaded palate.

'It's okay, sir, I manage,' I said. He noted my tone.

'Yes, I know it's an old bungalow, but the cook is good. I believe he makes good chops and cutlets. Some guests who have stayed there told me that his caramel custard is really good.'

That is all I had been eating for the last two weeks. If it was chops for lunch, it was cutlets for dinner, and vice versa the next day. The caramel custard was a constant.

'Unfortunately, Surat does not have many restaurants where an IAS officer can go and dine without loss of dignity. Kwality is there, but it is too expensive,' he remarked.

I wondered whether somebody had seen me at the Punjabi dhaba and reported it to him. I decided that the sooner I got my own accommodation the better for the preservation of the dignity of the civil service.

When I met Mr Dudani, he was in his mid-forties, with three young children. A handsome man, he could be quite attractive to the opposite sex, especially with the aura of power that hovered around the DM in his own district. At least it used to be so in the early decades after Independence. The acronym IAS had not yet taken root. People still considered the district officers to belong to the ICS, the old Indian Civil Service that had earned the reputation of being professionally irreproachable and personally unapproachable. That was in the early days of independent India.

Much later, Mr Shrotriya purveyed more gossip about the collector.

'Mr Dudani is a Sindhi, you know,' he said in a disparaging tone. For him, Sindhis, who ate meat and drank liquor, were at par with Muslims.

'He can't help it,' I remarked, rising to the defence of my absent boss.

'He is not a Gujarati. He migrated to India when you people started killing Hindus in Pakistan,' said Mr Shrotriya with a mischievous smile, hoping to provoke me into a retaliatory argument, but I did not take the bait. 'He was only a *mamlatdar* in Sindh. That is a step below the deputy collector, you know! But when he came over, he represented to the government that he was a deputy collector there. So, he was absorbed as a deputy collector here. Now he is a collector.' Mr Shrotriya sounded unhappy that a Johnny-come-lately, a meat-eating Sindhi refugee could get promoted over the heads of the local God-fearing Gujaratis. In the hierarchy of hates, Mr Shrotriya placed Sindhis after Muslims, followed by Jains, Sikhs and Punjabis, but preceded by Dalits.

'Do you mean to say that the government accepted the word of mouth on such matters?' I asked.

'No. He must have brought some document. He is a clever man. In 1947, who was there to check the authenticity of documents brought from Pakistan? You know, all those Sindhi refugees lodged documented claims that they had left millions of acres of farmland in Sindh, that they were big landlords and had to leave mansions in Karachi, Hyderabad, Thatta and what not. The total area of the land they claimed to have left behind amounted to more than the total area of Sindh itself!' Mr Shrotriya had guffawed at the end of this harangue.

Of course, the refugees on both sides of the border did inflate their losses, and, of course, Mr Shrotriya was exaggerating. Whether Mr Dudani was merely a *mamlatdar* in Sindh or a deputy collector there, he had come a long way. He had developed into a far more well-adjusted, liberal-minded man without any prejudices. He had many friends in Surat, especially among the Bohra and the Parsi communities. Two such were Roshan and Shehryar. Roshan was a very beautiful lady in her mid-thirties, always dressed in a printed frock that enhanced her complexion and emphasised her figure to great advantage. She had an outgoing personality, and whenever she came to the Gymkhana, she made it lively. One could easily see how Mr Dudani was enchanted with her presence. So were many others. Shehryar, an old-world Parsi in his seventies, was the secretary of the Gymkhana. Even he was enamoured with Roshan, though in a paternal way. For some reason, Mrs Dudani did not like Roshan at all. She was a regular visitor to the Gymkhana Club, whether her husband came or not.

When I was attached to the treasury officer, Mr Shah, I learnt how to count the notes and the coins kept in the strongroom. I even weighed the large cakes of a sweet-and-sour-smelling dark stuff. It was opium.

'But why do you keep opium in the strongroom?' I asked. 'You see, there are a score of registered opium addicts in the district. They cannot live without that stuff. Their health would be affected if deprived, so they claim. Since opium is a monopoly of the government from British times, we keep a stock here and issue it to the registered addicts on a monthly schedule,' Mr Shah enlightened me.

'But why keep it in the strongroom?' I asked.

'If we don't keep it under lock and key, the addicts will manage to steal it. And we will be answerable!' Shah explained.

I recalled that the British had fought two opium wars with China in the nineteenth century to force the Chinese to remain opium addicts so that the British could continue to make huge profits from the opium trade. I don't know whether the practice of keeping opium in the treasury strongroom and the regular issuing to registered addicts still continues. Viva Coleridge, Viva de Quincy!

One evening, Mr Shah invited me to dinner at his place. The Jains do not eat any root vegetables, not even onions and garlic, so they had developed a cuisine of their own without these seasonings. The food in Mr Shah's house was quite delicious even without garlic and onions.

'You had dinner with Shah,' Mr Shrotriya asked me accusingly the next day. It was less of a question than a disparaging statement, as much as to say 'See, what levels you have come down to!'

'You never invite me. So, what could I do?' I retaliated. But that did not rile him nor provoke him into inviting me for dinner at his house.

I knew that a thrice-born Brahmin would not commit the sacrilege of inviting a Muslim, a Jain or Baniya into the sacrosanct premises of his home.

~

'Now that you have completed your treasury training, it is time to learn how to manage VIP visits. The chief minister is visiting us, and the collector wants you to attend on him,' Mr Shrotriya informed me one day.

Dr Jivraj Mehta was the first CM of Gujarat after the bifurcation of the erstwhile Bombay State in 1960. He was scheduled to make an official visit to Surat.

The collectorate was agog. The collector called a meeting to review the arrangements and assigned duties to each of the officers. Mr Pai had completed his district training and had left to join his new assignment. As the only IAS officer left, the collector ordered me to accompany him as a sort of staff officer during the CM's visit. Mr Shrotriya, being the resident deputy collector, never moved from his chair.

Dr Mehta was a highly respected figure in Gujarat. Born with a silver spoon in his mouth to the diwan of the Baroda State in the heyday of the maharajas, he studied medicine in Bombay and went to London to get his FRCS and MRCP. Returning to India, he joined the freedom movement, participated in the satyagrahas of Mahatma Gandhi, went to jail more than twice and was a well-known leader in the Indian National Congress by the time India won independence in 1947. He rose to become the CM when Gujarat was spun off as a state from the old Bombay Presidency. When he came to Surat in 1961, he was already in his mid-seventies.

Dr Mehta was married to a very distinguished lady, Hansaben. She was a Brahmin, and he a Vaishya. In the Gujarat of the twenties, this marriage was a capital crime in the community, and the Brahmins excommunicated her. But intrepidly, she went ahead to fight for the cause of women, established several women's institutions, went to the United Nations (UN) and helped draw the Charter of Human Rights. She headed several universities as vice chancellor and became more famous than her husband.

Encountering such giants in their native habitat was a salutary experience for a novice who was entering the portals of the civil services at its lowest rung. I was in a nervous state anticipating meeting such a stalwart.

On the day when Dr Mehta was to arrive in Surat, Mr Dudani fell victim to a viral attack of high fever. It fell to my lot to receive the CM all by myself and conduct him around to various functions.

A rather cold, misty morning found me standing on the Surat railway platform. I did not see any political bigwigs, MLAs, MPs or party honchos crowding the railway platform. There were some police officers, inspectors and deputy superintendents, headed by Mr Deboo, the district superintendent of police (SP), all in uniform, looking very busy.

I was clad in a buttoned-up black jacket, called *bandh-gala*, and white trousers, the prescribed formal uniform of the civil servant, relics of the British Empire—the bush shirt and the safari suit had still not come into fashion nor accepted in civil society. Having the example of the collector before me, I safeguarded myself with a woollen muffler around my neck. Of course, Mr Deboo, a Parsi gentleman of the old school was in his crisp uniform, his chest adorned with all the colourful ribbons he had earned in his career. He was strutting around flourishing his swagger stick. His minions were scurrying around hither and thither looking important on unspecified errands.

In those days, we never had the benefit of the cellphone or even a landline phone you could use by yourself. You had to lift the heavy Bakelite handset and give the two-digit number of your proposed contact to the grumbling operator, who would take his time to connect you. If you had to make a call to another city, both in and outside the state, you had to book a 'trunk call' with the operator, who gave you a number on the waiting list. Sometimes it took a whole day for the call to 'mature'. There was a landline in the station master's office. That was, of course, exclusively reserved for 'official' calls. Hence, we all waited, not knowing the whereabouts of the expected train.

I was wondering whether the station master had received any message as to when the train would be in. It was already 6 am, and the train was a half hour late. Long-distance trains (any train that had to travel for more than a couple of hundred miles was long distance) were infamous for their frequent delays in those days, and numerous jokes were in circulation around the country about the notorious unpunctuality of the railway services. Even the first-class compartments were not air-conditioned. The CM, too, travelled without that comfort. But since we were all imbued with the spirit of Mahatma Gandhi, especially in his home state, we never felt any discomfort in travelling in such compartments.

That morning, I kept walking up and down the platform, with my hands in my pockets to keep them warm, inhaling the mélange of smells typical of all Indian railway stations—a mixture of engine oil, steam, rust, coal dust, stale urine and dried poop. Occasionally, I glanced at my watch to increase my nervousness. I saw Gopalji approach then.

'The train is at the next station, sir. It should be approaching Surat any minute now,' he informed me.

'How do you know that?' I asked. 'Did you check with the station master?'

'No. I didn't have to. Didn't you hear the bell ring?'

'The bell? What does the ringing mean?'

'There is the well-known formula, sir, about the bells in the station. *Panch ko teesra, teen ko doosra, do ko andar, ek ko bahar* (Five peals mean third, three means second, two means in, one means out).' Sure enough, just then the steam whistle blew its long blast, and the train rolled slowly in. All the policemen came to attention as the first-class compartment came to a halt just where we were all waiting. The door opened, and out stepped Dr Mehta, a dapper man of about seventy-five, clad immaculately in a white dhoti, a long white coat and a Gandhi cap. With his clean-shaven, wrinkle-free face, he certainly did not look his age. I stepped forward and introduced myself. There was a small police guard of honour. After that brief ceremony, we walked to the exit.

'I am to convey the collector's apology, sir, for not being here to receive you. He is down with high fever and has been advised not to go out.'

'That is all right. I understand,' said the CM in a gentle voice. He got into the Ambassador car—the standard workhorse that was the only vehicle provided to all officials.

He invited me to get in with him in the back seat while the personal security officer got into the front with the driver.

'How is your training getting along?' he asked.

'I am midway through it, sir,' I replied.

'And what have you learnt so far?'

'I learnt how the land records are kept in the village office, how they are maintained and updated, how they are inspected by the higher officers, and the entries verified and certified; how the problems faced by the villagers are ascertained and informed to the higher authorities by the *talati*, and so on.'

'That's all?'

'No, sir, I also learnt how the *mamlatdar* and the deputy collectors respond to the complaints they get; how the school, the public health centres, the cattle pens, the public distribution shops, etc., are inspected and the treasury operated.'

'That's quite a lot in six months.'

'Not in six months, sir. We also learnt the theory part behind all this at the National Academy for one year,' I clarified.

'And also a proper dress sense! I notice that you are wearing the right winter formals. But, tell me, is that muffler round your neck also a part of the formals?' He had a mischievous glint in his eye when he asked that.

He had caught me right on the wrong foot. Quietly, with an embarrassed air, I removed the offending muffler and thrust it into my pocket. Dr Mehta very well knew that the muffler was not a part of the formal dress. It was his gentle way of reminding me that when the dress protocol is observed, it should be done meticulously.

During the day, I accompanied the CM to several official functions—inauguration of a school, the commemoration of a freedom fighter's contribution, a valedictory function of some event and so on. He had his frugal lunch in the circuit house, where several MLAs and MPs joined him.

He had a meeting with the local Congress party workers scheduled at 5:30 pm. As we finished the last of his official functions at 5 pm and were in the vicinity of the Surat Fort, he turned to me and said, 'I will drop you at your office now.'

Still a novice, I said, 'But you still have a couple of engagements to fulfil, sir.'

'Yes, but you cannot come with me there. One is a political meeting, and the others are social engagements.'

So, he ordered the driver to deviate from the main route and left me at the collectorate. There was no pomp, no great hubbub surrounding the visit of the CM to the district.

Nawab Mehdi Nawaz Jung was the first governor of Gujarat, just as Dr Jivraj Mehta was its first CM. He was a royal aristocrat of the erstwhile Hyderabad State, and he had served in the civil services there as a municipal commissioner, secretary and so on. Later, he joined politics and was appointed a minister of the state immediately after it merged with India. I met him when he was in his sixties, a tall well-turned-out man with an aquiline nose and an elegant moustache. He was always clad in a sherwani and the Hyderabadi *dastaar*, worn by the aristocrats of Hyderabad. He spoke impeccable English, having been educated in an English public school. He was very fond of playing bridge.

The collector and the nawab got along very well. On his first visit to Surat, the governor was put up in a private bungalow belonging to Mr Deboo, in Dumas, a seaside holiday resort of Surat at that time. It was at a distance of some twenty kilometres from the city. I was in attendance with the collector during the governor's visit. After a sumptuous dinner, with many Mughlai and Parsi dishes, we all retired to the drawing room.

The governor took out a Romeo y Julieta cigar, rolled it between two fingers and carefully clipped it. Lighting it with a match stick, he drew a long puff.

'You can smoke, gentlemen,' he said. The collector did not smoke; but taking advantage of the permission so graciously granted, I lighted a cigarette.

'Do you play bridge?' the governor asked me.

'Passably, sir, but I make an excellent dummy,' I said. The governor smiled. That was no modesty but the truth. The collector did not smile, having heard that one before.

'That will do. Shall we make a foursome, Collector Sahab?' the governor enquired, getting up from the sofa and moving to the bridge table in the veranda.

'Sure, sir,' said the collector with alacrity, and it fell to my lot to arrange for the cards. Mr Deboo was called in to make up a foursome. We played a couple of rubbers, during which the governor regaled us with stories of the erstwhile nawabs of Hyderabad, including the tales of diamonds and rubies being used as paperweights by the nizam.

'What differences do you find between the Hyderabad State and Gujarat?' I asked him.

'Well, Hyderabad was a feudal state ruled by a hereditary aristocracy. The ruler introduced some forms of limited democracy in the last days under British compulsion. The state had its rituals and its inherited protocol. Gujarat, at least the British part of it, is a more professionally run democratic state. But I noticed many similarities between the two when I toured Baroda, Rajkot, Bhavnagar, Jamnagar, Junagadh and Kutch. Though it is thirteen or fourteen years since Independence, the mindset of the people and the officials here hasn't changed much, I note.'

'The people are happy, sir, that the one-man rule has given place to a democratic set-up,' said the collector.

'You would be surprised,' said the governor, 'There are a large number of people in these erstwhile native states who still venerate their maharajas and nawabs. For some of them, the former rulers are next only to the divinities they worship.' I realised how true this was when I toured the state in my capacity of director of famine relief and heard many of the people looking back to the benign rule of their erstwhile rulers.

'What about Junagadh, sir?' I asked. The former nawab of Junagadh had earned quite an unenviable reputation in Gujarat.

'He was reputed to have spent millions on the marriage of his male dog with the female dog belonging to the maharaja of Jamnagar. A whole trainload of *baratis* (the entourage of the bridegroom) accompanied the canine bridegroom from Junagadh to Jamnagar! In fact, at the time of the takeover of the state by the government of India in 1948, the nawab preferred to take with him a planeload of dogs, leaving behind some of his begums!'

'Yes, I have heard those tales. Some of the rulers did behave atrociously, spending public resources on frivolous pursuits, but there were others who governed their states quite well. Maharaja Sayajirao of Baroda, for example, is remembered by the people of his state with great affection. He opened schools, made elementary education compulsory, established a university, set up a Centre of Oriental Studies, built roads and bridges, and did more for the people than the British did in their territory.'

'Yes, sir, you are right,' said the collector. 'In fact, the peasants of Navsari taluka in my district are the most literate farmers in the whole district. Navsari was a part of the Baroda State.'

Some years later, I happened to be the collector of Bulsar district (now Valsad) that had been created after bifurcating the Surat district. Maharaja Sayajirao Gaekwad had the vision to appoint Maulana Muhammad Ali as the collector of Navsari. Maulana Muhammed Ali later joined the freedom movement and was one of the founders of the Khilafat Movement of India. It was supported by Mahatma Gandhi, laying the foundation of Hindu–Muslim unity in India. In his presidential speech on the occasion of he Kakinada session of the Indian National Congress, Muhammad Ali had talked of a federation of religions of India: 'I still dream that old dream of the United Faiths of India.' That old dream still remains a dream.

I met Nawab Mehdi Nawaz Jung one last time in Hyderabad after he had demitted office and settled down in his native city just a few months before his death in 1967. He invited me to his house in Banjara Hills and gave me a sumptuous dinner. I recently learnt that the beautiful heritage building where he once lived has been pulled down to make way for some monstrosity.

It was during my stint in Surat that I got married to Husnara, my cousin. She had just completed her eighteenth year. Leaving her large contingent of brothers and sisters in Madras to come and live with me in far-off Gujarat—an alien city, with its alien languages and alien people—must have been quite traumatic for her. But she adapted herself quite quickly to the Gujarati culture and cuisine. In a short period, she had picked up the local language enough to be able to read Saraswati Chandra and help me pass the Gujarati language examination. Walter Lawrence, one of the early breeds of ICS officers wrote in 1927: 'If one has the good fortune to win a wife who does not mind "roughing it", long journeys, constant transfers, sometimes a lonely life away from doctors, dentists and civilisation, a wife who likes India, the Indians and adventure of Indian life, a wife of noble patience and pluck—the sooner he marries the better.' My wife had these qualities and the strength to bear and bring up four wonderful children—educating them, settling them—all this while undergoing twenty transfers and twenty house changes. While so engaged, she completed her graduation in economics from Delhi University, in Arabic from Cairo and her postgraduate degree in modern Persian from the University of Baroda, the first two through distant education. She writes excellent Urdu ghazals. Some of them have been published in journals.

It was also during my training in Surat that I met Mr Fateh Singh Rana, the commissioner of Baroda (now Vadodara), who often came to Surat on inspection. Surat district, at that time, was a part of the commissionerate of Baroda. Thus, on my first visit to Baroda after joining in Surat, I called on him in his office. He asked me to join him for dinner at the club. I found Mr Rana to be a keen bridge player, and I was no match for him when I joined the opposing pair.

Mr Rana belonged to the native state of Amode, in Bharuch district of Gujarat. There was a large clan of erstwhile Rajputs in south Gujarat who got converted to Islam generations ago. Yet, they retained their custom of naming their children with Rajput names, and followed all the Rajput marriage customs, and family and personal laws. They were, and are till today, called Molesalam Garasiyas. Mr Rana, when I met him, was in his fifties and in fine fettle. Looking like a Rajput prince, he was hugely popular among civil servants of all grades and well-respected among the politicians as a competent, effective and honest officer. Since he came to the IAS from the army, he still retained his military bearing of an erect carriage, fierce moustache, strong discipline, deep commitment and two pegs in the evening before dinner. This last was known with disapproval among the political circle, and for a long time, they chose to ignore it. But there were several among the officers and social workers laying claims to the legacy of Mahatma Gandhi who openly frowned upon this. Gujarat was still under Mahatma Gandhi's influence as far as drinking was concerned, at least publicly.

Like many other states of India, the prohibition law was enforced in the state rigorously whenever the police needed pocket money. The higher echelons of the police force joined the corporate honchos in clandestine drink parties where smuggled scotch and single malt was served. The tribals, or to give them their correct appellation, the Adivasis of south Gujarat, never had to depend on imported liquor. They made their own stuff from the dried *mahua* flower, freely available in the forest, in homemade stills. The Adivasis mixed these dried flowers with jaggery and *nausadar* (ammonium chloride), and left it to ferment for three–four days until the alcohol develops. They then distilled it in earthen homemade stills in their huts. On all ritual occasions, such as marriages, deaths, holidays and whenever the village decided to pass the night in dancing and revelry, *mahua* liquor was specially consumed in copious quantities by both men and women. While the police let the elite and the royalty alone most of the time, the poor Adivasis were the usual victims of police raids.

Mr Rana was, however, careful enough to have obtained an official permit to buy, keep and drink liquor. He was entitled as an ex-military officer. Some Malvolios took every opportunity of criticising him, since they could not envisage a senior serving officer having his cakes and ale.

After completing my district training, I was waiting for a regular posting when I received summons from Baroda to meet the commissioner.

Mr Rana received me in his spacious office located in a palatial building, a legacy from the erstwhile Baroda State. It was perhaps occupied by the diwan in the heyday of the Raj. It still retained its opulence and ambience of power, enough to overawe any new entrant to the civil service, more so any poor supplicant who came to get redressal for his grievance. However, this impact was lessened to a large extent by the affability and affection of the commissioner's demeanour.

'So you have completed your training,' more a statement than a question.

'Yes, sir, waiting to get a *prant* subdivision,' I said. Normally, no expectant of a favour would have adopted a tone of banter with the commissioner. But having played several rubbers of bridge with him, I had perhaps developed a misplaced sense of familiarity. I never repeated that in my later career.

'Where would you like to be posted then?' he asked, ignoring my tone. This came as a pleasant surprise. Normally, in the cut-and-dried system of hierarchic indifference, no one ever asked a junior for his choice of posting. But here was the commissioner asking a mere supernumerary where he would like to be posted.

After a few moments of nonplussed silence, during which I thought over the available choices, I ventured, 'Sir, I shall be happy wherever you send me, but my preference would be for a *prant* that has a jeep attached and some potential for shikar.'

My native village in the south of India was located close to the forest of Karai, which abounded in large and small game. The large game included various kinds of deer, four-horned antelopes, mouse deer and various species of hares and rabbits. I had accompanied some of my elder relatives on shikar into the Karai forest. I did not like hares and rabbits, but venison and wild ducks were always welcome.

'Done,' he said. 'But one condition. When I come there, you'll organise a shikar for me.' Mr Rana, scion of a native state, was a keen hunter like most rajas and nawabs.

'With great pleasure, sir,' I said.

Though Mr Rana had promised me a posting where there was a jeep for the *prant* officer and some shikar in the area, he could not immediately find a suitable place.

So, I had to spend a short stint in a place called Kadi in Mehsana district. It was a newly created *prant* headquarter, with neither a jeep nor an official residence. I had to make do with a rented two-storey house in a highly congested locality. The local *mamlatdar*, Mr Bhutaiya, had to exert all his official authority to get that house, as the landlord was reluctant to rent his house to a Muslim, who would defile his premises by eating meat there. We spent less than a month there, during which we managed to survive on a purely vegetarian diet.

Kadi was known as a cotton-growing area, and the Patels were the most prosperous and powerful community of the *prant*. Since there was no jeep, I did most of the touring by bus. My *pattawala* would have to go in advance to the bus stand to reserve a front seat for me. During that time, Husnara's brother had come from Madras to keep her company during my tours.

During that brief sojourn, I had to face a minor crisis. There was a farmers' agitation in the whole district. Processions were being taken out, and, in some areas, the aggressive Patels had indulged in violence. The farmers, mostly Patel, announced marches to the subdivisional headquarters, culminating in a large procession to the collectorate in Mehsana.

The deputy superintendent of police (DSP) came to my office one morning, in a rather agitated mood.

'Sir, farmers from three talukas have gathered and are marching to Kadi tomorrow. The DM has diverted most of my police force to Mehsana. I am left with only eight policemen, four of them to guard the police headquarters. If the large procession of farmers enters Kadi, it will be difficult to handle it with only four policemen.'

I called in Mr Bhutaiya, who, too, was a new recruit into the revenue department. Between the three of us, we developed a plan to stop the procession on the highway itself.

The three of us got into the police jeep. Halfway down the road, we saw a large procession, shouting anti-government slogans, advancing towards Kadi. We stopped the jeep a hundred feet away. The deputy superintendent got down and, with the help of a portable megaphone, shouted at the procession that the SDM has declared the assembly as unlawful under Section 144 of the Criminal Procedure Code. Once an assembly of four or more people was prohibited to assemble under Section 144, every individual in such a group becomes liable to be arrested and punished. For a few moments, the leaders of the procession remained nonplussed. Perhaps they had not anticipated such a contingency. Then the leader stepped forward and called out, 'Where is the declaration?'

I then got down from the jeep, took out a sheet of paper and flourished it in the air. There was nothing on that paper. I had yet to pass that order.

The leaders then turned to the crowd and told them, 'The SDM has declared us unlawful under Section 144—*eksau chowalis lagadi didhi, khalas*—so let us all disperse and go home.'

Within half an hour, the crowd melted away. Those were the days when the British had recently left India, but the aura they had created during their rule still clung to the district officer like the smile of the Cheshire Cat. It was called *iqbal*—comprehensively meaning luck, presence, aura and an undefinable, unexercised authority that emanates from the very presence of a person. It was this *iqbal* that helped disperse the large crowd. It was with that residual *iqbal* that we administered India in the sixties and early seventies. The Emergency destroyed that aura. Today, unfortunately, that aura is mostly lost, except in some parts.

OF DAFERS AND DUFFERS

A few days later, I got fresh orders. The commissioner had posted me as assistant collector and SDM to Radhanpur subdivision in the Banaskantha district. (It has now been bifurcated and perhaps trifurcated in the last five decades.) In the early sixties of the last century, the whole of the Banaskantha district, bordering on the Rann of Kutch and the Thar Desert of Sindh (now in Pakistan), was classified as a backward district. The Radhanpur subdivision was in a remote corner of Banaskantha. It had four talukas—Radhanpur, with its headquarters at Radhanpur town; Deodhar; Tharad; and Santalpur, with Varahi as its taluka headquarter. The terrain was mostly flat, rocky land, and the rivers and streams that occasionally flowed through it in the monsoon season lost themselves midway in the desert, and if they survived, struggled to reach the Rann of Kutch, where they created a deceptive-looking marsh. And in this marsh, there flourished herds of wild asses, spotted deer and blackbucks, and the largest of Asian antelopes, the *nilgai*—the blue bulls—locally called *roz*. During my tenure in Radhanpur, the population of *nilgai* was estimated to be more than a lakh. Once they entered the vicinity of village farmland, they would wreak havoc and finish off acres of maize and bajra, and the farmers would be rendered destitute for a year. So, the government declared them 'vermin'. They could be shot without a licence. Many hunters, taking advantage of this dispensation, would go out regularly in the mornings and bag a couple of bulls. We used to buy a kilogram of *nilgai* meat for half a rupee in 1962. A single bull could weigh up to 250 kilograms—so a hunter bagging one could earn more than ₹100, a princely sum in those days when a maund (twenty kilograms) of aromatic basmati rice cost a mere ₹17 (so records my diary for 1962).

In the meantime, Husnara and I were expecting our first child. So, Husnara accompanied her brother to Madras. I took a month's leave to accompany her and see my family. Custom demanded that the first child be born in the maternal household.

On receiving my posting orders to Radhanpur, I packed my goods, all of a couple of suitcases, and took the train to Palanpur, headquarters of Banaskantha district. Mr Jaydev Vyas was the then collector of Banaskantha. Mr Vyas was in his forties and had joined the ranks of IAS through the State Civil Services. My first job was to call on him to report that I was joining my duties at Radhanpur.

When the native state of Palanpur merged with India, the then nawab, Sir Taley Muhammad Khan, shifted his residence to Bombay. The magnificent palace that he had built just before Independence was purchased by the government of Gujarat for a princely sum of ₹1.7 million. It became the collector's office.

When I called on the collector formally, he was sitting at the far end of a magnificent room, built as a banquet hall to seat a hundred guests. The false ceiling was made of plaster of Paris, adorned with arabesque designs and calligraphy in real gold, and a large chandelier of Belgian glass hung from the centre. The chandelier was lit and cast a soft glow on the golden ceiling. There was a row of imported lights adorning both walls, and the room was carpeted from wall to wall.

A month later, I learnt from the nawab of Radhanpur that Mr Vyas, who perhaps never cared for aesthetics or history, had called some merchants and goldsmiths and had got the gold in the roof assayed. He had proposed to the government that it may be auctioned off. The goldsmiths were to scrape off the gold ornamentation and recover the metal from the scrapings. The civil service harboured some insensitive individuals who lacked an aesthetic sense. Otherwise, how does one explain the dilapidated state of many of our heritage buildings and our prized Panchaloha Chola idols finding their way to the museums of the UK and US. At one time, it appears that the British government, too, under Lord William Bentinck, had planned to sell off the Taj Mahal after dismantling it block by block. Lord Elgin did vandalise the Parthenon and steal several marble panels that formed the frieze of the temple walls. Those panels still adorn the halls of the British Museum.

Palanpur was connected to Radhanpur by a metre-gauge railway. After Radhanpur, the line ran across the desert of Rann up to Kutch. After an overnight stay in Palanpur, I decided to take the slow train to Radhanpur. In any case, there was no faster alternative. I got into the first-class compartment. The first-class in those days was just four-seater coupes with a private washroom. I was dressed in a suit and tie, a most unsuitable dress for that clime and country but a de rigueur for a young entrant to the civil service. The hangover of the British Raj still reigned supreme. I found myself all alone in the compartment, engrossed in watching the dreary panorama of desert and rocky outcrops. Since Radhanpur was at a remote corner of the state and had no tourist allurements, the first-class coach hardly attracted any passengers.

When the train reached Deesa station and halted, the door opened to allow in a passenger, a Gujarati trader, clad in an immaculate white dhoti, white long coat and a white Gandhi cap. The Gandhi cap in Gujarat did not symbolise any adherence to the ideology of Gandhi but was a part of the normal dress of both the urban gentry and the rural peasants. In the case of the peasants, it was not so clean and not so white.

'Namaste,' greeted the newcomer politely, looking a little strangely at the suited and booted passenger—in contrast to his own traditional Indian attire.

'Namaste,' I responded, not to be outdone in courtesy. He sat down opposite me, still staring at me, curiosity dripping from every line of his chubby face.

'You are going to Bhuj,' he said, not able to suppress his curiosity. It was half-question, half-assumption.

'No, I am going to Radhanpur,' I replied in Gujarati.

My going to Radhanpur combined with my attire and my poor-accented Gujarati further excited his inquisitiveness, and I could see that he was not going to let matters rest there.

'Why are you going to Radhanpur, sir?' The 'sir' was in deference to my western attire and my strange Gujarati accent. 'I am the new assistant collector of Radhanpur, and I am going to take charge,' I said, hoping to satisfy his curiosity and put a stop to further questions.

'Ah, sir, many congratulations.' I noted that the enquirer was not to be put off by my abruptness. He was made of sterner stuff.

'But what happened to Rathod Sahab?' That was my predecessor in office who had been promoted.

'He has been promoted and transferred.' A short reply.

'He is a good man but belongs to the lower caste,' he said.

I noted the 'but'. Just being good was not sufficient for the high-caste trader, one should also belong to an upper caste.

I wondered how he assumed that I did not belong to a lower caste myself. Perhaps my western-style suit and tie may have convinced him that no Dalit would dare to wear such an attire. The gentleman introduced himself as Maganbhai Patel from Deesa. Patels, of course, belonged to the upper caste, just a rung below Brahmins and Rajputs. He was an isabgul trader. Banaskantha district was one of the largest producers of that medicinal husk, most of which was exported to the US and Europe.

'Where are you from, sir?' he asked, persisting in his inquisitiveness, his tone now somewhat deferential, having learnt my official position. After all, an assistant collector in independent charge of a subdivision was a collector for all practical purposes.

I told him I was from Madras in Tamil Nadu. Being a trader, he was, of course, aware of the country's geography. 'And what is your good name, sir?'

I told him my 'good' name. He tried to repeat it but could not get it right on his tongue. I noted in later years that in Gujarat I was always called Raja, but since Raja meant 'king', I never bothered to correct the mispronunciation. By now, I was getting a bit annoyed at the continued catechism. But since his curiosity appeared well-meaning and non-hostile so far, I continued to satisfy it.

'Sir, you are from the South. I have many trading partners from the South, both Brahmins and others. But since you are so young and going to a difficult place like Radhanpur, I want to give you some advice. Please don't mistake me. You must be very careful of the Muslims there. They are a very dangerous lot of people there.'

The gentleman assumed that since I was from the South, with a name like Raja, I must be a Hindu, perhaps a young naïve Hindu, ignorant of the local situation, walking into a den of cut-throat Muslims.

'How dangerous? In what way?' I asked, my curiosity aroused.

'Especially, there is a lawyer there called Kale Khan Pathan. He is the evil genius who almost persuaded the nawab of Radhanpur to declare a merger with Pakistan. The nawab was saved at the last minute by his *karbhari* (chief administrator), a Jain.'

'Kale Khan, as you say, may have played an evil role. But why do you term all Muslims of Radhanpur as dangerous?' I persisted.

'You don't know, sir, it is not only the Muslims of Radhanpur. All Muslims of Gujarat, in fact, all Muslims of India are dangerous. Look what they have done to our country. They divided it. I have heard their slogans just before Partition: "Pakistan *leke rahenge*." They got Pakistan but have remained in India. They should have all gone to Pakistan. It is all the fault of Gandhi and Nehru. It is they who supported the Muslims after Partition. Gandhi has paid the price, but Nehru still continues to rule us. The only one who stood against Partition was Sardar Patel. If Sardar Patel had become the prime minister instead of Nehru, he would have solved the Muslim problem.'

'How would he have done that?' I asked. I was to come across this assertion often later.

The gentleman frowned at my naïve question. His body language indicated that though I had passed the civil service examination and must have read history, I was still ignorant of some basic facts.

'Sir, Sardar Patel *kapi nakhyo* (slaughtered) 10,000 Muslims in Delhi alone in one night of August. He got the maharajas of Bharatpur and Alwar to finish of more than 40,000 Muslims. Sardar Patel diverted the weapons left behind by the British Army to the Hindus of Alwar and Bharatpur. He sent the army to clean out the Hyderabad State, and got 50,000 Muslims *safaya* (cleaned out). He would have done the same in Kashmir if Nehru had not held his hand. He died too early, sir, and we have that Mussulman-lover Nehru sitting as prime minister in Delhi!' For a mere trader of isabgul, Maganbhai's knowledge of the arcane history of India amazed me.

By the time Maganbhai Patel completed his account of Sardar Vallabhbhai Patel's unwritten and unknown history, the train had reached Radhanpur.

I never saw Maganbhai again. But I continued to wonder how many Hindus of Gujarat shared his opinions. I still wonder what his feelings would have been had he learnt that I was a Muslim.

As promised by Mr Rana, Radhanpur subdivision had a jeep attached to the office. Besides, every taluka headquarter was equipped with two horses and two camels. Most of the terrain was either rocky or sandy. Even a four-wheel-drive jeep often found itself unable to negotiate such a terrain. Only the camel or the horse could. Since we had been taught to ride horses in the National Academy, I could manage the docile horses of Gujarat. But the camel was a beast of an altogether different nature. As some wag remarked: 'On horseback you feel as if you are dancing in time to classical music, the camel seems to progress to the beat of a drum played by a drunk.' Maintaining your seat on the camel's back itself requires a Bedouin's skill and an Arab's endurance. I also agree with the writer who said that a camel is actually a horse designed by a committee. In all the literature I have read, I have not come across any description of how to get up on a camel. The reason for the remarkable absence of such a description is perhaps because the motions involved in getting on to the back of a camel beggar all description. One has to actually get up on the back of a camel to really learn what it feels like.

The camels attached to the taluka headquarter had two wicker panniers balanced on either side of the hump, tethered with a wooden *kujawa* (an intricate framework made of local timber). One of the baskets was meant for the officer and the other for the peon who carried water and other provisions required for the journey in the hot sun. The first time I rode a camel, I got into the basket, and my *mamlatdar*, who had ridden camels earlier, got into the other basket. Then the driver got up in front, perched almost on the neck of the camel (that is how it appeared to me). All this while, the camel was sitting with great insouciance in the sand, chewing the cud nonchalantly. Then the driver shouted '*hut, hut, hut*', and apparently that was camel language for 'get up, get up, get up'. (The thesaurus provides over 500 adjectives for the camel, most of them uncomplimentary.) The camel unfolded the lower one-third of its front legs, and I was thrown back in the basket. Before I could recover from my surprise, the driver shouted '*hut, hut, hut*' again. The camel then unfolded the front third of its hind legs, and I was jerked forward. The next step for the camel was to unfold the second half of its front legs, followed by that of the hind legs. I was thrown backward and forward I do not recall how many times before the camel stood erect and I became relatively stable in my pannier. All this happened in less time than it takes the reader to glance through the above description.

I travelled many a mile perched in the wicker pannier on the camel's back with a peon in the other pannier to keep me company and to carry my water bottle, books and bedding for the night halt. Since there was no shade for the traveller in the pannier, the peon also carried a couple of umbrellas to ensure protection against the sun and sudden squalls of rain. In summer, the temperature in the rocky terrain grew as hot as 46°C to 50°C. Even the umbrella often gave up its unequal struggle and one had to take shelter in one of those abandoned temples that dotted the vast desert landscape until it cooled down a bit. After a few such journeys, I grew quite accustomed to the swinging gait of the camel and the gentle swaying of the basket. Often, I have dozed off only to be woken up when the camel relieved itself of its flatulence with a loud fart. I could even read a book on longer journeys when I got tired of staring at the rocky outcrops relieved by clumps of *Prosopis juliflora* (known as *vilayti babool* in local language). The monotonous terrain was sometimes relieved by the vision of mirages where one could see castles, camel caravans and giants rearing their heads above the horizon. Sometimes, what I was convinced was a mirage actually turned out to be a herd of *nilgai* or wild asses, which scattered on our closer approach.

A remote part of my subdivision was inhabited by a class of people known collectively as the Daffers. The Daffers were a mixed lot ethnically, with strains of Sindhi, Arab, Pathan and Rabari in varying proportion. They followed their own brand of religion with deep-rooted faith in saints and tombs, and occupied a terrain that was part-desert, part-shingle and mostly barren. They cultivated a few patches of land, wherever some water was available, and hunted wild animals for their protein supply.

Because of the barrenness of the terrain and the hostile geographic and climatic conditions, the Daffers developed into a tough and hardy people, rode well and, I am told, used to fight well in the armies of the nawabs. With the advent of Pax Britannica and the disbanding of the state's armies, they were left to fend for themselves. With the main avenue of finding employment closed and faced with the grim prospect of wresting an existence from the barren, rocky soil, the Daffers became marauders and cattle thieves. Some of them would erupt out of their inaccessible territory, make a raid in the dark of the night on a preselected village and snatch away whatever cattle they could lay their hands on. The bolder souls among them would take advantage of opportune moments to rob travellers on the highway and commit a few dacoities. They could do so with impunity, for once they were back in their own territory, it was difficult to follow them in. The area was so rocky that no motorised vehicle could penetrate it. It was only a camel or a horse that could traverse that terrain, and on both these animals, the Daffers could compete on more than equal terms. It was impossible to catch a Daffer once he was on horseback or riding a camel. No policeman could outride a Daffer on either of these animals.

In the days of the nawabs, when the marauding became particularly obnoxious, the nawab himself would mount an expeditionary force and send in the cavalry, so to speak, and lay waste a few Daffer villages, punishing the innocent along with the guilty. For some time, the Daffer depredations would cease. But after Independence, this option had to be precluded. A constitutional government, bound by the rule of law, could not adopt the rough and ready methods of medieval ages. We had, therefore, to tackle the problem with more lawful means. But lawful means and democratic processes always take time, and people are not always patient.

So, complaints went up to the government, and I received a couple of strong letters from the DM. He accused me of doing nothing, while the Daffers were creating havoc all around in my subdivision. This was, of course, not true. I had, in fact, sent in police parties twice, but both times they returned empty-handed, as the culprits could not be caught. So, I decided that it was time for me to take matters in my own hand and go parley with the marauders of the Daffer villages to arrive at some sort of understanding with them. I realised that until the root causes of poverty and unemployment were removed, the Daffers would continue to remain a thorn in his neighbour's flesh. I was advised that reason was not a strong point of the Daffers and that they only acknowledged force, as was demonstrated in the old days by the nawabs. Some of my counsellors even advised me that the only way to bring the Daffers to heel was to march in and burn down a couple of villages, preferably while the Daffers were there. Others told me that the Daffers were so dangerous that they would not spare me if I went in without sufficient force.

After listening to all these counsels, I started negotiations with the Daffers through intermediaries. Their initial reaction was strongly negative, and they were not prepared to meet me. However, after a little persuasion, a compromise was arrived at. I was to come with not more than two companions, and the leaders of the Daffers would meet me in the village of Dungarpur. At first, the DSP, my police chief, ruled it out. There was no way, he said, he would allow me to go into that den of robbers with only two companions. I pointed out to him that there was no other way of bringing the Daffers to book. And if so, what solution did he propose? In the circumstances, he agreed, and I left with the *mamlatdar* and the toughest inspector in the subdivision to visit Dungarpur.

We had received full directions on how to reach Dungarpur. Knowing the absence or excess of landmarks, I had half a mind to carry a compass with me. But the *mamlatdar* was confident of his sense of direction. The inspector, Jhala, relied more on his brawn than on his brain, of which commodity he had short supply, and therefore, made sparing use. We wandered around shrubs, hills, rocky outcrops and crossed a couple of patches of desert before we rested our horses at noon in the meagre shade of a babul tree. We asked directions from a score of villagers, who, in all sincerity, assured us that Dungarpur was only a couple of fields away. Almost close to sundown, we hit upon Dungarpur, more by chance than any directional sense of the *mamlatdar*.

We were received by a dozen Daffer leaders a mile ahead of the village, over a dozen doughty warriors on horseback. Though they looked fierce, with bushy moustaches, sharp noses, swarthy complexions and large pugrees, they were quite friendly in their greetings. Surrounded by these outlaws, the party advanced to Dungarpur. Close to the village, I observed a hillock on which there was a small white tomb with a dome, over which a green flag fluttered. Gaur Khan, the Daffer leader, informed me that a great saint lay buried there, and as a mark of respect, we all needed to dismount and walk up to the village. Shaukat Khan, another Daffer leader, supplemented this by saying that the saint did not like anyone passing his tomb on horseback. Since I was coming to parley with the Daffers, I felt it diplomatic to go along with them. But Jhala, my muscleman, would have none of such superstitions.

'What will happen if we don't dismount?' he asked.

'No one in living memory has crossed the road here on horseback, Thanedar Sahab,' replied Gaur Khan. 'The saint does not like any disrespect shown to him.'

'Nonsense!' said Inspector Jhala, 'I don't believe in any such superstitious rot. I will show you that these are only old wives' tales.'

And before I could intervene, Inspector Jhala had spurred his horse into a canter. I wanted to restrain Inspector Jhala, more for diplomatic reasons rather than from any lack of faith in his equestrian skills. I knew that Inspector Jhala had been winning the state gold medal in the equestrian show for the last five years in a row. The horse was in mild canter, but just as it reached a spot opposite the tomb, it whinnied suddenly and reared up, throwing Inspector Jhala to the ground. Having done that, it stood quietly by.

Luckily, the fall had given the inspector only a few mild bruises. But the injury to his pride was grave, and to his reason, more serious. He joined the party on foot, rather quiet and subdued, and we proceeded to the village.

That night we parleyed with the Daffers over a delicious dinner of barbecued venison (almost certainly poached) and grilled kidneys, and the final agreement was arrived at by the evening of the next day.

A rehabilitation plan was worked out to settle the Daffers in more hospitable terrain, where they could cultivate their patch of land and be more accessible to police surveillance. We returned to Radhanpur with the successful completion of our mission. Inspector Jhala made several trips to Dungarpur for subsequent parleys, and he told me, 'Sir, after my first fall, I still was not convinced that the saint had anything to do with it. So, on three of the four visits, I decided to test my own skills. But I'm damned, sir. Every time I tried to cross that spot on horseback, I fell. It did not matter whether my horse was cantering, trotting or merely ambling. Every time, the horse would shy, my grip would loosen and I would find myself on the ground. How do you account for it, sir?' he asked me.

I tried various explanations. He was psychologically conditioned by the first fall, I said. Every time he tried thereafter, he was apprehensive and perhaps communicated his fear to the horse subconsciously. But Jhala was not convinced. Nor was I.

One of the highlights of my tenure in Radhanpur was the land distribution campaign. Since we were still close to Mahatma Gandhi's spirit, and the governments had still not come under the baleful influence of land grabbers, real estate sharks, mining mafias and corporate cabals, the district administration had not lost the 'milk of human kindness'. Governments still thought of the travails of the downtrodden, the landless and the bonded labourers.

In every country where freedom was won from colonial rule, the early rulers still believed in egality, fraternity and liberty—ideals that were lost once the lure of pelf and profit overtook. The second and third generation usually turned out to be even worse than the colonial rulers. I received a strongly worded government order in 1963 that according to the revenue records, there were thousands of acres of wasteland lying uncultivated in my subdivision, and that I should undertake a campaign to assess the quantum of all such lands, village by village, and distribute this land to the landless Harijans, and send weekly reports to the government at Ahmedabad of the progress of distribution. Apparently, my predecessor had started the work but only half-heartedly. Being a Gujarati, he was afraid of being accused of bias, since he himself was a Dalit. So, on receipt of the orders, I started this work in right earnest. After all, I was an alien and had no caste obstacles to overcome.

The bible for the revenue officer was the Bombay Land Revenue Code, as applied to Gujarat. The entire civil administration of the district, viz. the collector, the assistant collector, the deputy collectors, the settlement officer, the *mamlatdars*, the survey department, the treasury, and all other miscellaneous work, like elections, education, health, municipal administration and census, came under the jurisdiction of the revenue department. Hence, though the collector and assistant collectors handled supervision of even the local educational institutions, public health, police force and civil supplies, they were still known as revenue officers. That was a British legacy. In some states, like Uttar Pradesh and Bihar, they used the nomenclature deputy commissioner, and most of Gujarat, Maharashtra, Madhya Pradesh, Tamil Nadu and Andhra Pradesh used the terminology of collector and continues to do so to this day. Revenue collection during the later days of the British Raj was a miniscule part of their work—maybe less than a per cent. But the nomenclature, 'collector', gave the misleading impression that the official's job was to collect taxes.

The Revenue Code framed by the British in the nineteenth century governed the life of the revenue officers—from the village officer to the collector, commissioner and above. The code prescribed that the assistant collector should spend 15 nights and 20 days outside his headquarters, camping in the other talukas, villages and forests of his jurisdiction. In the areas governed by the British Raj before Independence, most villages had a village office, called the *chaura* or *chaupal*, where the *talati* kept his official records. The rural building had a fairly large room with a tiled roof and a veranda with trellised walls, where visitors could wait under the shade. Whenever the *mamlatdar* or the assistant collector visited the village, the *talati* would produce a camp cot to supplement the solid wooden cushion-less chaise longue, a deep armchair with a cane back and seat. It used to have extendable and foldable arms, which the British officer used to put his feet up, and wide arm rests for him to balance his whiskey glass. The cot was to make your night comfortable. After a couple of such 'comfortable' nocturnal sojourns, I carried my own folding camp bed, a thin cotton mattress, a pillow and a blanket for the cold nights. But, unfortunately, in the villages of the Radhanpur subdivision, the nawabs who had ruled for a couple of centuries never thought of visiting the villages of their dominion, much less of camping there. If at all they ventured into their uncharted territory for shikar, they sent in their luxurious well-equipped tents. So, these villages had no such *chauras*, and the officers had to spend the night on a raised platform (open to the street) at the entrance of the house of the village headman. This was called a *chabootra*. The headman would, of course, provide a couple of cotton sheets tied across the wooden pillars to isolate the platform from public gaze. He would also be hospitable enough to provide a camp cot. The subordinate officers, like the *mamlatdar*, the police inspector, the revenue inspector, not to speak of the camel or the horse, too, would be accommodated by the villagers. The headman would also be generous enough to provide a simple meal of *bhakri* (a dry unleavened hard bread) with a glass of excellent unpolluted sweet milk to soften it. Sometimes, if the village happened to grow vegetables, he would have a potato or beans curry. But this was a rare luxury for a lucky few. Potatoes were never washed of the earth adhering to their contours and crevices, and were never peeled before cooking. I often spent some time before a meal to peel off the skin from each single piece, pile up a sufficient quality and then break bread.

Most of the villages in my jurisdiction were inhabited by Rabaris, with a minority of Patels and Rajputs. There was, of course, a ghetto of Harijans located on the outskirts of the village. They were not allowed to use any of the common facilities of the village—school, drinking water well, dispensary and other institutions. They rendered all the menial services to the villagers, such as cheap or free labour on the farms, removal of manure and dead cattle from the backyards, skinning the carcasses and disposing them, and such other miscellaneous lowly jobs that the upper castes considered taboo. In exchange, they were given some wages in kind, mostly in the form of food grains, like millets and so on. All men may be born free but not equal. The Harijans fell, and fall to this day, in the unequal category. The Rabaris, of course, belong to the upper class.

There were diverse theories about the origin of the Rabaris—they descended from the Huns when Toramana and Mihirakula ruled over large parts of northern and western India in the sixth century. Since they were known as worshippers of Shiva, the Rabaris, as descendants of the Huns, got absorbed and integrated into the Indian ethnic mélange. They retained their facial characteristics and were staunch Hindus. Both their men and women were tall, well-built and fair-skinned. Many a morning, I have sat on the *chabootra* and watched the Rabari girls, tall and handsome, with water-filled brass pots on their heads and their stately progress in single file down the village street. Some of them had blue eyes and brown hair, betraying their mixed racial ancestry. Most of them had their chins tattooed, beauty spots to ward off the evil eye.

My mandate under government orders was to determine the quantum of wasteland available in each village and distribute it among the landless Harijans who lived on the outskirts of the village in their ghettos. I examined the records of the first village I visited and found that it had 140 acres of wasteland. Sitting on the *chabootra*, I called a meeting of all the villagers. I asked the Harijans to gather around as well. The Harijans came and sat separately in a group.

'The government has ordered me to determine the available quantum of wasteland in this village and distribute it among the deserving landless Harijans of the village. All those Harijans who possess any land please raise their hands,' I announced.

There was a long silence, both among the Rabaris and Rajputs sitting to the right, and the Harijans sitting to the left. No one raised a hand. I thought perhaps they had not understood the purport of my announcement. My Gujarati was still in a state of immaturity, so I asked the *mamlatdar* to repeat my announcement in clearer terms. He did.

'There is no wasteland in the village,' said the oldest member of the Harijan community. I was taken aback. The village records very clearly showed, survey number by survey number, the extent of wasteland apart from and in addition to common pastureland, known as *gauchar*. So, I asked them to explain their assertion. It took long investigative research and probing enquiries to discover that all the wasteland had been illegally usurped by the Rabari and Rajput landlords, and they were merrily enjoying the usufruct of that land for the last several years, illegally and without even paying any land revenue on it.

'But that is illegal. They cannot simply appropriate government wasteland when they have plenty of land of their own,' I said. 'They will have to vacate that land and hand it over to the government. I will then distribute it to the landless.'

'But, sir, the land was lying fallow. We have made it cultivable,' one of the usurping landowners intervened. He obviously believed that wasteland lying idle should be put to good use. There was a point in what he was saying.

'That was no justification for usurping government land.' I was rather angry. 'It didn't belong to you,' I said firmly. My tone was quite acerbic. Perhaps unjustifiably so. The assembly of the upper-caste farmers turned sullen. Some of them were frowning, some glowering and most were giving me dour looks. I could get away with that approach in 1963. Today I would be lynched.

That night, the headman, on whose *chabootra* I was camping, served me the usual *bhakri* and milk for dinner but did not sit down to give me company. That was a polite indication of his hostility to my mission. Most of the villagers did not accompany me to the forest with towel, soap and bucket of water as they used to do earlier when I went to perform my morning chores.

The next morning, I went to the fields with the *mamlatdar* and other revenue officers to locate and demarcate the identified wasteland and hand it over to the nominated landless Harijan labourers. It took me the whole day to get the ownership document, the *patta*, made out in the names of the reluctant new owners and put them in possession. It was lucky for the Harijans that since it was off season, there were no standing crops on the fields. Else there would have been stronger protests from the usurpers instead of a mere sullen boycott.

After completing the work in this village, having dispossessed the usurpers and putting the landless in possession, I proceeded to the next village with my team. I was patting myself on the back sincerely believing that I had accomplished an act of social justice. By now, I had become savvy and did not expect to find smooth sailing. In the next village, too, the same scenario repeated itself. Most of the wasteland had been usurped by the upper castes, and they were sitting snug. When I started the proceedings, I found greater resistance in the second village. The revenue inspector, Hussain Khan, informed me that the culprits of the first village had already sent word to all the surrounding villages about my portended visit and its 'nefarious' purpose. I was becoming persona non grata among the upper castes. It was the surviving *iqbal* of the erstwhile feudal regime that I was provided a *chabootra* for my nocturnal sojourn and a *bhakri* and glass of milk for dinner. But those were the days when the shock of power and awe of authority created both by the British and their minion maharajas and nawabs had left the villages sullenly subdued. No one openly rebelled against the diktat of the collector or the SDM.

Though the palpable hostility of the villagers was obvious, neither the revenue officials nor I was ever overtly threatened by the displaced land grabbers. There was no open rebellion nor any violence. Today, the situation has drastically changed. The Harijans and the revenue officials would all probably be lynched in the fields.

I could cover over thirty villages in the next three months. The Harijans from some of the villages came later to Radhanpur and complained that once I had left the village, the landlords had thrown them out and repossessed the land. I instructed the police to register complaints against such landlords and proceed against them under the law. I did not have enough police force to station in each village. I thought that since those lands had been officially mutated in their names, the Harijans would get physical possession eventually.

The nawab of Radhanpur was a fair-complexioned, clean-shaven, dapper little man. He had succeeded to the gaddi when his father-in-law was killed while spear-hunting. The nawab had three pastimes—rummy on Saturday nights, nightingale training and arranging fights for them with his *karbhari's* birds, and smoking a full tin of Craven. He was a very hospitable man, and occasionally, he would send me some specially cooked viands from his kitchen. Once, he took me out on a hunting trip into the Rann of Kutch. We took some twenty vehicles (many of them could have participated with great distinction in vintage car rallies) for the shikar, saw some herds of *chinkaras* (Indian gazelle) chased them and failed to hit anything. We returned to the fort in a single jeep that had survived the rigours of the chase into the marsh of the Rann.

Within a few days of this adventure, I had to leave Radhanpur.

OF COCONUTS AND CLAY FEET

Mr Vyas, the collector of Banaskantha in Palanpur, was a fairly competent officer and very pleasant to his juniors.

One fine morning, I received orders from Ahmedabad to immediately proceed to Palanpur to relieve Mr Vyas and take charge as collector. This came as a pleasant surprise, for I had completed less than four years in service, and one never got an independent charge of a district before seven or eight years. So, getting charge of a whole district within less than four years of service was something of a record in my career.

When I reported for duty at the collectorate, Mr Vyas was in a despondent mood. After the exchange of charge documents, I saw him off at the gate.

The first thing I did was to call for the papers Mr Vyas had drawn up to auction off the golden arabesque roof of the office and cancel the auction. I also recorded the reasons for my decision to prevent any future philistine from taking an insensitive decision. I do not know whether that heritage has survived the succeeding decades.

The collector's bungalow was a large sprawling edifice, built in the colonial style to suit the lifestyle and comfort of the British political agent. Palanpur Agency, established in 1819, supervised the four native states of Palanpur, Radhanpur, Tharad and Wav, and the minor principalities of Varahi, Santalpur, Kankrej and Deesa. In its heyday, the political agent, who was always an Englishman, acted as a session judge, a DM and a general administrator for an area of about 7,000 square miles, with scattered towns and villages, the largest ones being Palanpur, Radhanpur, Deesa and Tharad. The British had even established an army cantonment at Deesa, ostensibly to help the native states against marauders from Sindh but actually to ensure that the native rulers did not build up any military strength of their own and conspire together to challenge the British Empire. Throughout their rule in India, the British never trusted the native states, large or small, and in turn, the native rulers, too, suspected the Empire of perfidy in all their actions. There were, of course, exceptions like Sir Pertab of Jodhpur, who 'yearned' to die on the battlefield with the name of Queen Victoria on his lips. The British Empire, at that time, covered half the old world. In fact, it was not for nothing that Indians used to say 'the sun never sets on the British Empire', as even God did not trust them in darkness. The rulers did not trust them even in daylight. That is perhaps why the British were reputed to have the most rigid code of immorality. Other nations used force to subdue, but the British used chicanery. The British did not eschew force when it was needed.

The Agency House, which was now the residence of the collector, of course, had several bedrooms to accommodate not only the family of the agent but important guests, both from India and abroad. Old-timers serving in the house and gardens used to show me the vast bedrooms that had been honoured by the nocturnal repose of the governor of Bombay or similar other dignitaries when they came hunting deer and the great Indian bustard. There was a humongous banquet hall, housing a long teak dining table with a capacity to seat fifty guests. The roof was more than thirty feet high, and the lights and fans installed later were hung on long leads. An ancient cloth-covered fan, eight feet wide and four feet broad, still hung on one side, with a long-frayed rope passing through a hole in the wall on a pulley wheel. In the days of yore, it used to be pulled by an Indian servitor. A whitewashed ceiling served as a false roof. But long neglect had taken away the white gloss. Whenever I gave a dinner there—not for fifty but for a dozen guests sitting huddled at the far end of the table—I always used to hear scurrying noises above.

The large drawing room faced a wide covered veranda. The political agent would receive the visiting local royalty without stepping out of his drawing room, while rulers could retain their prestige without having to get off at the gate and walk up to the drawing room. Dignity of both was protected, and the protocol was not breached.

There were two hard tennis courts in a state of utter disrepair and a long-abandoned swimming pool, half-filled with earth and spouting weeds and vines. The lawns and gardens were restored to the extent possible with the help of the ancient, decrepit gardeners—survivors from the British Raj. We used to play tennis whenever the nawabs of Palanpur and Radhanpur dropped in for tea. Mr Sundaram, the supernumerary assistant collector, joined to make a foursome. There were also four large tortoises living permanently in the gardens. They would be discovered, now and then, sleeping in the shade of some bush or in the humid roots of some tree. Musa, the oldest living servitor in the bungalow, claimed that one of the long-dead political agents had brought them with him from abroad, maybe a century ago, and they have lived here since then.

My mother, who was psychic, took one look at the old agency bungalow, which was fairly well-furnished, with alcoves in each bedroom, fireplaces, curtains and draperies, and refused to live there. My wife, too, concurred with her. So, we occupied a comparatively modern annexe. This had no kitchen. We used part of the veranda as a kitchen.

Within a week of my taking over as the collector of Banaskantha, I was faced with a piquant situation. Mr Vakharia, an influential community leader of the district, wrote to me that there was an urgent need to call a meeting of the Ambaji temple committee to address a controversy that was raging between two groups of temple devotees. He was apprehensive that if not resolved quickly, the controversy would spill over into the whole community.

I learnt that the district of Banaskantha, more particularly the Danta taluka, had within its jurisdiction, one of the most famous pilgrim centres of Gujarat—the Shri Arasuri Ambaji Mata Devasthan. Ambaji is worshipped as one of the manifestations of Sati, the consort of Shiva. It is reckoned as one of the original Shakti *pitha*s, and its antiquity is proved by an interesting feature—the temple has no idol in its sanctum sanctorum. The goddess is represented by a triangular *Vishwa Yantra* with the syllable '*Shree*' in the centre, surrounded by figures and letters, indecipherable today. Legend has it that when Shiva was carrying around the body of his wife, Sati, her dismembered parts fell at various places in India. Her heart fell where the temple stands today. The temple itself is not very large as temples go and does not have any distinct architectural features as do many of the temples of South India built later, such as the Meenakshi, the Srirangam or the Hampi temples. The temple itself, as it stands, was built in the fourth century. But since Ambaji Mata is to Gujarat what Durga Mata is to Bengal, it attracts a large number of devotees throughout the year. The number swells to millions on special festivals. Until 1947, the temple management was directly under the maharaja of Danta. After Independence, the temple came under the management of the state of Bombay, and later still, under Gujarat. To regulate the flow of pilgrims and to create facilities for them, the government constituted an Ambaji Mata Devasthan Trust in 1955, with twenty members and the collector as the chairman. When the legislation creating the trust was passed, it was not envisaged that Banaskantha may one day have a Muslim collector who would have to administer the affairs of the temple in the best interest of the temple, its devotees and the Hindu community.

Mr Vakharia was an important member of the trust. On receiving his letter, I requested him to come and see me. He travelled up from Bombay, where he operated a flourishing business, to meet me. He explained to me the essence of the controversy. It appeared that inside the temple sanctum sanctorum, where the *yantra* was housed, was a very small chamber. The devotees who brought their offering, especially the coconut, broke it inside on a stone. The coconut water splashed all over the floor. Since thousands of coconuts were thus broken inside, the space was always slushy and slippery. One group represented by several members of the trust argued that coconuts should not be permitted to be broken inside the sanctum sanctorum, defiling the whole space and affecting the devotees, but outside, at a specified place. Another group of trustees argued that the breaking of the coconut before the deity was an act of devotional worship, and since it had been the practice since time immemorial, no one had the right to prohibit it. My predecessor, it seems, had called the meeting of the trust once or twice, with no decisions being arrived at. The controversy continued to simmer.

Mr Vakharia suggested I call a third meeting and persuade the trustees to arrive at a decision, one way or the other, to resolve the controversy that was affecting the faith of thousands of visiting pilgrims every day.

Before calling a meeting, I thought it advisable to visit the temple and get a first-hand view of the problem. Of course, I took this decision with some trepidation. After all, I was a Muslim called upon to take a decision affecting a faith that was not my own. Would it be acceptable to the others? Was I capable of understanding the feelings of the Hindus in this regard?

Mark Twain once remarked: 'Very often in matters concerning religion and politics, a man's reasoning powers are not above the monkey's.' I did not want to make a monkey of myself by venturing into domains where angels feared to tread. Instead, I decided to go on a pilgrimage.

I left for the temple with my wife, my mother, who was a keen traveller, and my year-old son. En route, close to Ambaji town, I learnt that there were some beautiful Jain temples worth seeing. So, we made a diversion from the main road into an unpaved village road. We passed through a thick forest with old tamarisk, acacia and teak trees. A few miles later, we reached a clearing with a pool of clear limpid water surrounded by a creeping forest. And then a cluster of five marble temples burst upon our vision. Four of them crowded together and a fifth stood a little apart as a sentinel. Legend has it that these temples were erected by one Vimal Shah, a Jain prime minister of a Hindu ruler of Gujarat. The word erected does not correctly describe those beautiful edifices. To me, it appeared that each was carved out of a single marble hill, like David emerging out of a large slab of marble or the Kailash temple of Ellora. The pillars, the walls, the gateways and the friezes that adorned them had such an unearthly artistic unity about them and so well-integrated were they that even after almost sixty years, the beauty of the vision has not faded from my mind's eye. I see, even today, the marble tassels with tiny marble bells that hung on both sides of the marble *torans* that adorned the entrance. Any moment, I imagined, a gust of wind would set them jingling.

These temples have been standing for more than a thousand years in the midst of a forest clearance, with no visible maintenance, no watchman, no guardian up to the time of my visit. There were no boards indicating the Archaeological Survey of India (ASI) was even aware of them. I was told that the forest of Danta abounded in tigers, panthers, bears and other predators. Perhaps the fear of these predators kept robbers away from despoiling these ancient temples, and the ASI's neglect had kept out the despoilers. Perhaps an invisible hand kept the creeping forest vegetation from insinuating itself into the walls and pillars, as had happened in the case of Angkor Wat and Borobudur. For a thousand years, these Kumbharia temples have stood unprotected, conserving their pristine beauty, a testimony to the skill of unknown artists who must have spent years over the delicate traceries.

I was received at the gate of the Ambaji temple complex by the priests. As the chairman of the trust, I received all the temple honours reserved for the erstwhile maharaja of Danta as the head of the temple. As I was conducted to the main temple to attend the special pooja that was organised in honour of my first visit to the temple, I admired the understanding, the tolerance, the large-hearted acceptance of a Muslim as the chief trustee of the most important Hindu temple of Gujarat. That was in the early sixties. In a similar case, an act was passed by the Jammu and Kashmir government in 2000 when the Amarnath Shrine Board was constituted with the governor as the chairman of the trust. Mr N.N. Vohra, the governor, informed me that, according to the act, no Muslim can be the chairman of the Amarnath Shrine Board. If a Muslim is ever appointed as the governor of J&K, the act lays down alternatives to bypass such an unthinkable contingency. We seem to have travelled a long way over the last six decades.

When I inspected the sanctum sanctorum after the pooja, I saw that the space was very constricted, perhaps not more than ten square feet. Undoubtedly, if a large number of coconuts got broken in that small space and all the sweet water splashed out on the floor, it would create very unhygienic conditions. So, the point of those who wanted the coconuts to be broken outside had some weight. But the argument that a tradition that has been continuously observed for centuries should not be set aside blithely also could not be overlooked. Religion lives on traditions and rejects innovations, however reasonable or rational.

We stayed at the well-appointed guest house of the temple, where the erstwhile maharaja used to stay whenever he had to make a night halt. The food was supplied from the temple kitchen—excellent vegetarian dishes cooked in pure ghee and served in gold and silver utensils. The comfortable stay and the good food did not, however, help me resolve the controversy.

I consulted Mr Vakharia and a few other members. They advised that I should call in some pandas from Varanasi, the real experts, to address this knotty issue.

Whenever an expert committee or commission is appointed, it is advisable to appoint either a one-man commission or a three-man committee. Somebody once remarked that the most effective committee should consist of three members, one of whom should be chronically ill and the other permanently absent.

I, therefore, wrote to Varanasi and invited three pandas to come over to the temple to advise me. But I received a response that five of them would come. I agreed. All of them duly arrived. Before starting their study, they all performed several poojas.

They stayed for a week as temple guests and studied the problem from all angles.

I summoned a meeting of the trust. This time, almost all the members from Gujarat, Maharashtra and the rest of India turned up. I opened the session by asking the pandits to present their recommendations.

'Before we do that,' said their spokesman, the senior-most panda, a well-fed priest with a clean-shaven head and hanging jowls, 'We have not received our *dakshina* (honorarium). We should all get that.'

I bent down and asked Mr Vakharia, 'What does he mean?'

'I anticipated this,' he murmured. 'In anticipation of your approval, I have bought five silk dhotis and five *angavastram*s, and drawn some cash too.'

The golden-bordered dhotis, *angavastram*s and cash were ceremoniously handed over by me to the guardians of the faith.

Now that the demands of the pandas had been met, it was time to revert to the business at hand.

'We would like to hear the opinions of the members, sir, before we present our recommendations.'

Mr Mehta, one of the members representing the traditionalists, advanced all the arguments on behalf of the status quo. The pandas nodded their heads in agreement. Mr Patel, on behalf of the progressives, put forward all the weighty arguments as to why the coconut-breaking should go out of the sanctum sanctorum. I was watching the pandas. They were nodding their heads in agreement.

'We have studied all the relevant shlokas of the scriptures,' said the pandits. 'And we have heard the views of the members of the trust. We find nothing in the scriptures that sanctions that the coconuts should be broken only inside the sanctorum. Nor do we find anything there that says the contrary. Both the options are well within the scriptural sanctions. So long as the coconuts are broken, both alternatives are acceptable.'

Having pronounced this solemn advice, delivered in Solomon-like tones, the pandas departed to catch the train to Delhi on the way to Varanasi. And we were left exactly where we were before.

So, I went back to myself for expert advice. We discussed the issues, went to the temple again and decided to isolate a small corner within the sanctorum, raise a one-foot-high wall around the enclosure, provide a stone slab and drainage pipe, and laid down that all coconuts should be broken only within this square enclosure. That was a compromise. It did not satisfy all parties. But that is the essence of a compromise. It never satisfies all parties, but it works.

Every DM (or collector) was provided a code book that was to be kept in his personal custody. Every month, he received a coded password, which was a sentence. He was to memorise this password, or rather sentence, and destroy the paper.

One day, I received a message that the issue of the Kashmir dispute was about to be aired in the UN. V.K. Krishna Menon was representing India at the UN. It was perhaps felt that his arguments would be strengthened by a large number of telegrams from prominent Muslims of India. They would add further ammunition to his already fiery oratory. I was, and remain, an admirer of Krishna Menon, who was an alumnus of Presidency College, Madras, from where I, too, had got my degree decades after his graduation.

The telegrams emphatically and forcefully supporting India's stand were duly drafted and dispatched. Since the whole operation was carried out secretly and in camera, so as not to give the impression that it was a stage-managed, government-sponsored effort, the press got no inkling of it. However, the fact that a large number of prominent Muslim leaders and organisations had been closeted with the collector could not be kept under wraps from all prying eyes. So, the local papers went to town the next day, questioning what a Muslim DM was doing in secret with Muslim leaders and organisations. Was he hatching a conspiracy? Was he planning a coup to once again merge the district with Pakistan? Or was he planning a communal riot against the Hindus? Some busybodies also wrote letters to the government against me. Since the government knew the truth, I never got these letters nor saw their contents.

Doubts about my patriotism and bona fides as an Indian IAS officer were further strengthened in the minds of some of the rabid elements when news leaked out that I had met some Pakistani officials from across the border. This, too, was an officially sponsored visit to discuss and settle some issues related to the borders between the two countries. It was organised by the Ministry of Foreign Affairs of India. The officers of the survey departments of Pakistan and India met in my office and under my aegis to compare maps and determine the true position. Under government instructions, this, too, was kept under wraps.

It was apparent, even as early as 1964, that something was brewing between India and Pakistan. Tensions between the two countries was building up inexorably. I received another coded message in April that Mrs Maragatham Chandrasekar, union deputy home minister, had been instructed to visit Banaskantha and travel to the border outposts in the desert, manned by the Border Security Force (BSF), to bolster the morale of the soldiers and officers there.

Mrs Chandrasekar hailed from South India. After completing her education in London, she returned to India to join the freedom movement. In 1964, when I met her, she was in her late forties and was serving as the deputy home minister in Nehru's council of ministers. When I received her at the Palanpur railway station, she was a bit under the weather and looked tired. Having made her comfortable in the guest house, I called in my officers to plan the next day's trip to the border outposts in the desert.

The Thar Desert forms the border between India and Pakistan. It is perhaps the largest desert of the subcontinent. A larger part of it lies in Pakistan Sindh, but a substantial part of the advancing sands constantly threatens the states of Rajasthan, Punjab and Gujarat. The Rann of Kutch, too, is believed to be part of the Thar Desert.

Even in April and May, the day temperature in the desert sometimes soars up to 50°C. In an open jeep, with the hot wind blowing from any which direction, one would feel as though one is travelling through a blast furnace. Concerned about how the old lady—for a young man of twenty-six, anyone bordering on fifty would appear old—would stand this foray into the boiling desert, we decided to carry a fifty-kilogram ice slab kept in a tin tray, covered with wood shavings, in each of the three jeeps to provide some cool relief to her.

Mrs Chandrasekar sat in the front beside the driver, and I sat in the back with my peon on the opposite seat. The ice slab was placed between the two of us. As soon as we entered the desert, the minister started panting due to the heat. The jeep was stopped, and the peon dipped a Turkish towel in the cold water of the melted ice and tied it across the front window. This immediately cooled the front portion of the jeep; the back was cooler because of the ice slab. This manoeuvre was repeated every few miles, as the towel got dry within minutes from the blast of the hot wind. The desert was shimmering hot. As far as the eyes could see, it was a bleak landscape. From time to time, we saw camel caravans, fort walls and castle towers. They vanished on our approach. This was the first experience of mirages for the lady. She was amazed at the magical illusions.

'Perhaps this is the maya that is mentioned in our scriptures,' she remarked. 'It is a dream.'

It is the desert's dream, not mine, not hers, I thought. Mir Taqi Mir has put the situation so aptly:

Hasti apni hubaab ki si hai
Yeh numaish saraab ki si hai

(Our existence is just a mere bubble.
Its appearance is nothing but a mirage.)

Once we saw a herd of *chinkara*s from a distance. 'Is that a mirage too?' she asked. But the herd scattered on our approach. It was real.

The *khejri* tree is native to the arid areas of the old world. It grows wild in the Thar Desert. For eight to ten feet from the ground, it has no branches, it develops an evergreen canopy after that height. The Bishnois of Rajasthan hold it in reverence, and someone told me that many religious rituals are performed in its shade. The sight of this tree in the desert certainly provides great relief.

Mile after mile, we saw only the shimmering sand, with dunes sometimes rising up to a height of twenty feet or more. It was not so much the absence of man or beast that one's consciousness noticed in the desert but the presence of God. No wonder, the famous Urdu poet Iqbal remarked: '*Fitrat ke maqasid ki karta hai nigahbani Ya banda-e-saharaee, ya marde kohistanee* (the purposes of nature are safeguarded by only the desert dweller or the mountain man).' Perhaps this was the reason that all great prophets were born in the deserts and all rishis lived in mountain caves.

In the brooding hush that lulled our consciousness, Mrs Chandrasekar suddenly noticed that there were no tracks of any kind in the virgin sands.

'How does the driver know where to go? How does he steer?' she asked anxiously.

'He is an experienced driver. He has travelled many times on this route. He notices many landmarks that are invisible to us,' I reassured her.

After driving for four hours, we saw at a distance, a clump of some tall trees and a building standing in the midst of nowhere. The driver told us that we were approaching the oasis where the main BSF outpost was located. Within half an hour, we did reach an oasis, extending perhaps over a couple of acres. A few eucalyptus trees and a *khejri* tree gave some shade to the open area. Near a barn, there were a dozen camels tethered, lugubriously munching away their feed. There were a couple of forlorn jeeps, their paint scoured by the blowing desert sand, standing near the steps of an old and crumbling one-storeyed building.

Every line of it cried out that it was built in the colonial times. The army major commanding the outpost came out to welcome us with a small guard of honour for the minister.

Inside, there was a hall with a few wooden chairs scattered here and there. Two large fireplaces at both ends of the hall proclaimed their incongruity with the outside temperature hovering around 50°C. But the officer explained that in winter, the desert cooled to zero or sub-zero temperatures, which was when the fireplaces came alive.

My curiosity, as to why this outpost was established here in British times, was strengthened by the minister herself asking about it. The officer explained, 'It is true that we did not have a border with another country during those days. But this place falls right in the middle of the route from the once-native state of Kutch to native states of the Palanpur agency. A number of enterprising smugglers from the Trucial States of the Gulf would bring in gold, horses, Chinese bosky silk and other commodities here. Without paying any customs duties or octroi, they would smuggle them into British India. The British government, representing a nation of shopkeepers, never lost an opportunity to make money. So, it established this customs outpost here to patrol the surrounding area and ensure that no taxable commodity escaped their net. The camel corps you see over there is also a legacy from those days.'

'But now that there is no custom border what is the purpose of locating the outpost here?' I asked. 'Now, we have the border with Pakistan close by. We got readymade facilities here, so the BSF located the outpost here,' he replied.

'Who manned this outpost in those days?' I asked.

'The British, of course. They would not trust an Indian to collect the taxes for the state. A Scotsman would be posted here. He lived here alone with the Indian jawans—summer and winter. An orderly cooked his food in a shack outside.'

'No wonder the British could rule India with just 400 white dedicated officials,' I said to myself.

As we were talking, tea was brought for us in a tin kettle and tin mugs. The tea was salty. The officer explained that no freshwater was available in the oasis. They only found saline water in the shallow wells—called *virdas*. They cooked their food and made tea with this water.

The minister addressed the jawans who had assembled, talked to them of the threat from Pakistan, the need to be ever vigilant and not to slacken in patrolling the border. Thereafter, we left to visit a couple of other outposts where living conditions were even more difficult. The drill was repeated.

To my surprise, I learned from the *mamlatdar* that there was a village in the middle of the desert, close to the Pakistan border. We decided to visit the village and enquire after the welfare and well-being of its inhabitants.

It turned out to be a small hamlet with about fifty or so mud houses with thatch roofs. The *mamlatdar* assembled the villagers in the open space in the centre of the commons, under the canopy of a large tamarisk tree, with its slender branches and small overlapping green leaves giving a deep shade.

It was interesting to see these sturdy, strong-bodied and well-built men and women, dressed in the traditional attire of the Rabaris, eking out a difficult existence in the middle of that inhospitable terrain. What little patches of cultivable land they could snatch from the threatening fangs of the advancing desert was farmed diligently to yield perhaps a few vegetables and a few grains of cereals. Any habitation established in this arid desert was an act of indomitable human will imposed on a relentless soil, ever unwilling and resistant to yield. It is from such stock that pioneers are born. The minister addressed the villagers in her broken Hindi, half-understood by them. But accustomed to authority and inured to the occasional and rare visits of officials, they sat and listened courteously to her speech on the concern of the PM in Delhi for their welfare.

'You must have heard of the leader, our beloved PM, Shri Jawaharlal Nehru,' she intoned. The wooden expression on their faces told her they had not. They had not heard of any beloved leader of the minister. Noticing their blank stares, she changed to another rhetorical question.

'Of course, you have heard of Mahatma Gandhi, the Father of our Nation,' she remarked in exasperation.

The wooden expressions became, if anything, more wooden. They had not heard of Mahatma Gandhi either.

In sheer frustration, she rebuked them. 'I am sorry to note that you have not heard of Jawaharlal Nehru and Mahatma Gandhi, who have brought us freedom from the oppressive British Raj.' Then turning towards me she said, 'I am requesting your collector here...' Before she could complete her request, the audience came alive at the mention of the collector and the sudden realisation that he was present in flesh and blood among them. There was a flurry, and half a dozen elderly men got up and said they wanted to present some petitions about their urgent needs to the collector.

The minister sat down heavily. 'They have never heard of Nehru and Gandhi, but they certainly have heard of the collector,' she remarked ruefully. 'So much for independence and the passing of the British Raj!'

For the simple folk of a remote village in the middle of the desert, freedom, British Raj, heroes of independence and even a minister had no meaning. For them, authority—the highest authority—meant the collector.

During my tours in the district, I often had to make a stop for a cup of tea by the wayside tea stalls. I would get down from the jeep, stroll to the kiosk under the cool shade of a jamun tree, where there would be a couple of old, rickety benches thrown around, where the customers sat to enjoy their strong brew and crunch the *farsan* the kiosk-owner fried fresh every morning. These long strips of fried lentil flour batter, called *fafda*, eaten with pickled green chillies, were the staple snacks all over Gujarat. I still enjoy them.

While standing around waiting for the tea, I would chat with the customers sitting around, who did not recognise me, on local matters. A lot of useful information on the many happenings in that locality would be freely provided to a passing stranger. On one such visit, while travelling in the Deesa taluka, I noticed that the tea-stall owner kept a separate set of glasses and cups in a corner of the platform where he brewed the tea. Some of the customers would be served in those cups only. The owner would pour the tea from the aluminium kettle directly into the cups. The customer would take the cup and sit on his haunches away from the bench-users, and after finishing his drink, take the cup to a bucket of water kept near a bush, rinse and replace it on the allotted corner of the counter.

On enquiry, it was revealed that these customers were the untouchables whom Gandhiji had blessed with the sobriquet Harijan—literally meaning 'Children of God'. Like the oyster, uncomfortable with the grain of sand entering it, covers it with nacre to make it more acceptable, Indian society, uncomfortable with such terms as pariah, untouchable and *dhed*, covered them with names such as Scheduled Caste, Harijan and Dalit. Young and immature, still unaware of the ways of the world and labouring under the hangover of all the books of liberal philosophy and idealistic sermons dinned into my ears in the National Academy, I was furious to learn of how the Harijans were treated even in the tea stalls. I revealed my identity to the tea-stall owner and told him in no uncertain terms that untouchability was constitutionally abolished, and that he could be prosecuted and punished with imprisonment for keeping separate utensils for Harijans and not allowing them to sit on the benches along with other customers.

'But, sir,' pleaded the man, 'I do not prohibit them. They do so voluntarily. They wash the utensils on their own.'

'Why do the other customers not do so?'

'I don't know. As they don't, we do the washing and cleaning.'

Then I asked one of the Harijans whether this was true. 'Sir, we have been doing this for generations. We do not require to be told where to sit when we are in the gathering of the *savarna*s (the upper castes). We know our place. We have been washing our own glasses, cups and plates in all public places.'

But my anger was not abated at the docile acquiescence of the downtrodden at this blatant discrimination. I asked my *pattawala* to take out all those offending utensils, smash them and grind them into the dust—very high-handed indeed. The mix of idealism, authority and immaturity often is the precursor to self-destruction. That is what happened to Joan of Arc and Robespierre and Danton.

After that, I started a campaign against this kind of discrimination. No doubt, there must have been a simmering anger at the back of my mind against what happened to the landless labourers in Radhanpur and Deodhar talukas, whose lands were snatched away the moment my back was turned. On all my official tours in the district, I stopped at every tea stall on the route and got the offending utensils smashed. Normally, I should have followed the law—the The Untouchability (Offences) Act, 1955. But I did not have the patience nor the time to waste making out legal cases against the offenders, for some clever lawyers would have found loopholes in the evidence and got them off. Since the offenders believed that laws were made only to be broken, I did not want justice to be tainted by mere legalities. After all, as wisely remarked, laws are like cobwebs. They only catch the flies. The hornets and wasps break through.

The news about my campaign got fairly wide publicity. Some favourable. Mostly unfavourable. The local media was in the hands of the upper castes. No doubt, this was reported to the higher-ups in Ahmedabad, especially to the political leadership.

Balwantrai Mehta was the then CM of Gujarat. He was believed to be a Gandhian. He was elected to the Lok Sabha in 1957, and later succeeded Dr Jivraj Mehta as the second CM of Gujarat.

I met him when he came to my district at the behest of a local social worker to address the courtesans of Guddanpur, and had long discussions with him on the ways and means of rehabilitating them.

One day, a delegation of the Harijans of the district came to call on me.

'Sir, we have come to request you to stop this campaign against the tea shops.'

'Why? I am doing this because the law dictates that there shall be no discrimination against you. I am cancelling the licenses of all such restaurants who keep separate cups and saucers.'

'But, sir, we are suffering as a result of your well-meaning campaign. The *savarnas* believe we have instigated you to undertake this campaign. So, in the villages, they are taking it out on us. They are stopping all essential supplies to us from the shops and withholding our wages for fieldwork. They are boycotting us. Sir, please give up this campaign. Our time will come. And when it comes, we will deal with these *savarnas* ourselves. You cannot protect us in each and every village.'

The early sixties were years of great shortages in food grains, sugar, jaggery and even edible oils. Most of these items were rationed and supplied in specified quantities and subsidised prices to the vulnerable sections of the population, mostly Harijans and other depressed classes, through a public distribution system (PDS). All the poor were issued ration cards, and they were to draw the prescribed quanta from the authorised shops, which, in turn, received their supplies from official sources. The PDS was a misnomer because most of the shops under this system were run by licensed private individuals—all *savarna*s. These were at first called ration shops and later 'fair price shops', which supplied wheat, rice and sugar to holders of ration cards, issued by the district civil supplies officer (DCSO), who worked under the collector. Elaborate rules and regulations, framed under the Essential Commodities Act, 1955, governed the operations of this system. The shop owner was required to maintain detailed stock registers, receipt books, full accounts of inflows and outflows, etc., and was required to produce and submit them to the DCSO and his staff at the time of inspections.

All rationing systems, the world over, are prone to corruption and misuse, whether run by the government directly or through private shops. The PDS system in India, then as now, is no exception. Whenever new ways of channeling the commodities for commercial purposes were discovered by the minions of the civil supplies department, the government introduced new rules and regulation to plug the loopholes. But a thief is always two steps ahead of the policeman. The more elaborate and complex the rules to prevent misuse, the more imaginative were the shopkeepers' ruse to get around it.

There was this well-to-do and well-known political leader in the Palanpur district who was fairly high up in the hierarchy of the ruling party and also an articulate member of the coordination committee of the district. This committee—consisting of all the MLAs representing the various segments of the district, the MPs representing the district, the district panchayat chief and other important officials of the district—

met every month under the chairmanship of the collector to discuss the problems of law and order, development projects, issues of health, education and civil supplies. This important dignitary, let's call him SS, used to be foremost in raising such issues, especially relating to civil supplies—tardy receipt of food grains from the Central Depot and sugar from the government stocks and inadequate quantities. SS also operated several ration shops in Palanpur and Deesa talukas. I received a spate of complaints about that gentleman. Even after full supplies were made from the government stocks, his shops never had enough to meet the demand. Most of the poor had to return empty-handed from his shops, as supplies ran out after a few customers received their quota. Preliminary enquiries revealed that most of the supply was diverted by him to his own wholesale godowns, from where he sold it to the retailers of his choice at market prices and made substantial profits.

'You are a political leader, holding a high position in the state hierarchy, Mr SS,' I told him when he came to see me after several summons. 'I am receiving these complaints against you. These supplies are meant for the needy and vulnerable people of the district, not to earn profit out of the sufferings of the poor.'

'All this is crap,' he vociferously denied the allegations, 'My political enemies are spreading these canards against me. Some of my own local party members are conspiring to blacken my reputation.'

'Why would they do it?' I asked.

'Because the chief minister is considering inducting me into the Cabinet in the next reshuffle. These enemies want to prevent that.'

'But I am not going by what they are saying. I have made my own preliminary enquiries, and what I am telling you is based on those enquiries.'

'I am not bothered by what enquiries you have made. I deny every one of your allegations,' he asserted and walked out of the office in a huff.

I called the civil supplies officer (CSO) and his senior inspectors and organised a simultaneous raid on all the shops and godowns owned by SS in the district. The evidence of the forged stock registers, the fake receipt books and the physical checks revealed wholesale misuse and diversion. I, therefore, sealed all his shops and godowns, after issuing him due notice, and lodged a prosecution in the court. The punishment for such offences, if proved, could range up to seven years of imprisonment.

There was utter consternation in all the political and official circles of not only the district but also the state. That a young inexperienced officer, in his very first posting as DM, could take such a rash step, amazed them. The nawab of Radhanpur, over sixty years of age and having actually ruled over a state, was very sympathetic but commiserated with me for the consequence I would have to face. But I was unfazed.

Today, I stand amazed at my own audacity. I had read Chanakya's *Arthashastra*, Machiavelli's *The Prince and the Discourses* and Sun-Tzu's *Art of War*, but their lessons had not been learnt by me at that age. Capital punishment for the kind of *lese majeste* I committed was not in the law.

Later in my career, I continued to tilt at giants, disguised as windmills or vice versa. But I took precautions and safety measures in advance to avoid being hurled off my Rosinante. Sancho Panza called Don Quixote a muddle-headed fool with frequent lucid intervals. In my lucid intervals, I built ramparts, towers, citadels and drawbridges. They helped a lot to save me from my follies.

Much, much later, I wrote a couplet in my diary:

Woh din ke uthate the har uftada alam hum
Ab khak basar walwalae saf shikani hai

(Those were the days when I picked up every fallen flag. But now my courage to break ranks is weltering in the dust.)

Within a day of my action against SS, I received a call from the civil supplies department that Shri Vajubhai Shah, the civil supplies minister, was coming to Palanpur, and I should make myself available. By noon, the minister was in my office.

'Do you realise what you have done?' He asked in quite an angry tone, even before he took a sip of the tea placed before him.

'No, sir,' I said, 'I think I have done my duty as required by the law.'

'Yes, but before closing down all the shops and sealing all the godowns you should have considered the repercussions. The poor cardholders will be victims.'

'Sir, I have allotted all the cardholders to other shops, so they will face no inconvenience. I am also making additional allocation of food grains and other essentials to these shops.'

My defence was airtight.

The minister was a bit nonplussed. By repercussions, he was considering the political repercussions, which were strictly not my concern.

'Mr SS is an important state functionary of the party. He is an honest man working for the welfare of the poor and the downtrodden of the district. That should have been considered when you took such drastic action.'

'But the available evidence does not bear out that he had the interests of the vulnerable people at heart. He was not working for the downtrodden and the depressed. He was only working for himself. You must have read the detailed report I sent to the government, sir, stating the overwhelming evidence which formed the basis of my action.'

'That's alright,' he said, brushing aside my explanation perfunctorily. 'What is to be done now?'

'Nothing by me, sir, the law will take its own course.' The minister stared at me for a long moment; 'His career will be ruined if he is convicted. He will be debarred from contesting any elections for six years. He will lose all his current positions in the party. He is a victim of some conspiracy.'

'If he is innocent, he can appeal against my order to the director of civil supplies, sir. I am sure, he will be exonerated if he has not committed the acts,' I said.

'Oh, I have seen the papers. You have made a watertight case against him. There is no use going for an appeal. Can you do something? Let your cancellation of his licences for PDS shops stand. That is punishment enough for him. But can you withdraw the prosecution? That will be good. It will save his political career.'

'I am sorry, sir,' I said, 'I cannot withdraw the prosecution because that addresses the main offence. If I withdraw the prosecution, the whole case has to be withdrawn.'

He stared at me with despair in his eyes and left. I knew then that I had not heard the last of the matter. Sure enough, the next day, I got a summons from the CM's office.

Balwantrai Mehta is, even today, honoured as the architect of the panchayat raj in the country. The Panchayat Raj Act, devolving power on the elected representatives of the people at the grassroots level, was enacted on the basis of the Balwantrai Mehta Committee report. Some months before, one of the social workers had persuaded him to visit a village in my jurisdiction where the *savarna*s led by an ex-bandit, Zalam Singh, were preventing Harijans from entering the temple. I was asked to visit the village, persuade Zalam Singh, the headman and the upper-caste villagers to join the CM in a procession of Harijans for a formal temple entry. Zalam Singh simply told me to go climb a tree.

I was quite confident that with his Gandhian background and his reputation for honesty, Balwantrai Mehta would understand and appreciate the action I had taken. Oh, the atrocious folly of being young and credulous. I used to believe in six impossible things before breakfast, when young.

The CM kept me waiting for over an hour when I reached the secretariat in Ahmedabad. Perhaps he was busy. Or perhaps it was to soften me up and make me more malleable, more amenable. When I was called in, he was pleasant enough but brusque.

'Vajubhai has spoken to you. Have you thought over what he suggested?' He asked without many preliminaries.

'I have, sir. But I see no way to accommodate his suggestions,' I said, politely enough.

'SS is a useful and important member of our party. We can't have him disqualified from politics. It will be a loss to the state.' He meant his political party. *Le etat ce partie.*

I had to wait for years to learn that the needs of the state, in reality the needs of politics, overrode many ethical considerations. And also the truth of Dr Johnson's remark about patriotism being the last resort. That day, Balwantrai Mehta, who I had held in high regard, fell from the pedestal of honesty and patriotism and shattered his feet of clay.

I remained silent. What could I say?

Vajubahi, who was present, added, 'I thought I had explained all this to you when we met in Palanpur yesterday. Why don't you agree?'

'Do you have any solution?' This from the CM.

In desperation, I said, 'There is a solution.'

Both of them looked expectantly towards me. Perhaps they thought I had softened enough to agree to withdraw the prosecution launched against SS. Perhaps it was impulse, perhaps it was bravado, perhaps it was thoughtless youth tinged with vanity.

'Sir, you could transfer me and post someone there who may act on the suggestions of the honourable minister,' I said, concealing my trepidation and my disappointment at seeing his clay feet.

'Hm,' said the CM, with a thoughtful puckering of his brow. I knew he was considering that as a possible solution.

I returned to Palanpur that evening in a pensive mood, having made the mistake of believing that everyone who publicly professed his devotion to Mahatma Gandhi was a Gandhian.

A week later, I received my marching orders. Someone more mature, more amenable was posted as collector in my place. Mr Bhamri, an ex-army man, was a mature, suave man, well-versed in the ways of the world. My wife, in an irreverent vein, said I was an '*ek din ka sultan* (king for a day).' Perhaps she was referring to the story of Benbuka in the *Thousand and One Nights*. At least Benbuka was rewarded well for his one-day administration by Haroun-al-Rashid. I had no such luck.

A few months after my departure from Palanpur, war did break out between India and Pakistan. CM Balwantrai Mehta, along with his wife and secretary, decided to visit the war front on the border of Kutch district in a four-seater plane. The Pakistan Air Force shot down the small aircraft, and all the four occupants lost their lives. Hitendra Desai, known as Hitubhai, succeeded him as the CM. Hitubhai was a protégé of Morarji Desai. They belonged to the same Anavil Desai caste and came from the same district.

Years later, I had occasion to meet SS in Delhi. By then, he had become a member of the union council of ministers, a cabinet minister.

OF BLOODSUCKERS AND WILD ASSES

In 1964, CM Balwantrai Mehta posted me as the district development officer (DDO) in Surendranagar, a district in Saurashtra. The district panchayat president under the Panchayat Raj Act was, in theory, a very powerful individual indeed. The DDO was the chief executive officer of the district panchayat. My predecessor in that office was one Mr P.V. Bhatt, a rather soft-spoken and apparently mild-mannered Brahmin. Under his mild and benign exterior, I learnt, much to my advantage, he concealed a Machiavellian brain. I discovered that before the members of the panchayat could read the Act and become aware of the powers that had been vested in them by the Act, Mr Bhatt as the first DDO had sat down to study and note every single section, clause, subclause and proviso of the Act where the word Act, power, authority was mentioned directly or indirectly. Then, in the very first meeting of the district panchayat, he had put up a comprehensive resolution before the panchayat.

Under this, all the powers vested in the panchayat were delegated to the the DDO. Effectively, the district panchayat was converted into a debating society where they could discuss and pass various innocuous resolutions, but the real power was vested with the DDO. Mr Bhatt ensured that the elected members never came to learn of their powers. In any case, they were too engrossed in their local politics. The district panchayat president was apparently quite happy with this arrangement, as it freed him to take care of politics. If the relationship between the district panchayat president and the DDO were cordial and their mutual understanding was not strained, the system worked well.

During my tenure in Surendranagar, I saw no reason to interfere with Mr Bhatt's resolution. No one questioned the delegation, and few were even aware of it. Since the then district panchayat president, Mr Dave, was an honest and straightforward politician, I had no hesitation in keeping him in the loop of all the important decisions I took, often seeking his advice and counsel beforehand. As he had his hands on the pulse of the people and was fully *au fait* with the demands and needs of the district, his advice was always sound and sensible.

Every department of the government—public works, roads and buildings, primary and secondary education, public health, hospitals, agriculture and animal husbandry, irrigation and water management, and forest—were all under the DDO. The collector was left to manage law and order, PDS and treasury.

At that time, Surendranagar was a drab and dry district, though it had had a very colourful history before Independence, when most parts of it were ruled by Rajput rajas and maharajas. The native states of Dhrangadhra—one of the eight first-class states of the Kathiawar Agency (with 13-gun salute)—Limbdi (9-gun salute), Sayla, Wadhwan, Lakhtar, Muli and Chuda had all been ruled by the scions of the Jhala Rajputs. Though the founders of all these states traced their origins to common ancestors, they continued, for centuries, to fight among themselves, especially Dhrangadhra, Limbdi and Lakhtar. They devastated each other's territories, looting, rustling cattle and capturing women for rape and rapine. The Baroda State, under the Gaekwads, assumed some kind of loose suzerainty over these states. But it was not until the advent of the British into Kathiawar that some kind of order was imposed on this internecine warfare. Under Pax Britannica, the states were not permitted to keep any militias or heavy artillery; only small arms for policing were allowed. The boundaries of each state were defined and fixed. The rulers collected all taxes, administered local laws and lived a lavish life—eating, drinking, playing tennis, cricket and polo, building palaces, in short, leading a sybaritic life. The British enjoyed the power and the authority, and therefore, left them alone, except when they wanted to relax with shikar and hospitality.

Then, after Independence, when the state of Saurashtra was created and districts were formed, all the erstwhile states became talukas. Hence, the Surendranagar district contained more than a dozen old native states that now were all talukas of the district. During my two-year stint in Surendranagar, later as director of famine relief, I had occasion to visit many of the palaces of the maharajas and nawabs and enjoy their hospitality. Some of them, despite having lost the revenue of the state along with the sovereignty, still set a good table and maintained a well-stocked cellar in spite of the law of prohibition. Others took the loss of sovereignty to heart, retired to their citadels, drew up mental drawbridges and sat at their wailing walls to lament the loss of power and prestige. Though they, too, for old time's sake, invited the collector or the DDO for dinner, their table was more impressive for its monogrammed crockery and silver cutlery than for what was served on it.

Dhrangadhra Maharana was an impressive figure when he appeared in his full regalia. But since he lived mostly in Bombay, such appearances were rare even in his state. But Dhrangadhra boasted of a major industry, the Dhrangadhra Chemical Works (DCW), one of the first soda-ash factories of India. Its founder and owner, Mr S.P. Jain, was one of the most suave and polished gentlemen I have come across during my career. The well-designed and well-maintained guest house of DCW was one of my refuges when I had to tour the desert of the Rann of Kutch. DCW also maintained a very fine and well-stocked aviary with multitudes of exotic birds—from the multicoloured Chinese pheasants to the large and impressive golden eagle of the Himalayas. My mother, who in her childhood had been brought up on deer, rabbits, partridges, wildfowl and wild ducks, was more impressed by the pheasants, particularly the multicoloured Chinese pheasants. 'How does it taste when roasted?' she asked innocently. 'Madam, we have paid a thousand rupees each for those birds,' said the horrified curator.

My visit to Halvad, the first capital of the native state before Dhrangadhra, has left a deep impression on my mind for an altogether different reason. Halvad in Saurashtra is the equivalent of Umreth in the rest of Gujarat. For in a state ruled by Rajputs, it remained the bastion of the twice-born Brahmins. Over centuries, they had managed to retain their genetic purity and pride. They are also a very hospitable lot. On my very first visit, the *taluka pramukh*, a Brahmin of the old order, invited me and my entourage for dinner at his house. We all sat against the walls of a large hall on wooden planks. Another set of similar but slightly taller planks were placed before us.

In Gujarat, it is the general belief that eating should commence with sweets—dessert in the beginning and rice last. The Gujarati believes that the sweet made of wheat, lentils, ghee and sugar was a more nutritious food than mere rice, lentils and vegetables. Hence, it is healthier to fill up your stomach with more nutritious food than mere cereals. That is perhaps why they added jaggery to most curries, especially to dal. Consequently, the Halvad laddu became the king of all main dishes.

The laddu, served as the first course, was delicious, and I enjoyed eating it. I knew that I could comfortably digest all the fat and sugar in that laddu. As I was savouring it, I noticed my officer, sitting opposite, making frantic but indecipherable signals to me. Just as I was about to finish, a young and comely lady put another laddu in my plate. I protested. The *pramukh* introduced the lady as one of his granddaughters and urged that I accept the serving.

'You have accepted a laddu from my younger sister. If you don't accept mine, she will tease me for months,' said the young lady at my protests. So, perforce I accepted. I was halfway through the second, when another lady, this time the *pramukh*'s daughter-in-law, brought a third laddu. She was followed by the eldest daughter of the house, whose claim on the capacity of my stomach was even greater. And the last straw on the camel's back, or the last laddu, was brought to my plate by no less than the formidable wife of the *pramukh* himself.

That evening, I was coiled like an anaconda in the easy chair of the guest house, trying to digest the partially consumed heavy laddus. My officer had been trying to warn me not to finish the first laddu. With his experience of Halvad hospitality, he anticipated the challenge I would be facing. My taluka development officer (TDO) ventured into the sitting room of the dak bungalow just then.

'Sir, close by lives the granddaughter-in-law of the diwan of the last maharaja of Dhrangadhra, with her two sons. The family would be greatly honoured if you pay them a visit.'

'But we have a full day's work tomorrow,' I protested.

'It's only in the evening, sir, after we have finished,' the TDO pointed out.

Noblesse oblige, I said to myself, and agreed.

So, I went to call on the old lady, the scion of royalty. I was really sorry to see the bad days the family had fallen on. The diwan of the Dhrangadhra State must have been one of the grandees of the regime, one of the richest persons in his days. He had built a palace of his own on the outskirts of Halvad, his native place. The palace was now in utter ruin. Only the two rooms on both sides of the arched gateway had survived in a dilapidated state. I got down from the jeep without any fanfare and was ushered into one of the rooms. In one corner, the Rajput lady of the house was sitting at a kerosene stove, making tea for me. The room was furnished barely, with a single ancient rosewood chair, in which I sat and sipped the tea. As I was looking out, I saw two strapping young men clad in dhotis and red pugrees driving a herd of cattle into the gateway. They were the great-grandsons of the diwan. After giving me the traditional greeting, bowing down and touching my feet, they took the cattle into the ruins of the palace to tether them in the open space where once the reception hall and the large banquet room stood.

'Sir, the other room contains some old rosewood almirahs filled with books that my grandfather had collected. He was said to be a great scholar in many languages,' she remarked. 'My sons could not finish their schooling. As I was widowed when very young, I did not have enough resources to educate them further.'

Oh, what a fall! I thought to myself. The great-grandsons of a diwan, who was a scholar to boot, had been reduced to herding cattle! *Sic transit gloria mundi.*

'We are unable to sell those almirahs because we don't know what to do with the books,' she said, 'If you can get them transferred to some library in Surendranagar, we will be able to get some money by selling the almirahs.'

I went across to the other room. There were four large, ornate almirahs, beautifully carved in rosewood and teak. They housed the complete works of Dumas, perhaps first editions and Morocco bound, the entire set of Scott's Waverley novels, a set of Shakespeare's plays in a variorum edition in thirty volumes, essays of Montaigne, works of Corneille, Racine and Moliere in French with English translations, Goethe, Faust in German, and a cornucopia of classics—what a treasure there was!

Though I got most of the books transferred to the district library of Surendranagar, I do not know what happened to them after I left Surendranagar.

An interesting encounter and a friendship I made during my stay in Surendranagar, which has remained fresh in my memory, is with Madhavsinh Solanki, the then revenue minister of Gujarat, who visited Surendranagar and was staying in the guest house. I met him in the evening to have dinner and talk about Urdu poetry, especially Ghalib, in whom he was deeply interested.

'Do you know that there is a famous Gujarati ghazal poet working under you here, Moosa?' he asked.

'No, sir,' I said, 'Who is he?'

'I am surprised that with your interest in poetry, you have not discovered the talent that is flourishing right under your nose,' said the minister in a disparaging tone.

The poet was none other than Amrut Ghayal, who has some ten collections of Gujarati ghazals to his credit. Amrut was working as an accountant in my office and had occasion to meet me almost every other day. But he kept his poetic identity well-hidden. Of course, he had no occasion to reveal it, as I had not revealed my interest in poetry to him either. Moreover, in office, he was known as Amrutbhai Bhatt. Ghayal was his *takhallus* (*nom de plume*).

Amrut was invited to the guest house the same evening, and he regaled us with some of his choicest poems. Many of the poems were directly or indirectly critical of the government of the day. Mr Solanki, a highly polished and suave personality, was quite amused. Though he was a pillar of the very same government, he took no umbrage at Amrut Ghayal's barbs.

Amrut Ghayal was an accountant, fairly low down in the hierarchy. But he had the heart of a poet and the courage of conviction to tell a minister his sincere beliefs.

Another of the erstwhile native states, Chotila, had been ruled by Kathi durbars, a clan of Rajputs who were somewhat looked down upon by the other Rajputs—the Jhalas, Jadejas, Gohils, Vaghelas, Chauhans and other Suryavanshis. Chotila was notorious because Bhupat Baharwatiyo, the notorious outlaw of Gujarat, was said to have found refuge in the hills of Chotila and carried out his depredations from there. When the nascent state of Saurashtra was formed immediately in the wake of Indian independence as a Part C state, U.N. Dhebar, a freedom fighter, became its first CM. He had promised the peasantry freedom from the clutches of the landlords and petty zamindars once independence came. U.N. Dhebar passed legislation to hand over the tenanted land to the tiller. Naturally, the landlords and zamindars resented this deprivation. One of their ilk, Bhupat, rose to fight for the rights of the landlords. He went about looting and killing the peasants who dared to assert their legal rights. Near Chotila, he once lined up some eighteen peasants and their political supporters and shot them dead.

Ultimately, the government had to call in a tough police officer, Ashwini Kumar, from Bombay to tackle the menace of Bhupat the outlaw. Ashwini Kumar organised a tight cordon to corner Bhupat, who then fled to Pakistan.

When I joined Gujarat, both Bhupat and Ashwani Kumar had become legends. The landlords and zamindars hailed Bhupat as the Robin Hood of Saurashtra. The peasants hailed Ashwani Kumar as the avatar that came to drive away the *rakshasa* from their land.

During my travels, I called on the Kathi durbar of Chotila, who entertained me to dinner. He talked nostalgically of the days of Bhupat the Baharwatia who feared none, a hero who was driven into exile by an oppressive state.

One of my inspection tours took me to Zainabad, a small native state situated on the very edge of the Rann of Kutch. I had brought my wife along to see the famous wild asses of the Rann of Kutch, as she had missed the sight during my posting at Radhanpur.

Since there was no official guest house in Zainabad, I was invited by the Begum of Zainabad to stay in the palace. When we reached the modest palace, we found the household in a state of emotional tension. The heir and de jure ruler, the talukdar of Zainabad, Malek Shabbir Khan, a young man of twenty-four then, had just married a Hindu girl, much to the chagrin and discomfiture of the begum.

That day, we drove into the Rann. It was early winter, and the surface of the Rann had dried, making it easy for the jeeps to drive on the flat surface. As far as the eye could see, we saw a flat surface, unrelieved by even a clump of bushes or a mound of sand. But it was a mystery to us how the driver's instinct led him unerringly to the small patch of grass on which a herd of wild asses were grazing. They spotted us from a distance and started to move away.

As the jeep picked up speed and gained on the herd, we saw the magnificent creatures in motion. They did not run. They flowed. Their sleek grey bodies, with partly covered haunches of a deep chestnut colour, their erect dark mane, running from the back of the head down the neck, the dark brown stripe that ran across their back to the root of the tail, belied the name of ass. This *Equus hemionus khur*—*khur* means ass in Persian—had found its last refuge in the little Rann of Kutch. When they ran fast, our jeep could keep pace with the herd only with great difficulty, for the ass could run at speeds of up to seventy-five to eighty kilometres per hour. I asked the driver not to drive the wild asses to such speeds when they may collapse with a broken heart. After all, when we saw them in the Little Rann of Kutch, disease, usurpation of their habitat by Rabaris and the Maldharis, and *Prosopis juliflora* had reduced the population of these magnificent creatures to less than 400. I have recently learnt that with the wild ass sanctuary having come up in Zainabad and the measures taken by the government, the population of wild asses has now gone up to 4,000.

Ranagadh, in Limbdi taluka, is about forty-five kilometres from Surendranagar, situated on the banks of the wetland reserve of Nalsarovar (now a famous bird sanctuary), shallow for most of the 140 square kilometres area, with a maximum depth of four feet. Padhars use kayak-like narrow boats to maneouvre through the reed channel. There is a variety of freshwater fish in the lake on which the birds thrive. The Padhar chief of Ranagadh, Shyamal, took us on a kayak ride through the reed-bordered channels of the lake into the open waters. We saw a large variety of exotic migratory birds, rosy pelicans, flamingos, white storks, brahminy ducks, herons, purple moorhens and bitterns.

I had received representations from some of the villages of Patdi taluka, so I decided to visit them. Naturally, the only place to camp for three days was the palace of the erstwhile rulers. The ruler was a man well-advanced in years. He and his wife received my wife and me graciously, and put us up in a well-furnished guest room. Strangely, the ruler of Patdi, I found, was not a Rajput but a Patel. I was to meet his daughter and son-in-law, Jaykrishna Harivallabhdas Patel, chairman of Gujarat State Fertilizers & Chemicals Limited (GSFC), when I was posted as the managing director of that company twenty years later.

After visiting various villages for two days and suffering a sunstroke, which laid me low for a couple of days, I recovered enough to resume my visit. The thakur of Patdi told me that having come all the way to Patdi, I should not miss a visit to the Zinzuwada Fort, which was just twenty-five kilometres away.

The fort of Zinzuwada was built by the famous king of Anhilwad, Siddhraj, who was born in the very village. He perhaps built the fort to commemorate his birth. It is a magnificent fort with four large gates with historic names. Its very isolation, the dry air of the Rann and the absence of creeping vegetation had preserved it for centuries. I hope the influx of tourists there in the last few years has not destroyed its serene beauty.

CRYING OVER SPILT MILK

From serving people at the grassroots level in the districts, I went to Ahmedabad to serve the state government. The departments of agriculture, animal husbandry, cooperation, fisheries and forests were, in those days, headed by a single secretary and a single cabinet minister. With proper time management and competency, it is possible even today. But with the expansion of the bureaucracy and the ministries, we have, today, four secretaries, joint secretaries and four cabinet ministers supported by ministers of state, deputy ministers and what have you. All of them are now manning the departments, which in my time was managed by Shri Thakorebhai Desai as cabinet minister, Mr S.M. Dudani as secretary and myself as deputy secretary. Jonathan Swift said that whoever could make two ears of corn grow upon a spot of ground where only one grew before, would deserve better of mankind than the whole race of politicians put together.

In the districts, I knew what I was supposed to do as a chief executive officer, and I did it as well as I could, sometimes to the chagrin of my bosses. But in the secretariat, I had no idea of what I was doing as a deputy secretary, much less what the department was doing.

The forest department had been established during the British regime in the areas under their control. In the erstwhile native states, the department was a post-Independence creation. The native rulers preserved the forests not for any love of the flora and fauna but primarily as hunting preserves. Some of the erstwhile rulers were very fond of decimating the tigers, leopards, panthers, bears, boars, cheetahs, deer and other fauna. In the tiger sanctuaries of today, one can see proud proclamations of Maharaja so-and-so having shot six tigers during a single shoot. The evidence can be seen in the trophies that adorn the walls of their drawing rooms and banquet halls, now converted into government guest houses, in Baroda, Junagadh, Jamnagar, Bhavnagar, Dhrangadhra, Lakhtar and other states.

Many of the other rulers were themselves not interested in hunting. Publicly, they professed ahimsa much before Gandhiji made that term popular. They created the forest reserves and protected the animal life there to attract and entertain their British masters—the viceroys, the governors, the army chiefs, the political agents and such other miscellaneous marauders. The British loved to receive invitations from the rulers to come and kill their tigers and leopards. And they had quite cleverly devised a competitive incentive system to keep the native rulers running after them—the gun salute. The territorially larger states were their favourites. The rulers received a salute of twenty-one guns when they visited the governor or the viceroys. Rulers of the smaller and petty states received from one to nineteen gun salutes. And many of them would have been willing to sacrifice their right hand just to hear an additional blank charge fired in their honour from the ancient cannon during their visits.

I was not very happy pushing files in the department. The director of agriculture, a technocrat, was not very amenable to the advice of a generalist in the secretariat, nor was the chief conservator of forests, who believed himself too senior to interact with a mere deputy secretary, even if that officer belonged to the IAS. The situation became more embarrassing because Mr Dudani believed in full delegation of all his powers. Since I was the only deputy secretary in the department, I became the sole 'beneficiary' of his delegatory largesse. So, while the day was spent in pushing files, the evenings were spent house-hunting.

There was a great dearth of government houses in Ahmedabad for the officers, especially for the junior newcomers. The government paid just 10 per cent of the salary as house rent—an allowance rarely adequate to rent a single-room flat in a decent locality. So, I went around house-hunting in the distant localities. I would locate a suitable house, arrange a meeting with the landlord, finalise the rent, when he would ask for my name and address to enter into the rental agreement. The moment he saw my name, I would see a dark cloud pass over his brow, and he would look up speculatively at my face and close the discussion by saying he would get back to me with the agreement the next day. He would never turn up.

After several futile attempts and fed up with the guest house cuisine, I did manage to locate a decent house in Swarajnagar Society. I rented the house in the name of Raja, which was easier on the tongue.

Mr Shah, the landlord, dropped in a few months later to collect the rent. We were just a couple of days away from the festival of Bakra Eid.

'Sir, you never told me you are a Muslim,' he said accusingly.

'You never asked me,' I said, with a smile.

'Not that I have anything against Muslims, you know,' he said defensively. 'You see, this locality is mostly tenanted by vegetarians—Brahmins, Baniyas and Jains. They don't much like Muslims, Christians, Sindhis and Punjabis living among them, eating meat and fish. I myself don't mind you eating meat discreetly.'

'We don't beat drums about what we eat, you know,' I said, 'We even bury the bones in the backyard in the dead of night, to not hurt the feelings of our neighbours.'

He laughed at that. 'I know you cook biryani on Bakra Eid. I have lived for some time in Muhammad Ali Road in Bombay. My neighbour was a Muslim. He always invited me on Ramzan and Bakra Eid to enjoy *sheer korma* and *biryani* at his house,' he said slyly. Then, accepting his cheque, he left, promising to call on me on Bakra Eid to wish me Happy Eid.

In the meantime, I was made to learn another lesson in the management of committees. Mr Dudani, the secretary, informed me that the past schemes of our department were to be examined by the Public Accounts Committee (PAC) of the legislative assembly. I burnt the midnight oil, so to say, for several days, studying all the files, anticipating all possible questions that could be raised by the members of the committee, who were all MLAs, and readied replies to all of them for the benefit of the secretary.

In the conference room of the assembly building, we met the chairman and members of the committee. The secretary went around greeting most of the members and shaking hands with them. It appeared that he knew them well, having served in several districts of the state.

After some preliminaries, the chairman opened a new issue.

'Mr Secretary, the accountant general reports that the cooperative fertiliser plants your department has been running made a loss of ₹3 crore in the year 1964. It appears that there was no proper monitoring by your registrar of cooperatives nor by your department. Can you please explain?'

The issue related to a year when neither I nor the secretary were in office. However, I had prepared and briefed the secretary of the reasons for the loss and the actions that the director and the department had taken.

'Sir, it is like this,' said the secretary, with a confident look on his face. 'You may recall when you were in Visavadar in 1963. I also happen to have been camping there. I met you in the guest house. Chaganlalbhai too had come...'

'Mr Secretary,' called out a member, 'we are talking about the losses suffered by the cooperative fertiliser mixing plants in 1964. Please answer that question.'

'I am coming to that, sir,' said the secretary, unperturbed by the interruption. 'When we set up the plants, sir, you may recall that the agricultural production in the state was at a low level. Sir, when we met in Sanand, and I recall that the durbar had invited both of us for dinner. Sir, I felt guilty accepting that invitation. Sir, I believe we have no right to fill our stomachs when the common people do not have enough to eat. Sir, you were heading the Anand Welfare Society then, and you were kind enough...'

'That is all very well, Mr Secretary, we appreciate your sentiments. But that does not answer for the losses suffered by the fertiliser plants,' a third member interrupted the secretary's flow.

'Certainly, sir, I am explaining the losses suffered by the plants. It so happened that when we set up the plants, the sites selected for them were found to be unsuitable. The plant in Panchmahal, in particular, was, if I recall, located in Shri Rathod's constituency.'

'Mr Secretary, for the last one hour we have been discussing everything except the reasons for the losses of your department,' said the chairman in an exasperated tone.

'I am very sorry, sir, if I have been remiss and got diverted. But, sir, the presence of so many friends in this room has been somewhat distracting. They bring so many pleasant memories to mind. As I was explaining...'

He was interrupted again by another member. During the entire proceedings, I tried now and then to pass on chits stating the facts to help him reply to the queries, but the secretary would have none of them. He would not even glance at them, brushing them aside negligently.

The lunch break came to our rescue.

Much later, in the privacy of his chamber, he explained his behaviour in so many words, 'Moosa, you must remember that in your briefing, you had pointed out many sticky areas, for which we had no satisfactory or acceptable explanations. If I had attempted to defend those vulnerable areas of the department, those twenty wolves would have torn me to pieces. So, the best way of tackling them was to divert their attention to other irrelevant issues.'

The lesson that Mr Dudani taught me was that when you are in the field and are not in a position to score a goal or to defend your goalpost, then steer the ball out of the field. That is a lesson all senior civil servants learn, use and pass on to their juniors.

A few days later, Mr Dudani got transferred, and Mr F.J. Heredia took over as secretary of the department. Mr Heredia was cast in an altogether different mould from Mr Dudani. Though he did not ever make a disparaging remark about Mr Dudani's style of working, his body language and the occasional comments he let slip in careless moments were evidence enough of the concealed, subdued contempt all regular recruits held for those who had risen from the ranks. Mr Heredia, in addition to being a regular recruit to the IAS, had won the Nuffield Scholarship and got trained in the United Kingdom in economic administration.

I had been recently saddled with the additional responsibility of setting up an agro-industries corporation of the state (known and flourishing today as the Gujarat Agro Industries Corporation Ltd.).

It was to be set up as a company under the Companies Act. With a deep knowledge of Shakespeare's plays, Renaissance poetry and Anglo-Saxon prose, and with just three years of experience as a district officer under my belt, I knew as much about setting up corporations, memoranda and articles of association, Companies Act and such arcane subjects as I knew about cattle feed. In my day, corporate economics, company law, stock markets, etc., were not taught in the National Academy. Just when I was floundering about, trying to find my feet in the quagmire of the Companies Act, its clauses, subclauses, provisos and even more the morass of the commentary on each proviso and sub-proviso, I received a summon from the secretary. Mr Heredia's first reaction to our meeting was not very positive. Anyone who has served under Mr Dudani, he thought, would not account for much, though he didn't say it in so many words.

One day, the Cabinet took a policy decision to set up fertiliser mixing plants for each district under the aegis of the district cooperative federation. By this time, I had learnt enough to calculate and indicate the economics of each plant. My note naming all the eighteen district cooperatives that should be allotted the mixing plants was put up to Thakorebhai Desai, the minister of agriculture. It came back from the minister with a note in Gujarati, that in the district of Kaira, in addition to the district cooperative federation, a plant should be allotted to the tobacco federation also. I returned the note to the minister informing that the Cabinet's decision was to allot only one plant to each district. So, allotting two plants to one district would affect the economics of both and would be against the current policy as approved by the Cabinet, but if the minister felt strongly, the matter should go back to the Cabinet for a change in the policy, permitting two or more plants in each district, at the discretion of the minister, and in that case, the implications of allotting more than one plant to each district and the economic viability of two instead of one plant would have to be re-examined.

The note came back with a laconic remark in the neat Gujarati handwriting of the minister. 'I withdraw my note. Have it your way.'

Thakorebhai had started his career as a lawyer in the British Raj. He served in several Gujarat Cabinets and rose to become the deputy CM in CM Hitendra Desai's Cabinet.

I recall that when I served as the collector and DM of Bulsar district, he visited Navsari, his hometown, for the first time as the deputy CM. I went to call on him at his house as convention required.

'Navsari is my hometown and constituency. I shall be visiting this place quite often. I thank you for calling on me this time. But do not come every time I visit Navsari. If I need your presence, I shall inform you in advance,' said the minister.

Thereafter, as long as I remained in Bulsar, he never summoned me to Navsari, though I met him frequently on his official tours in the district. Only once, I recall, he had occasion to write to me. It was a recommendation to appoint someone to one of the posts of assistant public prosecutor. The letter started: 'I am writing this letter not in my capacity as a minister but as a domiciled citizen of Bulsar district familiar with all the lawyers of the area. I know and believe that Mr so-and-so, because of his professional integrity, is best suited for the post.'

Thakorebhai was a staunch believer that Gujarati should be the official language of the state, and Hindi should be the lingua franca of India. English should only be a second option, to be taught only from the secondary stage of school education. Like a sincere man, as defined by Remy de Gourmand, he raised his individual belief into a universal law. Hostility to English became a state policy, much to the detriment of two generations of Gujaratis. The flexible and resilient Gujaratis, with immense entrepreneurial capability, managed to get around the official policy, established private English schools and sent their children to learn English there. Most of the politicians who opposed the teaching of English in school sent their children to English-medium schools. It was only the poor, the underprivileged and the minorities who sent their children to Gujarati-medium schools. And those are the classes that lost out in terms of employment in the private sector, in participating in the boom of information technology, in getting employment with the BPO and call centres, and so on. They have not yet caught up with their fellow Gujaratis, who, with the benefit of English education, found jobs in the Middle East, Europe and the US, and today form a powerful segment of the Indian diaspora, calling the shots even in the US administration. Yet, I consider Thakorebhai Desai as a great son of Gujarat, who enjoyed the regard and respect of both the people and bureaucracy of the state. But even giants sometimes stumble and the pygmies in the vicinity get crushed.

Another object lesson was taught to me by Dr Verghese Kurien, the founder of Amul and the father of the White Revolution in India. I first met Dr Kurien at the beginning of my career. When I was still under training in Surat, Mr Coelho, the assistant collector at Anand was promoted and posted to Surat as additional collector.

One day, Mr Coelho had to go to Ahmedabad on some official call and took me along. The jeep journey from Surat to Ahmedabad was quite long and boring but was relieved by a halt for lunch at Anand. Mr Coelho and Dr Kurien were great friends, and Mrs Kurien was a gracious and very hospitable hostess.

'You know, Dr Kurien is a most impressive man. And you would love to meet him,' Mr Coelho briefed me on the way.

'You said he is from Kerala. He is perhaps a Christian. So, how did he find acceptance by the Patels of Kheda, who are said to be a bit conservative in their outlook?' I asked Mr Coelho.

'That is a wrong impression. The Patels of Kheda district are a most pragmatic lot. They don't let their personal beliefs come in the way of choosing and supporting the best professionals, so long as that professional does his job efficiently. And Tirubhuvandas Patel is a pragmatic idealist. He knows when idealism is required and when pragmatism will pay.'

We drove straight to the office of the Amul Dairy and joined Dr Kurien in his cabin.

By 1962, Dr Kurien's achievements had already been recognised, both nationally and internationally.

Dr Kurien was not very tall. Medium dark in complexion, with worry lines around his eyes, he appeared a man much given to thinking, planning and execution. He was already a legend when we met him, much appreciated by Morarji Desai, Lal Bahadur Shastri and Jawaharlal Nehru, who all embraced him when they came visiting the Amul Dairy. They appreciated the fact that it was Dr Kurien, ably supported by Tirubhuvandas Patel, who converted India from a milk-deficit state into the largest producer of milk and milk products in the world. And Taya Zinkin, the journalist and writer, had already made Dr Kurien famous both in India and the world in a biography.

Dr Kurien and his wife, Molly, gave us a modest but excellent lunch. Then he took us on a round of the dairy, where milk was collected from hundreds of centres in the district, mixed together, pasteurised and put into containers. Dr Kurien also introduced us to Dalaya, his right-hand man who succeeded in making milk powder out of buffalo's milk when the world experts had said it was impossible.

'Would you like to meet the founder and the man behind the cooperative effort—Shri Tirubhuvandas Patel?' Dr Kurien asked.

Of course, we had to meet Mr Patel. Dr Kurien drove us in his jeep into the narrow lanes of the town of Anand and stopped at a modest, traditional Gujarati rural house. Mr Patel was convalescing from a fever, so we climbed a narrow steep wooden staircase to the first floor, where Mr Patel was reclining on a string cot without a mattress. That was the way giants lived in the immediate aftermath of India's independence.

Much later, when I was serving as the deputy secretary in the state government, I received a call from Dr Kurien asking for an appointment.

Of course, I asked for his convenient date and time. He came on the dot. After we had discussed the issue pertaining to the dairy development schemes, he lowered his voice and said, 'Can you please check whether Karsanbhai Desai is in his cabin?'

'Which Karsanbhai?' I asked.

'He is the section officer in your office who is dealing with a file of Amul, which has been stuck with him for a month,' he replied.

'Oh, you mean that Karsan. I will call him here and check,' I said.

'Please don't do that. He will think I am using my acquaintance with you to pressurise him. I would like to call on him in his cabin and request him to expedite. After all, it's my problem and I should be going to him rather than you calling him to your office.'

That was a salutary lesson I learnt from Dr Kurien. I have used that lesson very effectively in my career. Often, even as secretary to the Government of India, whenever I found that a particular file was stuck in finance, environment, law or another department, I would ring up the concerned officer and ask for an appointment so that I could come and explain. Rarely did I actually have to go over. Mostly, the file moved fast enough or the problem was resolved on the telephone.

I have often wondered why a man like Dr Kurien was not conferred the Bharat Ratna. Most people just existed. Kurien lived, and his life impacted millions of people not only in India but in the world. He improved the living conditions of many Indians for the better. And millions of lives will continue to be affected for a long, long time to come. If a cricketeer, who has entertained those who are interested in the game, can be conferred the highest national award of India, a person who has changed the life of millions for the better, who has contributed towards India becoming the largest producer of milk and milk products in the world, deserves the Bharat Ratna several times over.

OF FOREST CAMPS AND SEMI-BOMBLAS

Mr R.K. Anklesaria, a suave, soft-spoken Parsi civilian was the secretary to CM Hitendra Desai. One day, he called me to his office to congratulate me, 'The CM has approved your posting to Surat, his hometown and his constituency, as the collector.' I was pleasantly surprised.

'Actually, I had not proposed your name. I had proposed three other more senior officers. But the CM has simply written: Moosa Raza *ne mukvi*.'

With those three words, my career for the next six years was sealed as the collector and DM of three districts—Surat, Bulsar and, concurrently, Dangs. Those three districts have now become seven.

The colonial-style collector's bungalow in Surat, a legacy of the British Raj, was located on the bank of the river Tapti. Its vast grounds had been left to seed, as the state could not afford gardeners to maintain the lawns. The bungalow had a large drawing room, sparsely furnished, a guest room and a dining room. On the ground floor, there was a detached veranda for the police security guard, with a secluded resting room. Three fairly commodious bedrooms with high ceilings were located on the first floor, with dressing rooms and ensuite bathrooms. There were, of course, miscellaneous staff quarters at the back, where the personnel of the collector's residence lived. I recently visited the bungalow, five decades after leaving Surat. The government has built a more modern and less pretentious residence for the collector close by. But it does not have the ambience or the charm of the old colonial structure, which is now abandoned, haunted by the ghosts of memories, looking forlorn. Since it is more than 200 years old, it deserves to be preserved as a heritage structure.

There was an ancient tamarind tree on the high bank of the river Tapti, spreading its branches to shade a large area of the high ground and the stone steps leading to the river's edge. The estuary of Tapti came within the tidal range of the Indian Ocean. On one occasion, I watched a fisherman walking on the lower bank, close to the edge of the rising waters. He had a fishing net slung on one shoulder and an earthen pot slung from the other. He stopped just below where we sat, bent down and picked up some moist earth. Rolling it into a ball, he dipped it into the pot and then flung it into the rising river, not too far from the shore. Then he broke a twig from the low-slung branch of the tamarind tree and stuck it as a marker against the spot where he had flung the mud ball. He then walked a few yards upstream and repeated the process.

Having marked about eight or ten spots in the mysterious manner, he came back to the first spot where we sat. Unslinging his fishing net, he flung it on the spot where the mud ball had fallen, spreading it in a wide circle. When he drew it in, I saw half a dozen wriggling large prawns caught in the net. He disentangled them and put them in a basket on his back. He repeated the process at all the marked spots. The mystery was solved. It was a novel way of fishing for prawns. An evening's fishing would net him two dozen or more large prawns.

Surat, of course, was familiar ground to me. Having been trained in that district, I knew much of the geography and demography. The local vernacular newspapers were a bit unhappy with my appointment, and they received the news with some reservations. It so happened that the posts of the district Congress chief, the mayor, and the district SP were occupied by Muslims. The four most important positions in the district being occupied by Muslims was a rare coincidence not palatable to certain sections of the local journalistic community.

Chorasi taluka, in which the city of Surat is located, was the pocket borough of Morarji Desai, then finance minister of India. He fought all his elections from that constituency. He would nurse the constituency with frequent visits, and I had to receive and accompany him on all such occasions. On long drives in the district, I would be the only one accompanying him in the back seat of the Ambassador car. Clad in his white khadi kurta, white sleeveless khadi jacket and immaculate dhoti, he would sit stiffly throughout the journey. I, in my white closed-collar jacket and trousers, would fidget around, feeling quite uncomfortable in the non-air-conditioned vehicle with the windows closed to keep out the dust. We would disembark at many dusty villages by the roadside to greet the waiting people, get jostled around a bit by the milling enthusiastic crowds and then get back into the car. I would find nary a speck of dust on the minister's white clothes, maintaining their pristine immaculateness, while I would silently bemoan my bedraggled cotton jacket and crumpled trousers. I noticed that most political leaders of that era maintained their faultless sartorial style and their sangfroid while walking through the dust and heat of the rural crowds, often hearing provocative slogans. I never found out how they did it.

One day, I received a high-powered delegation from Bardoli. Bardoli of the famous satyagraha so successfully led by Vallabhbhai Patel, his daughter, Maniben Patel, and Gandhi's Parsi disciple, Mithuben Petit. That was in 1928. The people conferred the title of Sardar on Vallabhbhai after the satyagraha. The delegation told me that they were planning to hold a one-day seminar on panchayat raj in Bardoli.

'We have already invited Morarji Desai, Hitendra Desai, several cabinet ministers and political leaders from Maharashtra and Madhya Pradesh. Jayaprakash Narayan is the guest of honour, he is billed as the star speaker,' they told me. Jayaprakash was a great proponent of grassroot democracy embodied in panchayat raj.

However, one of the requests of the Bardoli delegation was to exempt them from the Guest Control Order (GCO) in operation at that time so that the participants could be served wheat bread and rice.

The Guest Control Order was passed in 1960 when the country was facing a severe shortage of food in the aftermath of the various wars, famines and failure of monsoons. The order laid down limits on the number of guests who could be served cereals, rice and wheat products, so as to prevent conspicuous consumption and ostentatious parties and functions. The collector in the district and the commissioner of civil supplies at the state level were authorised, under special circumstances, to exempt certain occasions from the operations of the order.

Knowing Morarji Desai and Jayaprakash Narayan (popularly called JP), I had the gut feeling that they would not like to have the guests of the Bardoli seminar exempted from the order. They were both stalwarts in establishing norms of austerity and modest consumption. With regret, I refused the request. The organisers were deeply disappointed.

However, they appealed against it to the commissioner of civil supplies in Ahmedabad. Perhaps they even met CM Hitendra Desai. The commissioner overruled my refusal and gave them the exemption.

I received the VIP guests, most of whom arrived by two large helicopters at Surat, and drove them down to Bardoli. The inaugural function went off in an orderly manner. JP spoke about his thesis on the reconstruction of Indian polity—replacing the prevalent system of state assemblies and the

Parliament with state panchayats and national panchayats. Morarjibhai emphasised the need for developing a civil service that was more in tune with the ambience and ethos of the people of free India. He criticised the national government policy, a government of which he was a minister, of still producing civilians trained in the National Academy but maintaining the British traditions.

'They wear emblazoned blazers and English suits, and are taught to eat with knives and forks. I am told some of them even drink liquor and play cards. How can such officers relate to the village folk, understand their problems, empathise with them and speak their language?' he asked.

After all the speeches were over, we repaired to the adjacent tent for lunch.

First a round of vegetables, then a round of lentils. Then came wheat chapatis. The moment Morarjibhai saw wheat chapatis, his hackles were raised and he flared up. His face reddened. 'How can you serve chapatis? Don't you know there is a Guest Control Order in force?' he asked the hosts. The chief organiser, who was serving rice to JP, ran up and explained, 'Sir, we have got exemption from the GCO for the function.'

This added to Morarjibhai's anger. 'Who gave you the exemption?' He leaned across the CM towards me and asked, 'Did you exempt them?' Luckily for me, I had not. I could simply answer, 'No, sir.'

The host intervened. 'We got the exemption from the commissioner of civil supplies, sir.'

Morajibhai then looked accusingly at Hitendra Desai.

Squirming on his seat, the CM said placatingly, 'I don't know how it happened, Morarjibhai. I will look into the matter after I return.'

Morarjibhai understood how that had happened. 'Please do,' he said sternly. 'If we do not set the right example, those who hold large marriage functions and invite hundreds of guests will ask for exemption and quote this precedent.'

Without touching the food, Morarji Desai got up and announced that he would not like to be party to this breach of the GCO. Naturally, JP, the CM, and other VIP guests, all got up in deference to Morarjibhai's walkout and left the hall in a hungry exodus. It fell to my lot to scour all the restaurants and lodges in Bardoli to muster enough sustenance to feed the hungry men in authority. Lao Tzu, the Chinese philosopher, remarked centuries ago, 'The people go hungry, because people in authority eat too much in taxes.'

While JP and the CM stayed back to attend the afternoon session, Morarjibhai, accompanied by me, left for another engagement at Songadh.

Songadh taluka was to the east of Surat, a little over fifty kilometres away. With the prevailing state of roads then, it would take a little over two hours to reach Songadh from Bardoli. I sat with Morarjibhai in the back of the Ambassador car, silently ruminating on the speeches heard in the forenoon. But how long can one sit silent even in the presence of royalty. So, I ventured, 'Sir, may I make a comment on your speech at the panchayat convention?'

'Yes, you may,' he responded.

'Sir, you criticised the government policy of training the new breed of civilians in an anglophile atmosphere, wearing English dress, eating with a knife and fork. Sir, you are a part of that government at the highest level and have been so for several years. Why was it not possible for you to change the culture—the dress code, and the system of training in the academy?'

Morarjibhai remained silent for several minutes. Perhaps he was caught off guard by my embarrassing question. Then he said, 'I am only a part of the government as a minister. It is the whole Cabinet that takes such decisions.'

'Sir, did you ever raise this issue in the Cabinet and attempt to persuade them to your viewpoint?'

'Discussions in the Cabinet are confidential. There are often differing points of view. Decisions are made by consensus.'

'But, Sir, forgive me, if you felt so strongly, did you find it comfortable to remain as a member of that Cabinet when you were overruled?'

'Young man, once a decision is made by consensus, we all fall in line. There is no question of being comfortable or uncomfortable.'

'Then, sir, in that case, would it be right to criticise that very consensual decision in public after you have been a party to it?'

Morarji Desai's face—he was fair-complexioned and retained his glow until the very end—went lobster red. I looked at him and thought that I had exceeded my limits.

There is a fine line between audacity and idiocy. Perhaps, I thought, I had crossed that line. But Morarji Desai's character had been tempered on the Gandhian anvil. He remained silent for quite a while. Later, I tried to analyse why I had been so impudent. Throughout his speech at the convention, I was smarting under his scathing remarks on the civil service of India. After imbibing the Anglo-Indian type of atmosphere that prevailed during our training in Mussoorie, we were cleansed of all such accretions once we reached the district. What with having to sleep on stinking cots full of bed bugs, eating dry *bhakris* with unwashed and unpeeled potato curry, and performing morning chores in the open forest, squatting on two wobbly stones, all the Western 'pollution' was washed out of you. I felt Morarjibhai was somewhat unfair to the training and culture in Mussoorie.

After an hour of travelling in silence, I apologised to him if I had in any way upset him. He smiled. Morarjibhai smiled rarely, and whenever he did, it was mostly a sardonic smile. 'In the legislative assembly and Parliament, a minister is subjected to so much questioning on his actions and so much criticism is levelled, mostly unwarranted, that if he were to get upset at such questions, then he would be permanently upset,' he remarked, looking out of the window at the arid and rocky landscape, as we approached Songadh.

A few months later, Morarji Desai as finance minister presented a budget in which he increased excise duty on viscose yarn. Surat city, in those days, had a very large number of power looms. It was known as a textile city before it achieved fame as a 'diamond city'. A substantial part of Surat's population was employed in this industry, and a large part of the economy of Surat subsisted on the textile industry. That industry used a substantial quantity of viscose yarn, locally called art silk. Within days, leaders of the power loom owners' community and employees started an agitation against the increase in excise duty. They were particularly resentful that Morarjibhai, in spite of being a son of Gujarat, whose very constituency was in Surat, should stab his very own people, as it were, in the back. Mr Chokhawala (the brother of the then education minister, Gordhandas Chokhawala) and Kashiram Rana (who later became an important leader of the Bharatiya Janata party (BJP), wore the mayor's robes three times and became a cabinet minister at the Centre) and others led the agitation. There was no question of Morarjibhai withdrawing the tax. Once he took a decision, he stood behind it like a rock. Knowing this, I tried to persuade the agitators not to create a law and order situation. But they were adamant. They threatened to take to the streets. I was caught between a rock and a hard place.

To compound the critical situation, it was around that time that the president of India, Dr Zakir Husain, accepted an invitation to visit the Vedchi Ashram in the district at the request of Jugatram Dave, a veteran Gandhian, to participate in a khadi promotion function. I had to make frequent visits to Vedchi to supervise the preparation and organise the logistics of over 5,000 participants from all over the state, who were to sit and spin yarns on charkhas in the presence of the president, himself a Gandhian.

The spinning wheel had been popularised as a symbol of Gandhian economics, self-reliance, self-sufficiency and self-employment. Yet, Surat and Ahmedabad in Gujarat; Bhiwandi, Ichchalkaranji, Malegaon and Sholapur in Maharashtra; and Salem and Kanpur in other states emerged as power loom centres.

Back in the sixties, khadi still commanded respect, as all politicians, from Jawaharlal Nehru and Morarji Desai to the village sarpanch, wore khadi. So, the DM, though wearing mill-made cloth that was easier to maintain, had to mouth the praises of khadi, howsoever hypocritically.

While I was busy making arrangements for the president's visit, the agitators were busy holding protest meetings. They chose Gopipura to hold violent demonstrations against the government. Gopipura was the place where the CM Hitendra Desai had his modest, traditional house and where he usually stayed whenever he visited his hometown. It was also where Morarjibhai camped when in Surat, as a guest of the family.

I was on the way back from Vedchi, having spent the night there arranging for two standby electric generators to safeguard against power failure and a strong and stable wooden stage that could hold a dozen politicians safely, when I received an ominous message on the wireless. The agitators had gone on a violent rampage in Gopipura and adjacent localities, burnt a couple of public transport buses, destroyed electric and telephone poles, and burnt down a police chowki. Instead of going to the office, as I had intended, I asked the driver to divert to Gopipura, where the SP was trying in vain to restore law and order and to disperse the agitators.

The large crowd was resorting to heavy stone pelting, and the police were bursting tear-gas shells to keep them at bay. As I entered Gopipura, a flying brick hit my jeep driver on the head. Severely injured, he fell unconscious in my lap. Stopping the jeep and getting out was not an option, as the stoning was too heavy to risk any exposure. So, I manoeuvred myself into the driver's seat while still holding him in my lap. When I reached the burnt-down chowki where the SP had made his stand and restored wireless communication, I found him in a state of demoralisation.

'Sir, the agitators have caught us at a most vulnerable moment. Most of my constabulary and some of my best inspectors are on duty in Vedchi for the president's visit. With this shortage, I am finding it difficult to hold back the crowd. I have summoned assistance from the neighbouring districts, but that will take time. So far, they have been attacking only public property. But once the riff-raff among them start looting private property, we will have a full-scale riot on our hands!'

'The problem is, this locality is a Congress stronghold. It is the CM's assembly constituency, and his house is located right in the heart of this mohalla. I even saw some of the second-rung party workers in the unruly crowd.'

'Call in some of the inspectors from the other talukas. Use your force as a battering ram. After all the agitators are hemmed in by the narrow street, hit them hard with lathis. They will have to retreat or go back home. Don't hold back because it is the CM's constituency and just because you see some party workers in the crowd. Once they feel the bite of the stick, let us see how they hold up.' I told him.

A sub-inspector ran up to me then and whispered that the CM was on the line, wanting to speak to me. I wondered why the CM would want to speak to me when I was in the midst of controlling a riotous mob. Apparently, someone from his own house had briefed him on what was going on.

In those days, we did our duty as laid down by the law. We neither looked up to the higher-ups to protect us if we did wrong, nor did we seek their permission to do what was right. The law was supreme, and no one was above the law. If we remained honest, maintained our integrity and worked competently, the worst that could happen to us was to be transferred from one district to another, from one post to another. But if you were from a far-off state, working a thousand miles away, what did it matter if you are collector of Surat or DDO of Surendranagar. We resented it if there was any back-seat driving.

I went up to that part of the police chowki that had survived the fire and picked up the phone. The operator told me to hold on for the CM to come on line.

'How is it going there?' asked the anxious Hitendrabhai. 'We are trying to prevent the agitation from turning into a riot, sir,' I said, 'We are hampered because of the president's visit and lack of adequate force.'

'I rang up to tell you that I am trying to send you additional police help. You may take all necessary steps to contain the law and order situation. My only request is, please do not resort to firing. You know Gopipura is my area and my constituency. If anyone dies there, I will never be forgiven by the people for the rest of my life.'

The CM only made a request. There was no hint of an 'order' there. My apprehensions were laid to rest, but I could feel the palpable concern in his tone.

'I will try my best, sir,' I assured him. 'So long as it remains an attack against public property, I will try to contain it with tear gas and lathicharge. But, sir, if it becomes a riot with looting private property, I may have to resort to firing,' I said.

He remained silent for a few moments. Then asked, 'Is that happening?'

'Not yet, sir,' I replied, 'But it may.'

'Very well. Do the best you can,' he said in a resigned tone.

In any event, I did not have to open fire. We could control the situation with the help of tear gas and the bamboo staff. One of the outcomes of my involvement in the Surat riot was my missing the visit of Dr Zakir Husain to Vedchi. The function had not gone off as planned. I learnt that not only did the power supply fail but even the generators failed. The president's speech could not be heard. The superintending engineer, in charge of the generators, in his overcautious approach, ran both the generators for too long to test them. When their need arose, they ran out of fuel. The engineer was suspended for six months.

I arrested five of the main agitators at the riot and detained them under the Preventive Detention Act. It had a salutary effect, as the principal instigators had been removed from the scene. The Act enabled me to keep them in jail without bail. Among them were the brother of the education minister, two leaders, including Kashiram Rana. They remained in jail for close to nine months. The minister, Mr Chokhawala, on one of his visits to Surat, requested me to accept the apology of the five and release them. I accepted the advice. They had served long enough and were in a chastened mood.

I was so incensed at the wholesale destruction of public property by the agitators—public transport buses, electric transformers, street lights, telephone poles, police outposts—that I told the various public agencies not to restore public services—bus transport, street lights and telephone poles—for many months. This and the preventive detention of the leaders of the agitators for a long period was a salutary lesson for Surat, and I faced no law and order problem for the remaining part of my tenure.

I was camping in the forest of Zankhvav when I met another interesting man of Surat district. One of the duties of the collector was to make a tent camp in a remote forest area of the district to enable the forest-dwellers and the Adivasis to meet him and have their grievances redressed by the highest authority. The collector had to do this at least twice a year, and this duty was a part of the Land Revenue Code enacted by the British in the nineteenth century. In retrospect, I suspect the British made this rule for their own benefit—to help them with their forays into the forest for shikar.

The Anglo-Saxon race has always been prone to decimating the fauna of every country they colonised. Other races mostly hunted to fill their pot. But the Anglo-Saxons killed just for the pleasure of killing and boasting about it. They decimated the lions, cheetahs, leopards, buffalos and even the innocent gorillas of Africa. They killed the elephant for the ivory, and they glorified mass killers with the title of 'Big Game Hunter', the 'Great White Hunter', and so on. I had read the novels of Captain Marryat (*The Gorilla Hunters*), Rider Haggard (*Alan Quatermain, King Solomon's Mines*), Jim Corbett, Anderson and even the recent addition to the tribe, Wilbur Smith. They all sing paeans of the white hunter who took his high-powered rifle, sat in the safety of the machan or stalked a lion stealthily and shot it, 'at grave risk to his own life.'

Even today, the hunting lodges of Bharatpur, Jodhpur, Jaipur are replete with stuffed tiger, antlered heads of a variety of deer on the walls and bearskin rugs on the floor.

So, I may be forgiven if I suspected the forest tent camp to be a means of enabling the British ICS officer to collect as many trophies as he could to adorn the walls of his manor house in Scotland, Sussex or Wales!

The collector's office was equipped with several large tents—one well-accoutred for bedroom, one for the office and to receive and deal with the petitioners, one for the staff, one for the kitchen, one for the security guards and an open one for the privy, where the thunder box was ensconced. Most of these were relics of the British Raj.

Every morning and every night, before bedtime, all the tents had to be carefully inspected. Often snakes, scorpions and sundry centipedes found their way into the nooks and corners, especially in winter, seeking warmth.

Late one night, when I had just put out the kerosene lantern after closing the book I was reading, I heard the sound of a jeep being driven into the camp. I heard the security guard's challenge, and then the voices of the *mamlatdar* and other staff members raised in a hubbub. My curiosity getting the better of my sleep, I came out of the tent to find a short-statured, dark-complexioned gentleman, dressed in bedraggled shirt and trousers, covered with red dust, being heckled by my staff. Seeing me, the *mamlatdar* stepped forward and said, 'Sir, this man says he is the assistant engineer of the town planning department. He says he has driven all the way from Surat, bringing some documents to be signed by you tonight itself. I said you will look at the documents in the morning, not in the middle of the night. But he insisted that the morning would be too late.' The *mamlatdar*'s tone had all the contempt of a revenue officer for a mere engineer. The young man tried to open his mouth to offer an explanation.

'First, tell me who you are and why have you brought these papers so late in the night to the forest camp?' I asked him gently.

'Sir, my name is Amarsinh. I am an assistant engineer in the town planning department. We have been preparing the town plan of Surat for the last three months. It got ready only yesterday. We discovered that if it is not notified in the gazette today, our efforts would go waste and we will have to update the whole plan before the next date, to be announced by the government. That will take another six months. Our superintending engineer asked me to bring these plans to you and get your approval tonight and return straightaway.'

I could see the anxiety in his face to get the task entrusted to him done successfully and return.

'When did you leave Surat?' I asked.

'Sir, we worked the whole of last night. The blueprints got ready only yesterday morning. "The collector is camping in Zankhvav. Get his approval and rush back," he told me. So, if you sign these papers, I will start for Surat immediately.'

I knew that most of the *kutcha* route fell in the forest area covered with rocks, fallen trees and potholes blocking the way. He must have traversed that difficult, non-existent route for several hours to reach here. I could imagine the long journey he had to make through the forest tracks in the middle of the night, passing through panther- and tiger-infested territory. And he was prepared to go back immediately on the same track—it proved he was a really dedicated officer. So, I instructed the *mamlatdar* to get Amarsinh some food and water to clean up. Meanwhile, I said I would look at the proposals that required my immediate signature. As I sat looking at the maps and the underlying rationale in the light of the petromax, I found that the proposals needed several amendments. Moreover, Mr Shah, the town planner, had not properly understood the requirement. There was still more than a month available for gazetting the plan. After Amarsinh had washed and fed, I called him in and told him that his boss had misunderstood the requirement and there was adequate time available to gazette the notification. I asked him to stop for the night and leave in the morning, and that I would also write out and enclose my comments before sending him back.

'Mr Shah would be sore with me if I do not return before lunch with your approval,' said a worried Amarsinh.

'Leave Mr Shah to me,' I said, 'I will explain everything to him in my note.'

Amarsinh gratefully retired to the staff tent. In the morning, after getting a bath and breakfast, I sent him back with my comments on the proposals.

A few days after my return to Surat, Amarsinh sought an appointment with me. He came with his wife, Gajraben. She was serving as a *gram sevika* (a woman employed to advise and assist villagers in matters of community welfare and development) in Vyara taluka. While those who had joined service with her or later had been promoted as *mukhya sevika*s with higher emoluments, she was stagnating in the same grade. Since Amarsinh was an Adivasi, there was undoubtedly some prejudice working against him and his wife, who had certainly been denied promotion, though eligible. I was able to sort out the problem. Amarsinh came a third time to thank me for my kindness to him in Zankhvav and to his wife later.

Less than two decades later, in 1985, Amarsinh Chaudhary became the CM of Gujarat, succeeding Madhavsinh Solanki. I was chairman of the GSFC at Baroda then. I called on him at the secretariat, and he came out to greet me and conduct me into his chamber.

It was during my tenure in Surat that the government decided to operationalise the set-up of the South Gujarat University, with its headquarters in the city of Surat. Prof. C.N. Vakil, an eminent economist and a good friend of Morarji Desai, became its second vice chancellor. Some of the well-known academicians hailing from the district of Surat, Bulsar and Bharuch graced its senate and syndicate. A large budget was allocated to acquire land and construct buildings for creating a permanent campus and other infrastructure.

One day, I received a request from Prof. Vakil for an appointment. He came with a few members of the syndicate with a request that I should allocate 400 acres of government land on the road leading to the seaside suburb of Dumas for the university campus. Dumas was a small village located in the delta of the river Tapti, about twenty kilometres from Surat city.

Prof. Vakil chose the 400 acres of land he wanted for the university right on the road leading from Surat to Dumas. I found that I had earmarked that land for extending the runway strip of the future Surat airport and had notified it in the gazette. A little further away from the main road, there was enough free government land with good connectivity. I offered 200 acres of that land to Prof. Vakil. He was, however, insistent that the land that he had earmarked alone was suitable for the university campus and no other land would be acceptable.

Prof. Vakil was an economist. Having invented the SEMI-BOMBLA, an unwieldy acronym for a solution for all the economic problems of India, he was convinced that once he got that piece of land, all the problems of setting up a university would be resolved. Not being an economist, I never understood what the SEMI-BOMBLA stood for, and if Prof. Vakil had to set about solving the problems of India, why he contented himself with a 'semi' and not a 'full'-BOMBLA! I learnt after a lot of investigation that the awkward acronym stood for Scheme of the Economists for Monetary Immobilisation Through Bond Medallions and Blocked Assets.

I explained that while there were only a few locations in the close proximity of Surat suitable for an airport, there were many where a university campus could be set up. Since the land he had chosen was the only topographically suitable location for an airport, I declined his request and tried to persuade him to accept the alternative.

There were many amateur economists in the journalistic field of Surat who supported Prof. Vakil, and the local press were not very happy with my refusal. The airport was in the future, but the university was now. I had not reckoned with the fact that the only thing more dangerous than an amateur economist is a professional economist. Prof. Vakil, bolstered by the press, wrote a long letter to Morarji Desai, accusing me of being recalcitrant, adamant and anti-education. Morarjibhai forwarded that missive to me with a handwritten marginal note: 'I would like to discuss this with you on my next visit to Surat.' And since Surat was his constituency, his visits were fairly frequent.

He stayed with Hitendra Desai on his next visit, and I was summoned to Gopipura. I repaired there, with all the maps, records and technical advice I had received. In the antechamber, I found Prof. Vakil with his cohorts, sitting silent and dour.

I explained why I had refused to allot the land chosen by Prof. Vakil. Morarjibhai spent almost half an hour trying to understand the situation. He asked me many questions on the feasibility of alternative locations, both for the airport and the university. Then, along with me, he walked into the antechamber where the syndicate was waiting. He greeted them rather perfunctorily, and without much preliminaries, he said, 'Chandubhai, I have looked into all aspects of your request. I am afraid I agree with the collector. While there are other feasible alternatives for locating the university campus, there are no feasible alternatives for the future airport, except the earmarked land. The collector has offered you two or three alternatives. I would advise you to choose one of them.'

Prof. Vakil was taken aback. He did not expect to be dealt with so perfunctorily and peremptorily. After all, he was a friend of the minister. But Morarjibhai was not one to hear the same arguments twice. Apparently, he had heard them fully before my coming. Then he asked, 'You are not one of those American land grant colleges. The state government will be funding your capital expenditure. So, why do you require 400 acres? I am advising the collector to have a second look at his offer of 200 acres. Personally, I think 100 acres should be more than enough to meet your requirement, in any of the alternate sites. Land is going to become more and more of a scarce commodity in the coming years—with our five-year plans, the country's development would depend, to a large extent, on the availability of land. We have, therefore, to use this scarce resource quite frugally.'

With that, the interview closed. Prof. Vakil refused even the 100 acres I offered him. I learnt years later that the university campus had come up on Magdalla Road instead of Dumas Road.

In September 1968, Surat district, along with Baroda, Bharuch and Navsari, was flooded with heavy rains. All the rivers were in heavy spate. Most of the bridges on the major rivers of south Gujarat—the Mahi, the Daman Ganga, the Tapti and the Narmada—were washed away, along with the railway tracks, roads, telephone and electric installations. The only means of communication left was a couple of police wireless sets, whose batteries, too, were running low. With the power source cut off, they could not be replenished. Surat city itself remained under fourteen feet of water. About 120 villages in the district were totally washed away, with loss of several human and cattle life.

As both the municipal commissioner and the DDO could not evacuate their residence before being cut off by the floodwaters, both their responsibilities had to be shouldered by me. They remained incommunicado for the duration of the flood and for long thereafter. Once the highways and other roads were brought back to some semblance of operability, help in the form of food grains and clothes poured in from private donors. Naturally, the politicians of the district wanted to hijack all this aid and divert it into their areas of influence. My effort was to ensure that all this aid reached only the deserving sufferers. I set up a centralised receiving station for all the incoming trucks and a foolproof system to send it onwards to the various devastated villages and camps where the sufferers had been housed. Naturally, the politicians were very unhappy and so was that section of the press that was under their influence. I had recalled my old friend Mr Shrotriya from retirement to help me organise the receipt, dispatch and distribution of the relief material. I trusted his honesty, sincerity and competence. He did an efficient and honest job of it.

While I was engaged in restoring normalcy in the district, there were certain elements who wanted to take advantage of the preoccupation of the civilian and police administration with rescue and relief operations to indulge in uncivil activities. They thought it was the right time to break into and loot those establishments whose occupants had shifted to the houses of their relatives and friends on higher ground for safety. If I had allowed such criminals to succeed, there would have been utter chaos in the city. Some harsh and perhaps extralegal steps had to be taken by the police, under my instructions, to curb and control the potential breakdown of law and order. Some of the criminally inclined but otherwise hypocritical second- and third-rung political workers, too, indulged in breaking in and looting closed shops and establishments. When the police caught them and thrashed them, I turned a Nelson's eye to the complaints of the leaders. This also became a bone of contention between me and a section of the political leadership. Letters were written to Morarjibhai, and even while rescue, relief and rehabilitation work was going on, Morarjibhai decided to visit Surat and oversee the work. After I had taken him around the city, he agreed to meet the press and listen to the local leaders in the circuit house.

Morarjibhai always had an uneasy relationship with the press. He had a high level of hubris and a somewhat inflated ego combined with an acerbic tongue. It had nothing to do with the positions he held. It was a part of his personality and character. Even when he had joined the Congress at the junior level, he was willing to take on no less a person than Sardar Patel. He also had an annoying habit of answering every question with a question of his own. Moreover, he had no patience with fools and foolish questions. The Surat vernacular press did not distinguish itself for its wisdom and acumen. And they would not refrain from asking personal questions of him.

'Sir, why do you always insist on drinking milk of only a white cow?' they asked.

'And what do you eat for breakfast? *Farsaan*, *fafda*, *sev* and *jalebi*? Do you think that is healthy food? Do you believe that *bhajias and pakodas*, deep fried in oil, is the best food for all?'

To compound all these exacerbating traits, Morarjibhai strongly believed in *shivambu kalpa*—auto-urine therapy. He believed that for the illnesses of the poor Indians, millions of them, the best remedy was to drink their own urine—so the press claimed. Morarjibhai set them a personal example. The press loved to make fun of these claims and write pungent articles ridiculing these theories.

On one of my travels with him in Surat, I ventured to ask him about a headline that had appeared in the local newspaper that morning.

'You are referring to the report that I drink a glass of my urine every morning, aren't you?' he asked. I remained silent, embarrassed to respond positively.

'All that is highly exaggerated. I do not drink a glass of my urine. That is not necessary. Just a tablespoon is enough. Ignorant journalists do not take the trouble to look up the research done on urine therapy. Fresh urine taken just before daybreak has so many beneficial chemicals, hormones and melatonin in it that it prevents and even cures cancer if taken at the initial stage.'

I was not sure whether Morarjibhai's claim had any scientific basis. But I remained silent, more in deference to his status and age than to his scientific knowledge.

During the post-flood press meet, the press, egged on by the local social workers and self-serving politicians, complained that the distribution of private aid was not being done equitably. This was a totally false accusation, for I had organised the distribution in a rational manner. Every affected village, with the total affected population and the number of trucks with the nature of the provisions, the dates when they were sent, were all entered into properly maintained registers and updated by Mr Shrotriya. Anticipating the self-serving complaints of the political leaders, I had briefed Morarjibhai before the press meet. He had himself seen the registers and noted how meticulously they were kept.

He listened to the journalists with a sardonic smile. Then said, 'Why don't you let the collector do his job in his own way? Why don't you all go out and bring additional aid and distribute it the way you want? Why do you want to distribute what Arvind Mafatlal, Naval Tata or Kasturbhai Lalbhai has sent to the collector? Why don't you go and raise additional aid?'

There were sullen faces all round. They expected to be given some sops. But they were knocking at the wrong door.

So, they changed tack, 'Sir, it is three days since the floods have receded. There is still a lot of silt and muck in the lanes and by-lanes of the city. The administration has only cleaned the main roads,' they complained.

Morarjibhai turned to me and said, 'There are so many of them here. Take down their names. Give everyone a spade and shovel. Let them go into those lanes and by-lanes and clean up the muck. That is the responsibility of concerned citizens.'

There were no more complaints.

Then it was the turn of the leaders to complain of my high-handedness with the criminal elements. I was a bit on shaky ground. My mistake was to have remained present at the police station when the political looters were being dealt with. But even there, Morarjibhai came to my rescue.

Several villages had been totally devastated by the floods. The huts and ramshackle houses had been completely washed away. Several voluntary organisations had come forward to adopt those villages, raise resources to augment the government grants and rebuild the village. Plans had to be submitted to the collector and approved by him before the villages could be assigned to such non-government organisations (NGOs). Obviously, there was money to be made in this rehabilitation job. Several spurious NGOs, backed by vested interests, jumped into the fray, and I was under pressure to assign at least some villages to one NGO or other, whose antecedents were not all clean and clear.

One organisation that worked diligently and sincerely was the Ramakrishna Mission. At that time, it was headed by Swami Atmasthanandaji, who much later rose to head an important position in the Mission headquarters in Calcutta (now Kolkata). Swamiji was a soft-spoken, pleasant-faced, ever-smiling worker. Highly intelligent, very well-read, with an excellent command of English; he made for delightful company. I found acceptable the Mission's plans for building good-quality houses for the affected persons in a well-laid-out and planned village.

I, therefore, assigned more than a dozen villages to the Mission. Swamiji met me from time to time to apprise me of the progress of the work. Sometimes, I dropped in at the Mission office, where Swamiji and his juniors were housed.

One day, as the work was well-progressed, Swamiji came to meet me. 'Collector Sahab. I require your intervention,' he said.

'Sure', I said, 'What can I do?'

'You see, I got all the concrete pillars for the twelve villages cast in Surat, now I have to get them transported to the various villages. I met the chief of the truck owners' association. He quoted a high price of ₹1.50 per mile per tonne. It took me several rounds of negotiations to reduce the charge. He has now very reluctantly agreed to bring it down to ₹1.20. I feel that is still too high. With our budget, nothing will be left to provide bathrooms in the houses we are building. If you talk to him, he may bring it down further. Any savings would help the affected.'

I rang up the president of the truck owners' association. Since the collector headed the district transport authority, Swamiji knew my word would help. But the president pleaded that ₹1.20 was the bare minimum cost of transport. He claimed that, at the insistence of Swamiji, he had agreed to forego all profits and was, in fact, suffering a marginal loss. However, I managed to cajole him with some use of *dam* and *dand*, and he, very reluctantly, agreed to bring down the quote to ₹1.05. Swamiji was very pleased. A saving of fifteen paise translated into thousands of rupees of savings in the transportation cost.

I met Swamiji a few weeks later, when he came to report the progress. 'How is the work going on? Have you transported all the pillars?' I asked.

'Some are still left.'

'Did the association honour the quote of ₹1.05?'

'Well,' said the Swamiji, 'Actually I am paying them only 95 paise.'

I was a bit taken aback. It had taken me one hour of cajoling and arm-twisting to bring down the quote. 'How is that?' I asked.

'Well, after you brought down the quote to ₹1.05, I went straight to the office of the association. I told the president, "You have given a rebate of fifteen paise on the intervention of the collector. He is only a temporal authority. We are doing God's work. Will you not reduce another ten paise for the sake of God?" And he agreed.'

After the visit of Morarjibhai to the flood-affected Surat city, it was the turn of the then prime minister, Mrs Indira Gandhi. Once I received notice from both the PM's and the CM's office, not only my office but all connected departments got into a flurry of preparation.

It was felt that the circuit house was too small to accommodate her and her entourage. A much larger private bungalow was requisitioned for her stay of two nights. Though the bungalow was well-furnished, it gave a lived-in appearance. That would not do.

Mrs Gandhi was to arrive from Ahmedabad by helicopter, in the afternoon, after lunch. Accompanied by Hitendra Desai, she was to take a round of the Surat city in an open jeep. Both the CM and the collector had to stand with her in the vehicle to give her a running commentary. So, we had to procure a sturdy, tested jeep, take off its canvas roof and cover the iron bars with cloth to ensure that her hands (and ours too) were not soiled. The police driver had to be experienced, well-balanced and well-trained to handle emergencies. No emergencies were anticipated or expected. Surat was by and large a peaceful city. The law and order problems were confined to a few looters who tried to take advantage of the floods. But that had been effectively dealt with.

Two days before the visit, Hari, the old faithful of Jawaharlal Nehru and Indira Gandhi, came to Surat. He was an old family retainer, having served both the father and daughter for many years. He looked old enough to have been recruited by Motilal Nehru.

'What does she like for breakfast?' I asked Hari.

'I cannot predict, sir,' he replied 'She comes to the table, usually in a hurry. Then she asks for eggs or grilled fish or cutlets. Sometimes she asks for idli and chutney or dosa and sambar. It all depends on her mood.'

That put me into a quandary. How was the kitchen to be stocked? One had to be prepared, therefore, with all the possible dishes she may ask for. Not being a hotel, that was a tall order. Arrangements had to be made for the dinner that was to be attended by the CM; a couple of cabinet ministers; the mayor, Mr Golandaz; the MPs representing the city; Mr Hussain Badri, the district Congress chief, and others. I gave a detailed menu to Kwality Restaurant, the only one in the city that could cater to the PM's requirement. As for the vegetarians, such as the CM, the ministers and MPs, their demands could be satisfied by providing vegetarian Gujarati thalis—two sweets, two *bhajia*s, a couple of dry vegetable curries and a couple of dals, puris, rice, *khichdi* and *kadhi*.

The PM took a round of the city, which went off very well. She was deeply impressed by the clean look of the streets so soon after the floods receded. At first, she was sceptical that the roads she was passing through had been under fourteen feet of water just a week before. I pointed out the straw, the plastic bags and the other flotsam and jetsam stuck on top of the lamp posts and telephone poles, left there by the receding waters. When the rehabilitation work done in the district was explained to her, she complimented the CM and the district administration. I was looking forward to a pleasant dinner, with all the meat, fish and chicken dishes I had ordered for her. As we sat down, the uniformed Kwality bearers approached her with platters of kebab, fish and tandoori chicken. Simultaneously, thalis were being placed before the CM, who was sitting on her right, and other ministers. She turned to me and asked, 'What is Hitendrabhai having?'

I said, 'He and the others are having vegetarian thalis.'

'I will also have the vegetarian thali,' she announced.

Immediately, Mr Golandaz and Mr Badri, too, opted for vegetarian thalis in deference to her choice. Who would dare to eat chicken and fish at a table where the PM and the CM were eating only rice and lentil?

There goes my elaborate menu, I said to myself. I was about to order a vegetarian thali for myself when the PM intervened. She called back the Kwality bearer who was taking away the kebab platter.

'Collector Sahab will take the non-vegetarian meal. That should not be wasted,' she said with a twinkle in her eye.

To the dismay of Mayor Golandaz and the envy of Mr Badri, I was the only one who enjoyed the chicken, fish and kebabs at that table.

Taking advantage of her indulgent mood, I spoke of the sufferings of the flood-affected people and their immediate needs and rehabilitation—118 villages had been wiped out. Though the state government and its official machinery were doing its best to rehabilitate and resettle those villages, the inadequacy of finances was certainly a major factor. On her return, the Government of India did send an appraisal team and sanction substantial funds.

But in all my experience then and subsequently, neither the state nor the Centre ever sanctions adequate funds for relief. The Government of India's Central Committee that visits the affected areas and appraises the proposals sent by the state administration always looks askance at the data submitted and rarely recommends an adequate percentage of the demands. Knowing this possibility, the state administration usually inflates the data so as to get at least the actual need.

I am reminded of a story which I heard when I was advisor to the governor in Lucknow many years later. During the British regime, a landlord of Oudh sent in an application to the DM for a licence to buy and maintain a cannon.

'But why do you need a cannon, Khan Sahab,' remonstrated the DM.

'You see, sir, when last I requested for a hundred bags of sugar from the rations shop, you had sanctioned only ten bags. Actually, I need and expect to get only a pistol, so I had to ask for a cannon.'

During my first tenure as assistant collector, Syedna Taher Saifuddin, head of the world community of Dawoodi Bohras, came to Surat to inaugurate Madrasai Saifiya. Surat being the original headquarters of the Dawoodi Bohras before it was shifted to Bombay, the first headquarters contained one of the finest libraries of Bohra literature. I had found, even as early as the sixties, that the Sunni and Shia Muslims of Surat, and by extension the rest of India, held extreme prejudices against the Bohras (and the Khojas, the other major branch of the Ismailis).

When the Syedna's visit was announced, Mr Hussain Badri, the leader of the Bohra community of Surat and president of Surat district Congress Committee, invited me, among others, for an audience with the Syedna and to join the dinner he was giving in his honour. Mr Badri had a magnificent mansion on Station Road, and when I reached the carpeted audience hall, I found Collector Dudani, Mayor Golandaz and other dignitaries already seated around the wall. The Syedna himself was ensconced in an ornate chair placed on a raised dais. Syedna Tahir Saifuddin was in his mid-seventies when I met him. His white beard framing his unwrinkled glowing countenance reflected his Arab lineage. Being the supreme head of the million-strong Bohra community, with followers spread all over the civilised world, he showed his self-confidence and the conviction of his mission in every word he uttered and every gesture he made. I saw his followers enter the audience chamber, barefoot, awestruck and nervous to be in his very presence, and then bow down, place a nazrana before him, and then perform a deep *sajda* (touching their forehead to the ground).

Before dinner, the Syedna retired to an inner chamber. Mr Badri had arranged for a private audience for some of us. The Syedna greeted me with a show of deep affection (as he had been informed that I had supported the educational efforts of the community and had helped in the progress of the Arabic Saifee College) and made me comfortable on a chair close to where he was reclining on a divan. After some desultory talk, I ventured to ask him a rather embarrassing question, 'Your Holiness, I have read in our literature that a Muslim is permitted to prostrate himself before Allah alone, and prostration before idols and human beings is haram. I noticed that all your followers performed the *sajda* before you. Is that permitted?'

He smiled at my question. Perhaps this issue had been raised before him by others also, so he was neither riled nor embarrassed by my question.

'You are right,' he said. 'No one other than Allah should be worshipped. But prostration, or *sajda*, is of several types. The *sajda*-

e-uboodi is prostration before God, *ta'zeemi* or *tahreemi* is the prostration of respect, *sajda-e-shukrana* is the prostration of gratitude. My followers do not perform the *sajda-e-uboodi*. They do not believe me to be God. Some of them do so out of respect and some out of gratitude.'

The Syedna then presented me with a signed copy of a Arabic qasida, a panegyric he had written, with an inscription in his own hand. I still have it in my library.

His successor, Syedna Burhanuddin, too, visited Surat in 1967–1968, during my tenure as DM of the district. Mr Badri, who had remained in office as the district Congress chief, gave a grand dinner this time, too, for the senior officials and political leaders. I learnt that when the Syedna visits Surat, a team of his chefs are sent in advance to the house of the host. They provide a list of the provisions that they require for his daily meals and for the banquet. The well-to-do host, like Mr Badri, arranges for all the provisions. Needless to say, that was one of the best banquets I ever attended—a feast for the eyes as well as the palate.

The Bohra community, under the strong leadership of the Syedna, has remained a monolithic sect, and the voice of dissidence, even though rare, could not go beyond a whisper.

Recently, Syedna Burhanuddin passed away at the ripe old age of 100. Eighteen people lost their lives in a stampede while attending his funeral.

The effort at rescue and rehabilitation and my constant alternating exposure to the sun and rain took a heavy toll on my health, and I fell ill with an attack of severe rheumatism. For more than a month, I was practically immobilised in bed, with every single joint of my body crying out at the slightest movement. It was my wife, Husnara, who nursed me back to health, applying Ayurvedic oil to my body and giving me a hot water bath daily. After recovery, I took leave to visit my mother in Madras. When I returned, an order transferring me to Bulsar, the neighbouring district, awaited me, and I packed up my meagre belongings and left for Bulsar with my family in tow.

OF SMUGGLERS AND RIOTS

While Surat had its rural, underdeveloped talukas like Vyara and Songadh, mostly inhabited by tribals and Dublas, the landless labourers still smarting under the landlord's yoke and exploited by the rich absentee landowners, Bulsar had its share of tribals in Dharampur and Bansda. In addition to Bulsar, I was put in charge of the adjacent tribal district of Dangs, its 300 villages populated entirely by Adivasis.

Since Bulsar was a newly created district, sheared off from its parent Surat, it had no colonial-style bungalow with vast sprawling grounds. My predecessor, who was the first collector, had bought a bungalow from a Parsi family on Tithal Road. It was a two-storeyed mansion, with four large rooms and an airy veranda facing the front yard on the first floor. By this time, my mother and aunt had come to stay with us for some time. The accommodation on the first floor sufficed the needs of my small family. I used the ground floor only to receive visitors and put up the occasional guest. Since this bungalow was located right on the road leading to Tithal beach, which had a colony of fishermen, we had no dearth of daily supply of fresh fish of every variety.

Bulsar also happened to be the birthplace of Morarji Desai.

I found Bulsar a more interesting district than Surat. Since the town itself was quite small, with a population not exceeding 20,000 souls, there was less of politics and little of prejudice. The chairman of the municipality, a Mr Shroff, was a suave, polished, old-world Parsi gentleman. I had to interact with Mr Shroff fairly often in regard to municipal affairs and found him courteous and prompt.

The southern part of the district was dominated by landlords belonging to the Anavil Desai and Parsi communities. They owned large tracts of both fertile land and grasslands. In times of drought, Bulsar supplied thousands of wagonloads of fodder to Saurashtra and Kutch.

In the very first week of my charge, Mr Bhutaiya, the *mamlatdar* who had served me ably in Mehsana, came to brief me. He was now a deputy collector.

'Sir, the Desai landlords of the district are a very tough lot. The success or failure of the collector of Bulsar is assessed by the government on the basis of how much land he has managed to get from these landlords and put the tenants in charge.'

'But what is the problem, Bhutaiya?' I asked. 'There is the Tenancy Act and the Land Ceiling Act. Why can't we apply these laws and take over the surplus land for the tenants?'

Mr Bhutaiya smiled indulgently. 'It is not so simple as all that, sir,' he said. 'Every landlord has divided and sub-divided his vast holdings on paper and put the various portions in the name of his sons, his daughters-in-law, his grandchildren and his wife. They have employed a levy of senior lawyers from Ahmedabad and Bombay to advise them on ways and means of evading the land tenure laws.'

These facts were confirmed a few days later when I sat for my first hearing on the land tenure cases. In Surat, I had seen senior, old, sedate lawyers appearing before me, addressing me respectfully: 'Your honour. I am a widow of seventy-five and hold thirty acres of old tenure land...' Though it sounded a bit incongruous to hear a sixty-year-old Parsi lawyer, claiming to be a Hindu widow of seventy-five, I had soon caught on and entered fully into the spirit of the arguments. But the lawyers who appeared for the Desai landlords had none of the deferential airs of the Surat lawyers. Their demeanour and body language conveyed a message: Ah, what does this provincial officer from Madras know of the law? We could produce umpteen case laws and precedents to overawe this bumpkin.

After the first few minutes of listening to their arguments, I realised their game plan. So, I interrupted them, 'You can give me all the case laws and the precedents in your written pleas. Now, please come to the point. I have framed a few questions. Please answer them briefly and clearly. I do not have all day to spend listening to one case.'

That approach took the wind out of their sails. Their strategy was to impress their clients with long-winded representations, use of strong and incomprehensible legal jargon. Once they realised that their tactics did not overawe me, they fell in line.

However, I realised that Mr Bhutaiya was right. Following the law strictly was not going to help the government obtain the required land for distribution to the landless. There is a common saying: If the ghee does not come out of the bottle with a straight finger, you have to bend it. All the landlords, I found on investigation, had either skeletons in their closets or hidden chinks in their armours. The trick was to find and use them. The administration started putting pressure on the landlords by threatening to expose the skeletons or widen the chinks. Slowly and surely, the landlords realised that I meant business and started voluntarily surrendering the excess land. I could do all that without overtly antagonising them, individually or severally.

Bulsar district, in the sixties and seventies of the last century, faced the grave menace of the smugglers' mafia. The enclave of coastal Daman is nestled in the lap of the district, and since it was directly under the jurisdiction of the Government of India, the writ of Bulsar administration did not run there. While Gujarat was a dry state with the prohibition law in full force, Daman was a wet territory, helping both the bootleggers in Daman and enriching the police outposts on the border. As a hangover from the erstwhile Portuguese colonial rule, its territory was dotted with quaint pubs and small restaurants serving Goan-style seafood. Even the church fathers offered beer when an officer visited them. It attracted numerous weekend visitors from Gujarat, who drove over into the Union Territory and patronised the pubs and bars. Graduating from smuggling liquor into Gujarat, some of the enterprising members of the fishermen and seafaring community brought in gold from Dubai and bartered it for silver. This posed a heavy drain on the national exchequer, and the smugglers of Daman and Bombay thrived on this illegal trade. While Bombay was ruled by the underworld dons—Haji Mastan, Karim Lala and Shetty—Daman was ruled by three notorious smugglers: Sukkur Naran Bakhiya, Lallu Jogi and Bhana Khalpa. They had become household names in Gujarat and were considered to be the Robin Hoods of South Gujarat. The local fisherman community of Daman fully protected them, while they, in turn, supported the community economically. The ill-paid local police of both Daman and the border areas of Bulsar fell to the lure of the huge caches of money the smugglers commanded.

One of my informers got the news that a large consignment of silver ingots was being smuggled into Daman in exchange for smuggled gold. Ashok Tandon, the district SP, and I waylaid the two trucks and captured more than twenty tonnes of silver ingots. That was one of the largest consignments of silver seized by the district administration. The gold had escaped our net. For the first few days, the drivers refused to divulge to whom the silver was consigned. But then, under intense interrogation, we learnt it belonged to Sukkur Bakhiya. I confiscated the entire lot and issued a notice to Bakhiya to appear before me. For quite a number of days, he evaded the summons. Instead, one of his henchmen informed my personal assistant that he would see me when I tour in Vapi and Umbergaon in my open jeep. It was a veiled threat against my life. I sent word that I shall be visiting Vapi and Umbergaon the very next week.

The collectors in the late sixties and early seventies had not yet become eligible for an Ambassador car and still travelled around in an open jeep, sitting by the driver, exposed to anyone who wanted to take a potshot at him. I did go to Vapi and Umbergaon in the open jeep, keeping my eyes peeled for any threat and my right hand on the automatic in my pocket, with the safety catch off. But nothing happened, and I returned to Bulsar after a three-day visit.

But then, a barrage of lawyers appeared before me, along with Bakhiya, laying claim to the silver. 'Your honour, the silver belongs to Mr Sukkur Bakhiya, and here are the documents to prove that.'

'But why was he carrying twenty tonnes of silver to Daman?'

'Sir, he was taking the silver to make silver utensils in Daman.'

'But has he set up a factory to make utensils in Daman?'

'No, sir, he was taking the silver to store it in his godown there. He is proposing to buy land and machinery to set up a utensil factory.'

'But why was he buying so much silver before he had even bought land, built a factory and got the machinery?'

'But, your honour, there is no law that dictates that you cannot buy raw material when it is cheap to convert it into a finished product at an appropriate time.'

Of course, he had me there. But I went ahead and rejected his request to release the silver, giving various arguments. The silver remained in the treasury for more than two years. Of course, Bakhiya preferred appeal after appeal until his efforts reached the Central Board of Excise and Customs. There, he managed to convince the appellate member that the silver he was transporting to Daman was raw material for a utensils factory for which he had no licence, no land, no building and no equipment. The board passed orders to release the silver to Bakhiya. The wooden planks of the boxes in which the silver had been stored were sagging with the weights. Bakhiya was happy to get his silver back. As a parting shot at the administration, he turned to me and said, with an unctuous smile, 'Sir, thank you very much for keeping my silver safe and secure for so long. Thanks to you, I have made a fortune. The price of silver has now almost doubled in the last two-and-a-half years!'

Sometimes you act without foreseeing the results of your action. But then it is not always possible to foresee results.

One fine morning, I heard a hubbub outside the bungalow gate. A milling crowd of Dalit men, women and children were clamouring to meet me. They were all in a state of agitated anxiety. Such a large number of distressed petitioners boded an emergency. So, I walked down to the front yard and asked them as to what was agitating them.

'Sir, we have some lands just outside Bulsar. None of us has more than an acre or half of land. We live for the whole year on the rice we grow there. Our lands are downstream of a large rain-fed water tank that belongs to Shantibhai Desai. He allows us to draw water from this tank twice or thrice a year. In return, we provide free labour on his large landholding. Since we have to work almost all year round on his land without any wages, we requested him to give us some wages in addition to the free water. He got very angry. He is so angry that he has stopped that last supply. Our crops require one last supply of water to survive and are dying. If not saved, we will starve for the whole of next year. Please intervene and save us.'

Their plea was genuine and pathetic. I telephoned Shantibhai. After some polite talk, I told him that, according to law, he was bound to pay the prescribed minimum wage to the Dalit labourers. He could, of course, charge them for the water he supplied according to the rates charged by the irrigation department. He refused to listen. His reply was couched in language that told me to mind my own business, as the matter was between him and his 'traditional servitors'. I asked the petitioners to come to my office at ten in the morning. I also requested Shantibhai to join me so that we could explore an amicable solution. Shantibhai refused.

When I went to office after having alerted the chitnis, who dealt with all issues relating to land, I was informed that Shantibhai was the nephew of Morarji Desai and managed the affairs of the minister in Bulsar, and that I should be careful in the way I dealt with the issue.

I looked at the records of the ownership of the water tank. While the current records showed his and his family's name as owners, the older records, going back fifty years, were ambiguous. There was an entry indicative of the tank having been a public waterbody. Under the Bombay Land Revenue Code, it was laid down that in such cases where there was a doubt as to whether a piece of land was private or public property, the collector should order an enquiry into the matter. I, therefore, ordered that the *prant* officer or deputy collector in charge of the subdivision should enquire and decide on the matter and, in the meantime, the bund that obstructed the flow of the water to the lands of the Dalits should be demolished immediately. This was done the same day under police protection, notwithstanding the strong protest from Shantibhai.

Shantibhai, of course, challenged my order in the civil court. He called it high-handed, irresponsible and without jurisdiction. While the arguments were going on, I happened to meet the civil and sessions judge hearing the case, across a bridge table in the club. I did not know that the hearings had been completed that very day and he had passed orders.

'How was your day?' I asked him in all innocence at the bridge table. He thought I was enquiring after the case.

'I read your orders and the arguments of the government lawyer defending it. You know you had based your order on insufficient and ambiguous evidence?' he asked.

'I believe justice is more important than mere evidence, ambiguous or strong. If I see a murder committed before my very eyes by a particular man I recognise, even if a hundred witnesses depose that he was in London at that time, I would still convict him.'

'I believe you. I have, therefore, upheld your orders today,' he said with a smile.

'Thank you,' I said and promptly lost the next rubber.

In September 1969, riots broke out in Ahmedabad between Hindus and Muslims. There were large-scale massacres, brutality on women and children, rapes, looting and arson. The official death toll was over a thousand, with hundreds of grievous injuries. Unofficial death toll was over 2,000. Thousands were rendered homeless and had to take refuge in ramshackle tent camps or municipal schools or dargahs. Many of them took refuge in Sarkhej and Shah Alamroza in Ahmedabad. Out of the eighteen districts of the state, small- or large-scale pogroms took place in seventeen of them.

Since the attack of Mahmud Ghaznavi on Somnath in the twelfth century and the highly exaggerated claims of later sycophantic historians like Barani, Isami and Ferishta, there had been a simmering undercurrent of communal hostility against the Muslims not only in Gujarat but also in most parts of North India. The situation worsened with the advent of another Mahmud as sultan of Gujarat. Mahmud Begda captured the

Hindu kingdom of Junagadh (and later Pavagadh, where the notorious Godhra is located) and kept its last ruler, Rai Khengar, in prison in the Bhadra Fort in Ahmedabad for more than two decades. Junagadh was never restored to Hindu rule even during the British period, and a nawab ruled there until the independence of India. Many of the Rajput kingdoms of Saurashtra and Rajasthan constantly faced raids by other Rajputs and Muslim marauders. The itinerant singers known as the Bhats and Charans—the troubadours of India—kept the memory of these events alive, visiting every village in Saurashtra. They sang of the cruel Turks, Mughals and Afghans, and the heroic but futile resistance put up by the Hindu rajas. That strengthened the Hindu hostility towards Muslims—a clear case of visiting the apocryphal sins of the ancestors on the current generations.

Once the British discovered this fertile ground of Hindu–Muslim hostility, they sedulously nurtured it with additional myths. Lord Ellenborough ordered the British commander in Kabul to uproot the gates of Mahmud's tomb and restore them to Somnath, from where they had allegedly been removed. When brought back, they turned out to be of Egyptian make. British historians like Henry Elliot and John Dowson added more fuel to the fire.

Nurtured on such heroic myths, one can imagine the mindset of the common Hindu in the village who had to migrate to the city in search of sustenance. K.M. Munshi, the stalwart of Hinduism who got the Somnath Temple rebuilt after Independence, wrote a book titled *Jai Somnath*, which became a classic of Gujarati literature in the forties. It was widely read in cities and villages and successfully perpetuated the myth of Mahmud Ghaznavi having killed 50,000 Hindus during his raid. Munshi was highly influenced by Bankim Chandra Chatterjee's *Anandamath*, which propagated that Muslims were the greater enemy of Hindus than the British. Romila Thapar, after painstaking research, has debunked this myth in her book *Somanatha: The Many Voices of History*. But even my most secular friends deprecate her research as 'Muslim appeasement'.

The advent of Mahatma Gandhi, a great son of Gujarat, and the philosophy of ahimsa and Hindu–Muslim unity preached by him, pushed the simmering communal tensions into the underground for a few decades, though there were sporadic clashes between the two communities. Godhra was one such event in the twenties when Morarji Desai, then posted as a deputy collector, was accused of playing a partisan role. The forties brought the simmering hostility into the open with Mohammad Ali Jinnah, another son of Gujarat, calling for the partition of India, and the actual partition itself, in which a million people lost their lives. Gujarat could not escape this maelstrom.

I joined Gujarat just twelve years after the assassination of Gandhiji. The Muslims were pushed into the background after Partition and had been left rudderless and jobless. Even worse, they found themselves leaderless, ever searching for a guide.

In the city of Ahmedabad, the poor, illiterate Muslims elected a bootlegger as their Robin Hood. This brought them into direct conflict with the already well-entrenched Hindu bootleggers. Clashes for territory, with the police mostly siding with whoever paid them, were not infrequent.

In this tinderbox of a communal cauldron, even a small spark would have sufficed. Visitors to the city added more fuel. Atal Bihari Vajpayee, the leader of the then Bharatiya Jana Sangh, visited Ahmedabad in early September and spoke of the need for *rashtrabhakti* and the threat of Pakistan. He was followed by Balraj Madhok, president of the party, who spoke of issues closer home, namely the Muslim threat.

Then a police jeep knocked a handcart on which a copy of the Quran was being carried. A Hindu police inspector was alleged to have trampled it, leading to an agitation by some hot-headed Muslims. A few days later, in a similar incident, a copy of the Ramayana was allegedly trampled upon by a Muslim police inspector. Both these events were obviously concocted by agents provocateurs. A few days later, an *urs* (religious commemoration) function was being locally celebrated by the Muslims of Jamalpur. Some cows belonging to the Jagannath temple being driven home through the gathered crowd allegedly injured some Muslim women. Some miscreants, allegedly Muslim, broke the windows of the Jagannath temple.

Of such flimsy stuff are communal riots made in India. The conflagration consumed 2,000 lives. Every city and town had its tale of atrocities. Attempts were made to engineer riots in Bulsar district also. The Hindu Dharma Raksha Samiti sent agents provocateurs to various taluka towns to make inciting speeches. But we managed to nab most of them.

By September 1969, I had developed a network of informers of my own from all communities and in all towns. I nurtured them with minor favours. I used all the strategies taught by Chanakya and Machiavelli to keep the law and order situation under control. When a newspaper in Navsari attempted to inflame the public with provocative articles, I checked and found that he had not maintained proper accounts of the newsprint quota allotted to his press. The press was closed down, and it took him two years of litigation to get it reopened. When some of the communal-minded journalists in Bulsar tried the same tricks, I discovered that many of them had let out their houses on rent without obtaining permission of the collector. Since Bulsar was a newly created district, the government had made the Gujarat Rent Control Act applicable to the district. When notices were issued to such journalists, they stopped publishing inflammatory news. Some of the local members of the Hindu Dharma Raksha Samiti had establishments of various kinds under operation in the district. Some had fair price shops under the PDS, one owned petrol pumps and gas agencies, some had encroached on public lands, some had arms licences not renewed in time and so on. I used *saam*, *daam*, *dand*

and *bhed*, in various combinations, to keep such elements under control. A few attempts in Bilimora, Gandevi and Navsari were nipped in the bud with a stern hand. The Muslims were warned not to react to minor provocations such as slogans and music before mosques. No religious processions were permitted. All suspected disruptive elements from both communities were put behind bars.

It is my firm belief that if the DM and the SP act firmly, no riot of any kind can take place in a district. I discovered that the DM had been empowered with drastic powers under more than 500 sections of various acts and laws passed during the British era. If the DM studies these laws carefully, he can administer the district effectively for the benefit of the common man. By a judicious use of these laws, he can keep the nefarious elements under firm control, giving him time to look after other developmental work—construction of schools, colleges, public health centres, sports stadium, agriculture, animal husbandry and fisheries. Of course, it requires diligence, hard work and commitment.

When the home secretary, Mr Rajpal, visited my district long after the riots, he did appreciate the fact that Bulsar had remained by and large peaceful, 'Moosa, you were lucky. The people of Bulsar seem to be a peaceful lot. They did not join the rest of the state in the pogroms.'

I regretted that I had failed to keep the state government informed of the vigorous steps taken by me to achieve that peace. But then, I was happy that the people of Bulsar got the credit.

A few months after the riots, I visited the tribal taluka of Dharampur. The area of Dharampur covered almost all of Bulsar district. The headquarters of this mainly afforested taluka is the small town of Dharampur, with a meagre population of less than 7,000–8,000 souls. It had been ruled for long by the Sisodia Rajputs—the last ruler lived in Bombay and visited his estate but rarely. The last palace his father had designed with the help of an Italian architect had been abandoned halfway by the son when the state merged with India. When I visited it in 1969, its abandoned rooms, dust-covered sliding-glass doors and jammed French windows had a forlorn look. It was designed as a modern palace in the middle of a forest. The elegant billiard table, not used even once, still looked in good condition.

The only two industries of note were an activated charcoal factory and a catechu (*kattha*) factory. Both were based on the supply of wood by the forest department. *Kattha*, used by the betel-nut-chewing Indians, is made from the wood of acacia catechu, locally known as *khair*. It was a highly priced commodity and was sold in retail in grams, while the factory produced it in tonnes and exported it all over India.

The government had built primary schools in many of the villages, but the teachers preferred to live either in Dharampur or Vapi, where their own children could enjoy better facilities. There was one primary health centre and some sub-centres, but during my visit, I found most of the government doctors and many of the nurses absent from duty. At only one sub-centre did I find a doctor actually living on the premises in a quarter built for him.

'Why are most of the doctors absent from the other centres?' I asked him. 'I propose to take severe action against all the absentee staff.'

'Sir, as it is, the department finds it difficult to attract doctors to serve in these forlorn tribal areas. If strong action is taken against the existing staff, the periodic visits they make to the PHC (public health centre) and the occasional medical help the Adivasis get, will stop too.'

'Since the government has provided decent quarters and special allowance for service in the backward regions, what prevents the doctors from their humanitarian duty?'

'Frankly, sir, we doctors do not enjoy credibility among the Adivasis,' he replied. 'You see, every village in Dharampur has a local witch doctor called the *bhua*. The Adivasis believe that all diseases are caused by a demon occupying the body of the patient. So, the family takes the patient to the local shaman's house. The *bhua* puts on all his finery and dances around the patient. Sometimes, depending on the ferocity of the occupying demon, the *bhua* beats the patient with his magic wand to drive away the unseen occupant. If the fever or diarrhoea is mild, the terrifying antics of the *bhua* drives away the demon and the patient gets well. But more often, if the condition of the patient deteriorates, the family then brings the sick man to the PHC. By the time the patient is brought to the doctor, he is close to death, while some die in the centre. "See, had you brought him to me instead of the doctor, I would have driven away the demon," the *bhua* would claim. Our reputation and credibility in the eyes of the Dublas and Warlis of Dharampur is zilch.'

After deep thought and study of the methods adopted by the British in Afghanistan and in other tribal areas, I thought of a possible solution. At the moment, the *bhua* was a part of the problem. The solution was to make him a part of the solution.

I wrote to the government that we should recruit a prominent and recognised *bhua* and appoint him as an attendant to the PHC. He should be a kind of resident consultant, and his job would be to persuade the Adivasis to bring their sick to the hospital. He should be allowed to perform his mumbo-jumbo on the patient while the doctor should do his diagnosis and administer the required medicine. The *bhua* could also be persuaded, since he would have gained government recognition and remuneration, to become an important propagator of public health schemes like hygiene, administration of vaccines and prevention of prenatal and postnatal complications.

My scheme was forwarded to the director of medical services. The professional health experts were horrified.

'What! Make the witch doctor a part of the health department! Allow him to live on the premises? Perform his mumbo-jumbo on the premises! The district magistrate is encouraging superstition,' they commented.

Long after I left Bulsar, I learnt that some enterprising health secretary involved the Indian Institute of Management, Ahmedabad, to undertake a study of the problems. The IIM-A produced an erudite report, full of statistical data and charts, essentially supporting my solution. I do not know whether the *bhua* has yet become a part of the solution or still remains a part of the problem.

Later that year, the governor, Shriman Narayan, and his wife, Madalsaben, were to visit Dangs. Governor Narayan enjoyed the reputation of being a Gandhian. He had functioned as Gandhiji's secretary in the Wardha Ashram. Madalsaben was the daughter of Jamnalal Bajaj, who had risen from a poor background to become a rich industrialist and businessman. He came under the spell of Mahatma Gandhi, gave up his British title of Rai Bahadur and persuaded Gandhiji to shift to Wardha, near Nagpur, from Sabarmati. Gandhiji had adopted Jamnalal Bajaj as his own and was known to call him his fifth son.

When Shriman Narayan, Jamnalal's son-in-law, became the governor of Gujarat, he used to get himself and Madalsaben photographed in the Raj Bhavan grinding their own wheat in the stone mill—a *chakki*. This was published in the newspapers. Unkind gossip had it that the first shot was not approved by the Raj Bhavan PRO as the governor and his wife were immaculately dressed in crisp white khadi. This was not in keeping with the image of a couple who ground their own flour. The officer then took another photograph with the couple dressed appropriately in crumpled clothes.

There was only an old, dilapidated forest guest house in Ahwa, the headquarters of the Dangs district, where the governer and his wife could to stay for their three-day visit. However, long neglect had rendered it almost uninhabitable. Even the toilets had become non-functional. Since the governor and Madalsaben slept in separate rooms, at least two well-furnished bedrooms with attached toilets were required. The only other building that could accommodate the governor, his wife and his secretary was the collector's bungalow, where I stayed for a week every month. This, too, had very minimal facilities, with old-style bathrooms, rusted taps and creaking fans, remnants of the British Raj. I had been asking the PWD to repair and make the bungalow habitable. The executive engineer always pleaded that he had no funds and that the work was not budgeted. So, I took this opportunity to invite the governor to stay in the collector's bungalow, and I myself would have to manage for three days in the forest guest house. Called upon to take care of the governor's needs, the executive engineer somehow managed to find the necessary funds not only to repair, refurbish and paint the bungalow inside and outside but to also install new bathroom fittings in the two bathrooms. He even installed two window air-conditioners. The governor's stay was comfortable, and, in the bargain, I got a decent bungalow for the rest of my tenure. The executive engineer, of course, later removed the two air-conditioners, which had been borrowed from the circuit house in Navsari. I managed to retain the rest of the fittings.

As we were driving to Ahwa, the governor and Madalsaben were talking of the recent communal riots in Gujarat. I was sitting in the front seat and could not help overhearing parts of their conversation. Madalsaben had just returned from Wardha, where she had gone to meet Vinoba Bhave, another well-known Gandhian. Vinoba Bhave, at that time, was engaged in collecting surplus land from the landlords in Maharashtra for distribution to the landless poor. This was known as the Bhoodan Movement..

'I told Vinobaji about the tragic communal riots in Gujarat,' Madalsaben turned to her husband.

'Hm,' said the governor, making a non-committal sound. 'And what did he say?'

'He didn't say anything. I told him that the unofficial death count amounted to close to 2,000, mostly Muslims,' Madalsaben said.

'And what did Vinobaji say?' asked Shrimanji, again. 'You know, he simply said, "*bas*!"' Madalsaben said wonderingly. 'What did he mean? Weren't 2,000 deaths a large enough number to shock him?'

'Perhaps it was a sarcastic comment,' said Shrimanji.

But Madalsaben continued to wonder. And I along with her.

Having been secretary to Gandhiji, the governor had a lively curiosity. But the problem was that he believed the collector should know everything, even the minutiae of the district, its flora and fauna, its ethnic composition, its soil characteristics and so on. On the way to Ahwa, he would look out the window and ask me odd questions, for example, the species of some large trees in the roadside plantations. I had to make a guess. 'They are teak, sir,' I said.

When he saw another grove, he asked, 'And what are those trees?'

'Eucalyptus, sir,' I said without batting an eyelid. 'And how old do you think those teak trees are?'

'About ten years old, sir,' I again made a shot in the dark.

Just before starting the climb into the mountain of Dangs, the conservator of forests was waiting by the road with his staff to meet us and pay his respects to the governor. Before the governor could get down from the car to accept his greeting, I jumped out from the other side, drew the conservator aside and told him sternly, 'The governor has seen some plantations on the way. I have told him they are teak and eucalyptus. And that they are ten years old. Please make sure they are teak and eucalyptus and ten years old. Not any other species.' The conservator understood and smiled. By this time, the governor had got down. When the governor asked him, the conservator confirmed what I had told him. The governor complimented me on my knowledge of the flora of my district as we resumed our journey.

When I met the conservator at dinner that evening in the forest guest house where I was staying, I thanked him for backing me up.

'I didn't back you up, Mr Raza,' he said, again with a smile. 'They are actually teak and eucalyptus plantations. Only, the teak is fifteen years old, and the eucalyptus, only five.'

Dangs has had a very colourful history. It is reported that even during the reign of the sultans of Gujarat and later the Mughals, the rulers gave Dangs a wide berth. The highly afforested and hilly terrain, familiar to the tribals, inhospitable to any invader, proved forbidding territory to them. Shivaji, the great Maratha warrior, is reported to have made peace with the five kings of Dang—Pimpli, Gadhavi, Daher, Vasurna and Linga—and used it as a base, with their help, for his forays into Surat. The British, greedy for the forest wealth of the district, tried to capture it by force. In 1842, the five kings of Dangs formed a confederacy and gave the British redcoats a tough fight. The defeated British were forced to enter into a treaty under which they agreed to pay 3,000 pieces of silver to the rajas and were permitted to exploit the teak and bamboo of Dangs. This compensation continued to be paid annually in a grand durbar even after Independence. The Government of India, in 1970, abolished the privy purses of the Indian rajas and nawabs who had ceded their territory to

India. But since the Dangs rajas had entered into a treaty with the British, the Government of India continues to honour it to this day.

Just before Holi, Ahwa became one big mela ground, with stalls selling eatables, gewgaws, bangles and bead necklaces. Almost the entire population of Dangs—men, women and children—gathered in the township, camping in the open ground and makeshift thatched huts. They came bedecked in their best finery and moved from stall to stall, window shopping or buying trinkets—bangles, necklaces, anklets, earrings and multicoloured fabrics. Of course, marijuana in various forms was consumed.

On the appointed day, the rajas arrived in their horse-drawn buggies (carriages). Generally dressed in white but wearing colourful turbans, they made an impressive show. I sat in the centre of the stage, with Husnara by my side. But none of the rajas brought their wives with them. I recalled that mention of their womenfolk before the rajas and nawabs was considered *lese majeste*, a breach of royal etiquette. I made a customary speech, lauding the love and affection in which the government held the rajas. Of course, it was nothing but keeping up the old colonial tradition, the *mai-baap* approach. Thereafter, the ceremony to handover the 'privy purses' started. One by one, they were called by their names and titles. As they came up, I handed over their purses to them ceremoniously.

In the evening, I hosted a banquet for all of them in my bungalow. This time, I noticed they came in a different headgear, accompanied by their *karbharis*, their ministers who stood behind them in respectful silence. Having been brought up in a different tradition, I tried to make small talk at dinner, enquiring after their domain, crops, flora and fauna. But they never answered my queries. It was their *karbhari* who answered. Whenever the raja felt that his *karbhari* had not given a correct reply, he made a signal. The *karbhari* bent down, and the raja whispered the correct information into his ear. Then the *karbhari* would straighten up, apologise and amend the reply given earlier.

'How was the crop this year in Pimpri?' I asked the raja of Pimpri.

'Well, the rains were not enough. We had to buy millets from the other villages,' replied the *karbhari* of Pimpri.

'Which other villages?' I asked. 'Oh, Gadhavi came to our help.'

At this, the raja of Pimpri made an invisible signal. The *karbhari* bent down, listened and straightened up.

'I am sorry, sir, it was not Gadhavi but Vasurna that came to our help.'

One fine morning, the government in its wisdom decided that Gujarat, too, like its neighbours, must have a hill station of its own. Maharashtra had Lonavala and Matheran; Rajasthan had Mount Abu. Gujarat had none. The tallest and coolest mountain of Gujarat was, of course, Dangs in the Sahyadari range, and the highest point of Dangs was at a village called Saputara—the 'Abode of Serpents'. It was so called because it had the carved image of a snake worshipped by the local tribals. Moreover, Saputara had a seasonal river that could be dammed to create an artificial lake. Work had been going on for the dam. As it neared completion, a tribal village was coming under the backwater and was threatened with submergence. It fell to my unfortunate lot to shift the tribal village to a different, higher location. The tribals had been living on the banks of the river for centuries, cultivating their small patches of land, catching fish from the river. So, naturally, they were most unwilling to be 'shifted' from their natural abode to go and live in a totally alien location. Though the new village I built for them, just a few miles away from Saputara, was well-planned, with a primary school, a public health sub-centre and other amenities, the tribals would have none of it and just refused to move out of Saputara.

As I sat talking with the headman, he came out with many arguments against the new village.

'You have built a cement floor in each house. Who can sleep on such hard ground? Every bone in my body aches in the morning when I sleep on such a floor.'

'How do you know that?' I challenged him.

'I went and spent a night in the pucca house you have built for us. We prefer our soft earthen floor.'

'That is not a difficult problem to solve. I can get the cement floor dug up and you can plaster it with earth and cow dung.'

'You have made brick walls. When the cool breeze blows, our reed walls allow the wind to pass through.'

'Okay, we can put a couple of trellised windows in each wall.'

'But what will I do when my old father dies, tell me?'

'Why, what is the problem if your father dies?' I asked him.

'When anyone dies in our hut, we know the soul remains in the hut. So, we burn it down, liberate his soul, move a few yards away and build a new one. Will you allow us to burn down this brick-and-mortar house and build a new one for us?'

I was stumped. I found it beyond my capacity to find a solution to liberate a soul without burning his abode.

Morarji Desai visited Bulsar and stayed at his ancestral house, which was in a village close to Tithal, the seaside resort, when he was invited to lay the foundation stone of the new building that was to house the collectorate and a new government hospital. The focus of his speech was on honesty in administration. He fulminated against all public servants who did not lead a life of austerity, honesty and integrity. He then quoted the example of Lord Ram and the ethical model of Ram Rajya. However, his speech did not endear him to the orthodox Hindus nor the press, which noted: 'Even Lord Ram failed in the high standards of morality he had set up. His asking Sita to go through the *agni pariksha*, the ordeal by fire, to prove her chastity challenged by the casual remark of an illiterate washerman was not right. Sita in that test emerged as an upholder of higher morality than Ram himself.' Such views publicly aired always got a hostile press. At the hospital function, he talked of a correct lifestyle that would obviate the need for hospitals.

That evening, when I called on him at his modest house, I found him busy with the village accountant, a public official, meticulously going over the records of his landholdings. I had earlier learnt that on the day of the Diwali festival, when the village accountant came to pay his respects and greet him, Morarji gave him ₹50—a lot of money in those days. That was to ensure that his land records were not tampered with.

On the way to Umbergaon, the next morning, I asked him as to the morality of paying money to the *talati* for keeping the records straight, which was in any case his duty. 'Is it not a bribe?' I asked.

'That is not a bribe. That is only a Diwali gift. It is a tradition of the senior to give a gift to the junior callers on Diwali day.' The issue demanded a debate, but I remained silent. But his assertion that leading a sober austere life, eating vegetarian food, consuming only fruits, both fresh and dry, would ensure that you would never need to go to a hospital provoked my argumentative spirit.

'What about accidents? If you are severely wounded, break your leg or injure an eye, don't you need a hospital?' I asked.

'You did not hear my speech properly. I never said we don't need hospitals. I would not have laid the foundation stone of a hospital if I had believed that. I talked of the right way of living that would obviate the need to go to a hospital. And with a right way of life and right conduct, all accidents can be avoided. And there are many diseases that can be treated through naturopathy, with a proper diet and conducive environment'.

'Such as?' I asked.

'When I was a deputy collector in the twenties, my younger brother fell ill with tuberculosis. In those days, it was a fatal disease. There was no medicine to affect a cure. So, I took leave, took my brother to a village in Kaira district and fed him with the milk of a white cow for six months. I gave him no cereals but fruits, nuts, vegetables and plenty of milk, day in and out. At the end of six months, he was fully cured.'

'Why a white cow? Why not a brown cow?' I asked. This was not a facetious question. I had heard that Morarjibhai always took a white cow's milk. That had aroused my curiosity.

'God has created animals with different sets of horns, bones, colours. There is a meaning behind that differentiation. The qualities of the milk of a white cow are different from the milk of a black or brown cow, just as the goat's milk is different from cow's milk.'

That appeared a rational response.

'What about cancer?' I asked. 'What is the natural cure for cancer?'

'A diet consisting of grapes, red, for three months will cure first-stage cancer,' he said.

'But if the man is in the third stage?'

'There is no cure for the third-stage cancer even in your allopathy.'

'Sir, all this appears so simple. If all diseases can be controlled or cured by diet alone, then all the doctors and vaids will go out of business,' I said rather facetiously.

Morarjibhai reddened. 'You have not read anything about naturopathy. You do not know its basic principles. You should never argue from a position of ignorance,' he rebuked me sternly.

After his return to Delhi, I received a parcel containing three volumes, with a letter from his secretary.

'The honourable finance minister has asked me to send you these books on naturopathy. Please return them to him when he next comes to Bulsar.'

I had to wade through those three tomes thoroughly, knowing that Morajibhai would put me through a catechism on his next visit.

In the beginning of 1971, when it was announced that Indira Gandhi was to visit three cities in Bulsar district, ostensibly to explain the rationale of her policies, the onus of preparing for her visit fell to my lot as the collector. She was to hop from venue to venue by helicopter, and I wondered how I was supposed to remain present at Navsari, Bilimora and Vapi simultaneously.

The Blue Book, which governed the protocol of handling presidential and prime ministerial visits, laid down in detail the dimensions of the stage, the material of its construction, the number of persons to receive her at the helipad and the number of persons to be allowed to sit on the stage. One of the stipulations was that an exclusive tent was to be put up as a washroom equipped with a toilet, washbasin, soap, towels, etc., at every venue of her meeting.

'But, sir,' said the executive engineer to me, 'The venue of her meeting is in the midst of nowhere. She is to land close to the stage, make a fifteen-minute halt and then fly off. Why do we need to have washrooms at all three places? I think since she is flying down from Surat, we should skip Navsari and set up the washroom at Bilimora alone. That should suffice. After all, each washroom costs a few thousand rupees.'

'You may be right logically, Mr Shah,' I said. 'But what happens to you and me if there is no toilet at the venue where she needs it? It is better that you err on the side of caution and follow the Blue Book to the letter.'

Shah muttered some imprecations under his breath but obeyed my instructions.

At Navsari, as soon as the PM got down from the stage after her speech, and I was walking her to the helicopter, she turned to me.

'Where can I wash my hands, Mr Collector?' She asked.

I took her to the tent, all the while thanking my stars that I had not succumbed to the niggardly advice of the executive engineer. I stood there wondering how I was going to make it to Bilimora in my jeep to receive the PM when she would be flying in the much faster helicopter. As we reached the helicopter, she turned to me.

'Please hop in. Aren't you going to accompany me?'

A much-relieved collector hopped in. She did not use the washroom tent in Bilimora, but in Vapi, again, she needed it. So much for cutting corners where the Blue Book is concerned.

OF PESTS AND PREDATORS

Jim Corbett and others of his ilk, I personally think, have romanticised the hunting of big game beyond all reality.

All those stories of Corbett wandering in the forests of the Terai for days, sleeping in the cattle pens in the midst of bulls and cows, walking for miles with a gun on his shoulder, stalking wounded tigers and so on, have to be taken with a large pinch of salt. For, believe me, I have slept in close proximity to cattle in the villages of Gujarat and have walked the forest of Dangs—not in search of wounded tigers but as part of my duty—and the experience was not pleasant, except in retrospect. For the fleas and the mosquitoes alone, not to speak of the unpleasant odours, kept me awake a good part of the night. My experience of hunting for cattle-lifters and man-eating panthers was no more pleasant.

One of my experiences relates to the period of my stay in Surat, when Dr Noman Mascati and I went out on a hunt. Noman was not only the most famous ophthalmologist of his day in Surat but was also a great hunter to boot. His palatial house was a veritable menagerie of stuffed tigers, for he claimed to have shot more than twenty man-eaters. He maintained a well-equipped Land Rover, specially strengthened with all sorts of steel pipes and struts, with built-in wooden drawers for spears, knives and weapons of all sorts. He was also the honorary game warden of the district.

When I received a bunch of complaints from the capital about a panther that had been harassing the cattle of the Maldharis in the forests of Songadh and orders that I should take all necessary steps to put an end to this menace, the best I could do was to call upon Noman's services.

The Maldharis of Kutch are rather well-known in Gujarat. They inhabit the extreme north-western part of the district of Kutch, bordering on the vast Rann, and are basically pastoralists. They maintain vast herds of animals—cows, camels and flocks of sheep and goat. In good times, the grazing lands to the north of Kutch and the fairly fertile islands in the Rann itself are able to maintain these vast herds. But when the rains fail successively for two or three years, both human beings and animals suffer. Before Partition, these pastoralists took their herds across the Rann into Sindh. But with the borders closing after the Partition, they had nowhere else to go but south. For the Maldhari and his cattle could never be separated. For him, his herd was not merely a means of livelihood but conferred status and prestige on him in his society. So, whenever there was a prolonged drought, the Maldharis loaded their donkeys or camels with their pots and pans, and their charpoys and household goods, and started on their long trek to the fertile southern districts of Gujarat. Driving their herds before them on the highway and the side roads, these tough and hardy pastoralists posed a threat to the standing crops en route. Often, by accident or design, they would allow their hungry cattle to stray into the unguarded wayside fields. This always led to friction between the Maldharis and the villagers, often ending up in grievous injuries to both sides. The government, therefore, attempted to make the migration as orderly as possible, usually without much success, by providing them with camps en route where fodder and food was made available. And when they reached their destination, they were sent over into the government forests, away from the villages, where they could not come into conflict with the locals.

In 1967, I had to play host in my district to one such group of Maldharis and their cattle, and I had sent them over into the forest of Songadh and Vyara. But these forests were the last refuge of the panthers and tigers of Gujarat. Just before the ingress of these vast cattle herds, the government had conducted a census of tigers and had announced that there were only eight of these magnificent beasts left in the whole state, and all of them were reported to be in the two southern districts of Surat and Bulsar. The tiger was declared a protected animal, and hunting the beast was an offence. However, there were still a few panthers left.

Within days of the arrival of the Maldharis, the panthers got active in Songadh and Vyara, and every now and then, a hungry animal would lift a sheep or calf, and a hue and cry would go up from the Maldharis. I received several complaints against the poor predators, but my sympathies were with the panthers. After all, what little of the forests that were left were their natural habitat, and if you provide food within fang's reach and expect the poor, hungry creatures to show restraint and self-control, you were expecting too much. I, therefore, ignored these complaints as long I could. But the government in Ahmedabad felt that I was not performing my duties as a host with due diligence, and I received clear instructions to terminate the depredations of the panther with 'extreme prejudice'. After all, the panther did not vote, but the Maldharis did.

Noman readily agreed to accompany me, and since the end of Ramzan was close, we decided to go to Songadh immediately after Eid.

One fine morning, we started for Songadh in Noman's old Land Rover. We reached the dak bungalow in the afternoon. The *mamlatdar* told us that there had been a kill the previous night, and the panther had not had his fill of the victim. He was sure to visit the carcass at sundown. Arrangements had been made to set up a machan near the kill, from where we would take a shot at the panther.

Since it was already four in the afternoon, we decided to go over and take position early so that if the panther was in the vicinity, it should not get alerted. We got down from the Land Rover about a kilometre away from the tree on which the machan had been set up. Noman, an experienced shikari, advised me that the sound of a Land Rover approaching the machan and sounds of human voices were sure to inhibit the panther's movements, so we had to walk. It was a fairly dense forest, and there was no pathway through the shrubbery. We had taken a tribal to guide us. He was leading the way with a long staff in his hand. We followed with a .306 each on our shoulders, plus a shotgun for defensive purposes. Within a few hundred feet, I was perspiring freely from every pore in the humid and hot air of the forest.

Another couple of hundred yards and a couple of litres of perspiration later, I discovered that all the mosquitoes of the forest had got scent of our presence and invited themselves. I looked up and saw a dark column of the bloodthirsty creatures hovering over my head. This halo accompanied me right up to the machan, by which time I had been scratching away my life's blood.

As soon as we had climbed up the machan and the guide had taken his leave, I began to feel even more miserable. The machan was a three-foot square, makeshift cubicle, made of broken branches and green leaves of the forest. The floor was made by criss-crossing the branches and covering them with fresh leaves. Every time I tried to shift position, I found some projecting piece piercing sensitive parts of my anatomy. In the meantime, the mosquitoes had entered the cubicle and resumed their interrupted dinner. As I tried to swat them away, Noman advised me, in a whisper, not to make any noise that would alert the panther.

Evening had fallen, and the bull's carcass, which was lying about fifty yards away near a bush, was getting gradually indistinct, as the forest all around grew darker. The panther had still not made an appearance. I tried to recall all the jungle lore Corbett had described so vividly. I tried to concentrate on all the distinct and vague noises of the jungle, hoping to track the movements of the panther from the sounds of the forest creatures. I heard no langur calling in alarm nor the nightjar imitating shrill bugles.

In any event, I completely missed the entry of the predator when he made his appearance. It was Noman's nudge in my ribs that alerted me to what was happening at the kill. I saw a rather huge animal standing over the kill. From the size, I subconsciously realised that it was no panther. Then I noticed the stripes. By this time, my vision was getting accustomed to the surrounding darkness. I realised suddenly that I was looking at a full-grown tiger, his muscles rippling, his ears erect, moving this way and that, his tail swishing. Without any conscious thought, I wriggled in my semi-prone position to take aim and looked through the rifle sight for proper alignment. I aimed at his heart, as being only a passable shot, I was not too sure that I could take him in the head.

As I zeroed in on the spot where, as Noman had explained to me earlier, a tiger's heart lies, the realisation struck me suddenly. I was aiming at a tiger, not at a panther! In fact, I was, with intent malicious, aiming to reduce the tiger population of Gujarat by more than 12 per cent with a single shot, committing an offence to boot. The temptation was sore. This would be, perhaps, my only chance to shoot a tiger in my life. I knew that once the deed was done I could always explain to the government that in my excitement I could not distinguish between a panther and a tiger in the dark. I also knew that this explanation coming from the DM who had been directed by the government to destroy the predators that were harassing the Maldharis' cattle would be readily accepted.

As all these thoughts were passing through my mind when Noman gave me another nudge. We had often discussed his exploits in the past, and I had openly envied him his luck several times. He must also have reasoned the same way I did and come to the same conclusion.

But in spite of the temptation, my finger remained immobile on the trigger. Here was a magnificent denizen of the forest, in the prime of youth, one of only eight in the state, a prospective father of many cubs. My desire to bag a tiger slowly died in my breast, and I gently took my finger off the trigger. To Noman, I nodded my head, a signal that the tiger was not to be shot.

By this time, the tiger had settled down on his prey. His body had now merged with the bull's, and I could see him but indistinctly. But the noise of tearing and crunching was loud enough to let us know that the tiger was enjoying his meal. Insects had crawled into my trousers and shirt—things unknown were wriggling around inside my undervest. But I sat through the whole torture, waiting for the tiger to have his fill. At some point, I must have made some movement, for suddenly, the tiger got up, alert and alarmed. Then, with one bound, he leapt over the bush and was gone, and simultaneously Noman fired two shots in the air to summon our party.

I have no desire to describe our miserable retreat from the machan and how we traversed that one kilometre back to the Land Rover. The return journey was no less hazardous, what with the fear of poisonous snakes being added to that of all others, in the dim torchlight that hardly illumined the shrubbery of the forest floor.

It was only when I reached the dak bungalow and had a bath that I could really feel that I had got rid of all the unwanted denizens of the forest who had found a home in my hair and my clothes. So much for Rudyard Kipling and Jim Corbett, I thought.

Bansda was one of the talukas in my charge. It was spread around the foothills of Dangs and deeply forested. Before Independence, it was ruled by the maharaja of Bansda, a Solanki Rajput who traced his lineage to the Chalukya rulers of South India. As a matter of fact, the river that flowed through the forests of Bansda was called Kaveri, in memory of the larger river of the same name in Tamil Nadu, from where a branch of the Chalukyas had migrated to this remote part of Gujarat and established a dynasty.

The maharaja of Bansda was in his mid-forties when I met him in the late sixties. He was a very pleasant man, given to all the old-world courtesies, quite polished in his behaviour, both with the officials and his old retainers. He lived in a vast sprawling palace, with a long façade, that gave the impression that some European palace had been physically transported from the heart of Vienna and erected in the wilderness of Bansda. It had all the usual chambers that one reads about in the books of Wodehouse—a large banquet hall, with refectories and gleaming silver behind glass cases; a private, smaller dining room; a vast reception room, with deep, old leather sofa sets; a gun room; a smoking room; an armoury; a huge library, with ornate bookcases covering the walls from floor to ceiling; an auditorium and so on. Everywhere, there was marble statuary adorning the nooks and corners, inside the rooms and passages and the gardens and fountains outside.

A little away from the palace was a villa, built in the Italian style, all marble and stucco, containing about a dozen rooms, which was used in the old days as a guest house for the English guests of the maharaja. Whenever I visited Bansda on official work, this was where I stayed. It was well-equipped, and in spite of the reduced staff and consequent neglect of upkeep in the post-Independence era, it still retained its charm in decadence.

The palace itself was crumbling, and the plaster falling from nooks and corners here and there. Maintenance of such a vast edifice required large sums of money, and with no state treasury and limited private income, it was obvious that the palace itself would not last long. The maharaja had been discussing a proposal with me for some time to persuade the government to take the palace off his hands and convert it into a forest training college. He himself would move into the guest villa. I was in sympathy with this move. To allow such a beautiful castle to go to ruin was such a waste of national wealth. After all, these buildings belong to our heritage, and I felt, and still feel, that the government should not allow them to vanish from the face of the earth. But then, India is a poor country, and we have so many such palaces and castles, and many pressing demands on our own resources that perhaps it would be too much to expect the government to look after such decaying palaces.

The taluka, which once formed the territory of the maharaja of Bansda, was inhabited mostly by tribals. There were about a hundred villages scattered about in the forest of Bansda, rather sparsely populated by Adivasis, who lived below the poverty line, growing a few crops of inferior millets and living off the fish from the river and the ponds. Yet, they were a happy lot, akin to their kinsmen in the nearby Dangs, until a man-eating panther intruded into this paradise. We never learnt why this panther turned a man-eater, but within a period of three months, it had lifted nine children, some of them, in almost broad daylight. The Adivasis had to abandon their nightly dances and their fishing. The more afraid the Adivasis grew, the bolder the panther got, until one night, it broke through the flimsy reed door of a hut and snatched away a four-year-old boy from the very arms of his mother. The parents and half the village followed the panther carrying away the pathetically crying child until his cries dwindled in the deep forest.

As soon as I got the news, I rang up the *mamlatdar* and maharaja, and reached Bansda the same afternoon. The half-eaten remains of the young child killed by the man-eater had been located and taken away by the parents for burial. The maharaja's shikari had constructed a machan some yards away from where the remains had been recovered and had tied a goat there instead. The maharaja and I left by jeep and reached the village, not too far from Bansda. The village consisted of a few thatched huts surrounding a clear area in the centre, plastered with a mixture of mud and cow dung, where the Adivasis threshed their corn and where the village children played when the threat of a man-eater did not hang over their heads.

Some old men came out of their huts when our jeep reached the clearing, and we heard the whole harrowing tale of the panther attack. We assured them that we were planning to sit over a goat that evening and bag the man-eater that was making their lives miserable.

We left the jeep there and started walking. But this time, I was better prepared, with thick boots, sturdy trousers and jacket, and a couple of tubes of insect repellent cream.

I found the machan comparatively more comfortable than the first machan I had sat in, in Surat. We settled ourselves in and waited. The poor goat, tied with a rope to the branch, was bleating piteously. Just as dusk was falling, it suddenly fell silent in the middle of a bleat and stood tense, its whole body alert to some unseen danger. Even without the maharaja's whispered warning, I realised the panther was in the vicinity. I glanced all round but could spot nothing. But I was sure that the panther was close by, since the goat had instinctively felt its presence.

As I was watching tensely, moving the barrel of my rifle gently this way and that, trying to spot some movement in the surrounding bushes, I saw the goat suddenly become tense and jerk its whole body pointing towards the machan. For a moment, the significance of the movement escaped me. Then the realisation hit me with a shock. The panther had made a flanking movement and was either already on our tree or directly beneath us. If it was already on the tree, it could very easily make a rush into the machan, crashing through the flimsy screen of twigs and leaves. And in the cramped space, we would not have time to even turn and bring the rifle to bear on the predator before it was at our throats. For a moment, all my senses were paralysed. The maharaja, a more experienced shikari, had realised, from the direction the goat's head was pointing, that the panther was directly below us. From a gap in the leafy floor, he pointed quietly, and I glanced down to look at the large animal staring up at the machan. I looked directly into his shining yellow eyes. For a second, we stared at each other. One moment, he was there, and in another, he had made a leap and was away. We heard him crashing through the bushes and relaxed, as did the goat. But we also realised, at the same time, that there was no chance of the panther returning that evening. Rather disappointedly, the maharaja fired the signalling shots. Within minutes, a large number of the villagers surrounded us at the foot of the tree.

'It will not come again, Sarkar,' said Dilawar Singh, the maharaja's shikari. 'It was not interested in the goat. It must have felt your presence and was reconnoitering the position. If it has realised the threat, a goat's bleating would not tempt him.'

'Then what should we do?' I asked.

'Sir, I have an idea,' said one of the villagers, 'Sir, the panther likes human flesh. It has become accustomed to human kills. If you permit, we can keep a village child there.' I was shocked. The idea of offering a human bait was so preposterous that for a moment I could not speak. Taking my silence for consent, the villager went on, 'There are so many children in the village. There won't be any difficulty in getting one.'

'What happens if the panther kills the child?' I asked, taking control of myself and holding my anger in check.

'Sir, you and the Sarkar are such good shots. You will kill him before he comes within leaping distance.' The villager's confidence in our aim was touching, but I was still not through with him.

'And how will the child stay where you put him? Or do you propose to tie him to a tree like a goat?' I asked, sarcasm dripping from my tone. Perhaps, I thought, poverty, pestilence, drought and disease had inured them to the idea of death, particularly the death of orphan children. But his reply came as a revelation.

'No, sir, you don't have to tie him at all. I would sit under the tree and hold him in my arms!'

The Adivasi, in effect, was offering himself as bait, along with the child. My anger suddenly evaporated, and I admired the courage and simplicity of faith the villager had.

Needless to say, we did not accept the offer. We tied the goat again the next day and sat on the machan for another evening. As feared, the panther did not turn up.

Night had already fallen as we were driving back to Bansda. The maharaja, who had wanted to see me in action, was rather disappointed. Since I had mentioned to him that I had been out on shikar a couple of times before, he thought I must be a good shot, and he had wanted to see my marksmanship first-hand.

He suddenly stopped the jeep, which he was driving, and pointing to the gleaming eyes of a nightjar, a hundred yards away in the field, asked me whether I would like to take a shot. My heart sank. I knew that I was only a passable shot. The chances of my hitting the nightjar at a hundred yards, with only its eyes visible, were extremely remote, unless I was a veritable Arjun. But a refusal on my part to take on the challenge would leave a poor impression on the maharaja's mind. So, rather reluctantly, I accepted the .22 he handed me, and sitting in the jeep, I put it to my shoulder, took careful aim and shot. A shout went up from the maharaja and the other occupant sitting behind me. The gleaming eyes were no longer gleaming. One of the retainers ran across and brought back the dead bird.

'You are a marvellous shot!' said the maharaja.

In the event, it was the maharaja who killed the man-eating panther after I returned to Bulsar. With the first shot, he broke the panther's spine. It was the second shot that it took in the heart. The skin bears both the marks visibly.

THE GREAT FAMINE OF GUJARAT

Even though there were pockets of tribal-populated areas in Bulsar district, such as Dharampur and Bansda, the district was, by and large, known to be fertile and well served by the monsoon. The southern part of the district contained large tracts of grasslands, mostly owned by the Desais and Parsis. Most of the districts of peninsular Saurashtra, however, had no irrigation facilities. This was before the Narmada Canal took the river water there and solved the problem of both irrigation and drinking, with the rare exception of Junagadh. I had served in one of the most arid regions of Saurashtra, Surendranagar—rich in history and political leaders and poor in soil fertility and irrigation facilities. Saurashtra was also poorly fed by the monsoons, and since no perennial rivers pass through the region, no large reservoirs, too, could be built to retain substantial quantities of water.

The year 1972 proved a very difficult year for both Saurashtra and North Gujarat. That year the assessment revealed that almost 12,000 out of the 18,000 villages of Gujarat had a harvest of less than 25 per cent. The government, therefore, declared famine conditions in those 12,000 villages, that is two-thirds of the state, and applied the Bombay Famine Relief Code to provide regulated relief.

Since the state faced a major calamity with two-thirds of its population of humans and cattle facing the threat of death by hunger and thirst, the

Cabinet met almost every day since the moment the assessment figures came to be known. They had known what had happened in the tragic historical famines in Bengal, Kashmir and Madras, where thousands had perished—parents sold their children, sons abandoned their parents and there were rumours of cannibalism in some pockets. A major famine in Gujarat was quite a scary prospect for the government.

One fine morning, in September of 1972, I was basking in the cool breeze of the sea blowing from the Indian Ocean in the west. After a great deal of persuasion and bribery, my daughter, Gazala, who was all of four years, had agreed to go to school.

Then the telephone rang. It was K.N. Zutshi, the revenue secretary, on the line.

'There was a Cabinet meeting this morning to review the scarcity situation. It was decided to post you as director of famine relief to take charge of the relief operations. You better pack up and move over to Gandhinagar. The chief minister wants you here yesterday. You have 48 hours to reach here. Handover charge to your resident deputy collector,' he ordered me.

Though I had been in Bulsar for more than three years, the normal tenure of a collector, still the sudden transfer came as a surprise. Bulsar was such a pleasant district to govern—open-minded and reasonable people, able and committed staff, and a flourishing club that I had established. When I announced my transfer to my officers as soon as I reached the collectorate, there was all-round consternation. By noon, the whole district had come to know of the transfer. As I was having lunch in my chamber, the peon announced that a delegation of MLAs from the district wanted to meet me.

'Sir, there are so many development works going on. All surplus land has not yet been taken over from the Desais. You cannot leave the task half-completed. You should not move,' they said.

'I have completed my tenure here. If the government wants me at Gandhinagar, I have to move,' I said. Left to myself, I would have liked to serve another four or five years in Bulsar.

I learnt later that all the MLAs of the district, including those from the opposition, had driven to Surat. They had persuaded Zinabhai Darji, the president of the state Congress, to accompany them to Gandhinagar to persuade the CM, Ghanshyambhai Oza, to cancel the transfer. One of the MLAs later told me that the CM had asked them only one question.

'Is Mr Moosa Raza unhappy with this transfer? Does he want to stay back in Bulsar?'

'No, sir, but we want him there in the interest of the district.'

'Don't you think that the larger interest of the state should override the interests of a single district?' the CM had asked reasonably.

They had no answer. The next day, after handing over charge to the resident deputy collector (RDC), I drove down to Gandhinagar to call on the CM. I had known him during my tenure in Surendranagar, his hometown. Having been a member of the Parliament for two terms, Mr Oza was a suave and polished politician, exuding politeness and bonhomie at every movement. He received me graciously, and as I was taking my seat, he pointed to a large pile of telegrams on his table.

'Do you know what they are?' he asked me with a smile. 'No, sir,' I replied truthfully.

'Over 500 telegrams from Bulsar district requesting me to cancel your transfer.'

'I had nothing to do with them, sir,' I said. But I would have been less than human not to feel pleased at this show of appreciation from the people I had served.

'But I had to disappoint your fans in Bulsar. The state is facing a severe challenge, and your work in Surendranagar, Surat, Bulsar and Dangs has convinced the Cabinet that you are the best officer to shoulder the task.'

'We have done a preliminary survey and made an initial assessment of the various requirements. A budget of ₹120 crore has been sanctioned. Your mandate is to ensure that not a single human life is lost for want of food and water, all cattle are provided fodder, and all villages supplied with water. The Land Revenue Code mandates that the able-bodied villagers are not given doles. That encourages a dependent mindset. You have to organise relief works through which all those who can work are provided employment. The wages should be paid every week. The revenue department will brief you on the organisational arrangements. So, get cracking.'

The next port of call was Mr Zutshi, the revenue secretary. Mr Zutshi, as his name indicated, hailed from a family of Kashmiri Pandits. An old-style civilian, with impeccable credentials, he believed in management by the book. He would not deviate an iota from the rules, and everything had to be put down in black and white before he would commit himself to a course of action. Though he used the telephone as a necessary evil, he would not trust any conversation carried out on that unreliable machine. One had to go over to his room to discuss even petty issues.

'Bhai, Deolekar has prepared an organisational chart for you. We think you will need around ninety staff to manage this huge operation. I think you should speak with him, and he will help you to get the necessary staff in place. We will ask the various departments to depute the needed staff. The PWD will provide the furniture and other necessary equipment,' he said.

The PWD would naturally dispose of its rejected furniture—broken, roughly repaired and not required by others. Also, the staff would be from those divisions where they had proved their dispensability. I would, therefore, start with a severe handicap, which would never be overcome during my entire tenure as a director of famine relief. Nor would I be able to successfully meet the challenge of the worst famine

Gujarat had seen in its decades-old history with rejected equipment and discarded staff.

So, the first thing I did was to persuade Deolekar, the deputy secretary and confidant of Zutshi, that I did not need ninety people. I would start with just fifteen. The larger the number of minions, the lesser the amount of work done. As C.N. Parkinson had remarked, a large bureaucracy creates enough paper to remain engaged within itself without requiring any external inputs or producing any worthwhile output.

My next job was to prepare a list of my seconds-in-command. I chose D.R. Bhutaiya, who had worked under me in Mehsana and Bulsar and had proved his mettle; Vasant Lekinwala, a most meticulous collector of data, expert analyst and articulator (this before the day of the computers, laptops, smartphones); Sumant Doshi, who had worked with me in Surendranagar as my deputy accountant, a most honest, diligent and hard-working financial wizard; K.T. Parmar, who could charm a cockerel into laying an egg with his dulcet tongue; and B.R. Patel, a most entrepreneurial go-getter.

Choosing a team is one thing but getting them into position is another. Zutshi or KNZ, of course, would have none of it. He could not imagine a chief choosing his own team. One works with the officials in place or allotted by the secretary.

KNZ, with a civilian's suspicious mind, could not countenance an officer surrounding himself with his trusted staff and forming a clique. As expected, he asked me to put up a note. I knew the note would go back and forth between me, Deolekar, KNZ and miscellaneous other unconcerned officers. And before that KNZ would use his pen to improve upon my English, correct the punctuation marks and typographical errors. So, I took the note to Madhavsinh Solanki, the revenue minister. He had no problem with Bhutaiya, Patel, Lekinwala and Doshi, but he got stuck with Parmar.

'I see from the note that Parmar is under suspension and an enquiry is on against him,' he said. The enquiry had been in progress, or no progress, for close to a year.

'But, sir, I have seen the charges against him. He allotted ten bags of sugar for a marriage function when he had the authority for only eight.'

'Then he has to pay the penalty.'

I thought two excess bags did not deserve such a penalty. 'Sir, Shakespeare said if you pay everyone what they deserve, would anyone ever escape a whipping?' I replied.

Mr Solanki was a well-read man, interested in literature, philosophy, poetry (especially Ghalib), film music and good food.

'Did Shakespeare say that? Where?'

'I think it is in *Hamlet*. That was my text in college. I remember it.'

The minister leaned back in his chair, with a thoughtful look on his face.

He called for Parmar's enquiry file, quashed the enquiry and released an able officer to work with me.

The collectors and DDOs of the affected districts proved most cooperative. In no time, we had prepared a master plan covering all the villages, listing out the various relief works needed, assessed the number of jeeps required, planned the purchase of water tankers to supply water to villages where wells could not be dug and located the sources from where water could be drawn. It was estimated that about eight million cattle will have to be kept supplied with fodder. The only place where fodder in such large quantities was available was from the vast grasslands of Bulsar, my erstwhile charge. We estimated the total requirements of fodder over the year at over several million tonnes. This would require more than 4,000 rakes moving between Bulsar and various destinations in Saurashtra and North Gujarat. This movement had to be coordinated with the railways.

The weekly Cabinet meet decided that I should immediately proceed to Bulsar and procure the required fodder.

There was clear and present danger in accepting such a responsibility. Whatever price I pay would be questioned, and I would not be able to escape unfounded accusations subsequently. Immediately after the meeting, I submitted a note in which I suggested that instead of entrusting the authority to a single officer, a committee consisting of the finance secretary, the revenue secretary and the director should be entrusted with the job. Both KNZ and Mr Sadhwani, the finance secretary, demurred. They pleaded that their hands were full, and since the Cabinet had reposed full confidence in me, I alone should proceed to Bulsar and purchase the fodder. This was giving a dog a good name and hanging him. Ultimately the matter went up to Ratubhai Adani, the minister in charge of scarcity management. He reluctantly agreed to my suggestion. All the way to Bulsar, the two secretaries, my seniors, were cursing me for dragging them out of their cozy corners.

In the meantime, the owners of the grasslands, a powerful group of Anavil Desais, had formed a powerful cartel. The committee met the association, and the negotiations dragged on for two days. The price was brought down from the initial quote of ₹80 million to ₹50 million. But I thought the price was still too high. On the third day, the association refused to meet the committee, saying that they had given their rock-bottom price. They walked out of the negotiations.

'Now what?' asked a frustrated Mr Sadhwani.

'Moosa, you are being too rough with them,' said KNZ. 'They have come down by almost 40 per cent. We think we should clinch the deal at ₹50 million.'

Mr Sadhwani agreed. But I did not. I felt that the cartel was putting pressure on the government, taking advantage of its dire straits. I knew that the Desais would be making enormous profits out of the naturally growing grass, where the landlords had invested no resources. So, I decided to twist their tails a bit. In the meantime, I rang up my colleagues in Madhya Pradesh and proposed to go down to Bhopal for buying fodder from the forest lands of Bastar. I allowed this information to be leaked out.

The secretaries returned to Gandhinagar, authorising me to buy fodder at a price of ₹50 million or less. I let the association know that since they had refused to come for negotiations, I, too, was returning to Gandhinagar to explore alternatives.

That evening, the association came back to the negotiating table suo moto. The final deal was struck at ₹40 million. When I returned and reported the matter to Mr Sadhwani, he remarked, 'You have saved almost ₹40 million for the government. For this, you deserve no less than a Padma Shri.'

'I do not expect that, sir,' I said, 'I shall be happy if I finish this job with no enquiry against me.'

'Don't be so cynical,' he said. 'Even governments sometimes appreciate good work.'

I had to wait almost forty years for that recognition to come through. The president conferred the Padma Bhushan on me when I was in my seventies, fifteen years after my retirement from service.

While we managed to provide jobs to about 1.5 million labourers on the various rural works, water scarcity posed a severe challenge. Saurashtra is a peninsula jutting into the Indian Ocean. Its soil is mostly basaltic rock, with hilly outcrops in some districts like Junagadh. No major or perennial river flows through the arid terrain of this peninsula. Groundwater levels are very low, and the water is mostly brackish and often saline.

During my tours, I visited the small town of Jamkhambhaliya in Jamnagar district. While I was sitting in the taluka office, reviewing the progress of the relief works with local officials, there was a loud hubbub outside the office. The *mamlatdar* informed me that a delegation of local women wanted to meet me.

'Sir, we are suffering for the last six months for want of water,' they said in chorus. 'None of us has had a bath for the last two months.' I had noticed that as soon as they had come in.

'But I am sending two tankers daily all the way from Rajkot,' I said.

'By the time the tankers reach us, half the water splashes out on the bad roads. And you have rationed out the water at the rate of one pot per family. That is barely sufficient for cooking and drinking. We are even burning our dead without giving them a ritual wash. Two tankers are just not enough. At least ten should be sent.'

I realised the predicament of the ladies, who had to stand in a queue in the scorching sun to get the one pot of water and manage so many chores with that. They, of course, augmented that supply by walking to the brackish water *virdas* on the outskirts of the town. But that water could hardly be used for any but non-essential purposes. I realised that satisfying the demand for ten tankers a day was not feasible. We just did not have enough water tankers to supply water to all the villages at that rate.

'Did I not sanction a borewell for this town?' I asked the taluka chief.

'Yes, sir. We struck saline water at a depth of eighty feet. Even at 300, it was the same water. We had to abandon the effort. But, sir, there is a feasible solution,' he said as an afterthought.

'What is that?' I asked eagerly.

'Some years ago, the Oil and Natural Gas Commission (ONGC) was exploring for oil here. They bored a deep well right here in Jamkhambhaliya, at a depth of some 900 feet, they struck a freshwater vein but no oil. So, they have capped the pipe, constructed a room over the well-head and have left it locked. If that well is handed over to us, it will not only supply enough water to Jamkhambhaliya but to the nearby villages too.'

'Then why didn't you ask the ONGC?' I asked in an exasperated tone.

The taluka chief produced a bulky file of correspondence. First, they wrote to the executive engineer of ONGC at Rajkot, the closest jurisdiction. He said he was in charge of only current operations and was not concerned with any old capped well in Jamkhambhaliya. Then they wrote to his superior. He wasn't even aware of the well's existence. The executive engineer in Ankleswar said he was in charge of exploration and not in maintaining old assets. After some more futile correspondence, they wrote to the head office of ONGC in Dehradun. Their several reminders elicited the reply that the request had been sent to Baroda. The request got caught in the merry-go-round, and no one was willing to take a positive view.

'If I get the well opened, do you have a pump to extract the water?' I asked.

'Yes, sir. But if you open the room, the ONGC will later put the blame on us and involve us in some criminal case.'

So, I summoned my steno, who always accompanied me (in those days the only way of instant communication between collectors and headquarters was to carry with me on my tours a wireless set and a police-operator).

I dictated a letter: 'To whomsoever it may concern. I, so-and-so, Director of Scarcity Relief, Government of Gujarat, hereby take the entire responsibility of removing the lock of the ONGC well in Jamkhambhaliya and utilisation of its water for the relief of the suffering public.' I signed it and gave a copy to the taluka chief.

Then, accompanied by a concourse of men, women and my officials, I proceeded to the well, broke the lock and got the cap removed. Perhaps it was an artesian well. The moment the cap was removed, a powerful stream of sweet water gushed out with great force. A loud cheer went up from the eager audience. Men and women, in fact, danced in the gushing water, unmindful of getting their clothes and bodies wet.

I never heard from the ONGC about that well. I don't know whether that well still supplies water to the people of Jamkhambhaliya.

I used to leave my house in Gandhinagar early, long before sunrise, to reach a scarcity work site in Rajkot, Surendranagar or Amreli before the heat became too intense and unbearable. On the way, at times near Chotila, I would stop at a wayside tea stall, where fresh *fafda* along with jalebis and pickled green chilies would be sold wrapped in newspaper. The flaky, crunchy snack would not only be my breakfast but would sustain me till late after lunchtime.

One day I reached a famine relief work site by noon, when the sun was beating down in all its glory. I saw more than 300 workers on the job. The half-naked men were digging the earth, perspiring profusely and using their scarves to wipe their faces from time to time. Some women were moving among the diggers with water-filled earthen pots on their hips to quench their thirst. All of them looked tired and listless.

When the British framed the Famine Relief Code in the nineteenth century, they developed an elaborate formula for paying wages to the labourers. They believed that the labourers on the relief work should be paid just enough to keep body and soul together. Their experts calculated that a man needed nineteen ounces of cereal, a proportionate amount of oil, vegetables and fuel to cook into an edible meal. This was the requirement for him to just survive, not thrive. They then converted this requirement into cash, and came to the conclusion that the labourer should be paid one rupee and two annas daily. To earn this, the labourers had to dig a certain number of cubic feet of earth, working for eight hours. But when it came to the women labourers, the British were motivated by two considerations—their misogynist attitude and their desire to pay out minimum cash. So, they fixed the women's wages at half the man's. After all, they did not do any digging, and perhaps their souls were strong enough to cling to their bodies with even lesser nourishment. And the poor dressers of the earth, the old men, were lumped together with the women. The succeeding governments, even after Independence, followed the same Famine Code. The wages were minimally adjusted to inflation. After all, the British were wise, weren't they? Everywhere I went on inspection, the women and the old men surrounded me with complaints on this issue.

'What crimes have we committed? Being born women? You need water carriers. You assign some women to that job. And we work in the same hot sun, supplying water to the diggers. So, why are we paid only half their wages?'

The old men were equally aggrieved. The local MLAs supported this plea.

The arguments had a lot of weight behind them. So, I retired to the shade of my jeep with a guilty conscience at leaving the labourers toiling in the sun. I drafted and sent out instructions on the wireless to all collectors that the women and old men, too, should be paid the same wages as the diggers, with immediate effect. These instructions were welcomed by all collectors and implemented.

I returned to Gandhinagar a week later and reported my action to KNZ. I had reckoned without KNZ's zeal and commitment to the British-framed Famine Code. He wrote a long note throwing the rule book at me. He pointed out that (a) I had committed a serious breach of the Famine Code, (b) I had placed myself in a position of superior wisdom to the nineteenth-century British civilians, who had arrived at that wage philosophy after very deep consideration, (c) I had taken an impulsive decision, (d) that the authority to override the Famine Code lay with the government, in the Cabinet, not with a junior officer and, (e) that calculated over a year, my unauthorised order would commit the government to an additional expenditure of ₹20 million.

In the light of these overriding considerations, KNZ ordered me to immediately cancel my instructions.

I pointed out in my responding note that since the decision had already been implemented by all the collectors, it would not be in the fitness of things to rescind the instruction, as that would place me and the collectors in an invidious position. Apart from affecting their morale, it would reduce their effectiveness and credibility. I suggested that the secretary might like to take the matter to the Cabinet and get my decision ratified. KNZ was horrified at this suggestion and shot back that since he himself did not endorse my decision, there was no question of taking it to the Cabinet. At least, let both our viewpoints go up to the finance secretary and the chief secretary, I suggested. As anticipated by him, both the finance secretary and the chief secretary agreed with KNZ. Then I suggested that KNZ himself may cancel my order instead of asking me to rescind it. It would be highly embarrassing to me to commit harakiri in public.

'Since you are the perpetrator, you better rectify the mistake,' he retorted. I knew that rescinding the order would elicit a severely adverse reaction from the sufferers and the people's representatives. I apprehended the next step of KNZ might be to recover the excess from the hapless recipients.

The next day was a Thursday, when the entire Cabinet met in the morning. There were several important issues on the agenda. The revenue secretary, the finance secretary and the chief secretary were all in attendance. Just as we were approaching the last items, Ratubhai Adani, the minister who chaired the Cabinet sub-committee on famine relief, interrupted the meeting and turned to the CM, 'Sir, I have been receiving calls from several MLAs complimenting the government on a recent order passed by the director of famine relief. I do not know the details. Shall we ask him to brief us on that?'

The CM turned to me questioningly. I gave a detailed report of the instructions I had issued as regards bringing the wages of all workers on the scarcity works at par. However, I confessed that I had committed an oversight in not having obtained the prior approval of the government before passing such instructions. For that, I apologised to the Cabinet.

'That can be easily rectified,' said Ratubhai, and the CM nodded. 'Let us pass a resolution endorsing the instructions of the director and amending the Famine Code accordingly so that the wages of all workers remain uniform in such future contingencies.'

'I think no apology is needed from the director, he deserves a compliment', said the CM. 'We should have passed this resolution right at the beginning of the scarcity season.'

The resolution was duly passed.

Usually, when the full Cabinet met to discuss the items on the agenda, the meeting ended in a cacophony of multiple voices. Every minister, instead of sticking to the issue on the agenda, would want to draw the attention of the CM to some specific need or grievance of his district. Since the government was spending huge sums of money in the affected areas, districts and talukas not affected by the famine felt left out. Many voices were heard from such talukas demanding '*amne pan dushkaal nu labh malvun joiye* (We too should get the benefit of the famine).'

The government was hard put to convince the MLAs and people from the unaffected areas that such 'benefits' could not be extended to those areas where there was no failure of crops and no famine had been declared!

The Kutch district was one of the worst-affected. The Maldharis maintained large herds of cattle. Right at the beginning of the scarcity, the government made elaborate arrangements to shift the Kutch cattle, along with their owners and their families, to the forest areas of Panchmahal, Surat, Bharuch and Bulsar districts. I decided to visit the Banni areas of Kutch to get a first-hand feel of the ground situation there.

The Banni Grasslands Reserve have been well-known to ecologists and wildlife experts. Some years before, the forest department had attempted to plant *Prosopis juliflora* to stop the ingress of the desert into whatever little cultivable area there was on the fringes.

My first halt in Kutch, before proceeding to the Banni area, was at the famous temple of Mata no Madh. This is the most holy temple of Kutch, dedicated to the goddess Ashapura Mata. Pilgrims from all over Kutch flocked to this temple on religious occasions. When I visited the precincts, it housed a complex of several temples, with a well-appointed guest house at one corner.

The chief priest, Mahantshri Raja Nenshiji Maharaj, was also the taluka panchayat pramukh at this time. I had known and interacted with him in the latter capacity earlier. The tradition of religious heads entering politics had started in Gujarat well before it did in other states of India. When I had asked what made him contest election as a sarpanch and then a taluka panchayat pramukh, the mahant had explained, 'You see, the temple has been the most important temple in this part of the country. And the mahants of this temple have been the most-respected priests of the community. In fact, for centuries, we have been the *rajgurus*, mentors to the rulers of Kutch. Once every year, the maharajas come to attend the seasonal puja. On such occasions, we sit on the high gaddi, the throne, and the ruler sits at our feet.'

'I didn't know that,' I said. 'But what about the common people? Why do they respect and regard you?'

'The temple has also been serving the people for long. We run a langar. We maintain a large *gaushala* for taking care of the cows and, during famines and droughts, the Maldharis leave their milch cattle with us. We feed them and take care of them until the rains. We provide medical assistance to the people, and we are planning to start a mobile medical van.'

I was impressed.

The mahant, a handsome man in his early forties, with a full head of dark hair held down under a silk pugree, bordered in gold filigree, and with the vermilion mark on his forehead, received me. He guided me to the small but well-appointed guest house. 'We will wait until you have had a wash. An open jeep is not the most convenient transport for the Kutch weather and terrain. In the olden days, we used to travel mostly on camels.'

I agreed with him, recalling my travels on camel back in Banaskantha districts and the soporific effect it had.

'We will have lunch as soon as you are ready. I have invited the *mamlatdar* and the BDO to join us. We can plan your visit to the Banni tomorrow with them.' He had taken charge of my itinerary.

'I thought we would go and visit the area after lunch,' I made a feeble protest.

'No, sir,' he said. 'Not in this heat. The sun may appear mild to you at this time of the year, but that is only deceptive. We always rest after lunch and take a short nap. Then I will take you around the temple complex.'

I had to fall in line with my host's suggestion. The lunch was sumptuous, with roast chicken, meat and fish. I was taken aback at the variety of the dishes, especially the non-vegetarian fare, in the temple guest house. The mahant noted my surprise.

'As I told you, we are the *rajgurus*, and royalty always wanted non-vegetarian dishes. And this temple has been accustomed to animal sacrifices. Whenever the maharaja came for special pujas, he sacrificed a buffalo. Ashapura Mata is a manifestation of Shakti, and animal sacrifices have been offered in her temple across India. We are, therefore, accustomed to serving meat and fish to our guests.'

Then he summoned the cook, one Hussain Shah, a venerable old hand, to introduce to me. The mahant perhaps thought that being a Muslim, I might hesitate to partake of animals slaughtered by a Hindu in a temple. The summoning of Hussain Shah was to reassure me that everything was kosher.

During lunch, the *mamlatdar* and the BDO briefed me about the relief work being conducted in the taluka.

After lunch, I was shown into the bedroom that the mahant had told me used to be occupied by the rulers whenever they camped at the temple. The bed was made of solid silver, with ornate moulded decorations, and the mattress was soft as eiderdown, fit enough for the delicate build of the pampered maharajas and their consorts. I had, of course, no scruples in using it. I had slept on *chabootras*, on string cots with no mattresses, and with bed bugs for company and a host of mosquitoes to lull me to sleep. I was accustomed to both the luxuries and hardships of travels in the civil service.

Ghazali, the famous twelfth-century Muslim mystic had advised that a man must live in this world like a civil servant. He should enjoy all the facilities his employer provided him, without attaching himself to any of them. And when the employer transfers him, he should leave the house, the facilities and the comforts to take up his new assignment without regret or compunction. He was, of course, talking of a sojourn in this world under God and transfer to the next world.

After the siesta, the mahant took me on a round of the temple complex. The temple building itself, as temples go, was not very large or impressive. Mata no Madh was a rather modest edifice occupying around 2,500 square feet.

'This temple is about 700 years old. Not the edifice but the house of the deity. It was perhaps repaired and rebuilt many times, though in keeping with our neglect of history, we do not have records of the early times. In the eighteenth century, the ruler of Sindh, one Gulamsha Kalora attacked the temple. Legend has it that Goddess Ashapura blinded his soldiers. Repentant, Gulamsha then donated a huge bell to the temple as an act of penance, and their vision was restored. The bell is still with us. Later, Jamadar Fateh Muhammad presented the temple with a silver *deepmala*. That, too, is in the treasury of the temple.'

The next morning, we left early to visit the Banni area. The small villages that dotted this vast arid tract, now devoid of any significant vegetation, were inhabited by the various tribes of the Maldharis. Most of the men had left with the cattle for the pastures of Kheda, Surat, Bulsar and Bharuch. Only old men, women and very young children were left behind. Since supplying all the villages with drinking water by tankers from a distance of a hundred kilometres through rough terrain was beyond the resources of the state, we had helped them by employing the women and old men in digging shallow pits in the soft, sandy soil. At a depth of eight to ten feet, brackish water oozed out of the soil. The quantity of water that collected in the pit was not sufficient to fill even two pots. So, they dug another pit adjacent. The whole terrain was thus criss-crossed by several pits, leaving narrow, crumbling ridges in between. When I ventured to cross them, the old men warned me to be careful, as they were so soft and narrow that they often collapsed, burying the person who ventured on them.

The mahant wisely stayed on the other side, but the *mamlatdar* and the BDO managed to cross with me using other bridges. The poor fellows had to follow their boss.

We then went to see the huts in which the Maldharis lived. A small earthen hearth occupied a corner of the hut, and some of the old ladies sat in the other corner stitching the famous patchwork handicraft of Kutch, the mirror-studded skirts and scarves and quilt covers, which the elite and fashionable ladies of Ahmedabad and Bombay wore to their parties, flaunting their ethnic wear. The artisans were paid a pittance by the middlemen, but the opulent ladies paid through their bedecked noses for the privilege. The famine-stricken women of Kutch had to wait for years before socially conscious NGOs set up cooperatives to help the artisans get a reasonable wage for their labour. The middlemen, of course, got the cream.

The eastern part of the Rann suffered the onslaught of the drought with equal intensity. Almost all the villages in this area were severely affected by the drought. With the total failure of the meagre crops that grew, starvation stared the villages in the face. While we could supply food and water to this area from Rajkot, providing employment to the labourers posed a problem. So, we pooled together all the geological, topographical and geographical skills we could muster, and decided to build a large water tank, covering a vast area somewhere near Rapar. The entire surrounding land would form a basin, the catchment area, if and when it rained. We could give employment to around 15,000 people to dig this tank. Of course, many of my colleagues laughed at my endeavours, asking from where I was planning to get water to fill up this vast reservoir. Even the Cabinet was not immune to this propaganda. In one of the meetings,

I was asked to explain the rationale behind this project. One of my bosses even made a snide remark suggesting that it could be called 'Moosa's Folly' when constructed. But I explained that the mandate was to provide employment so that the labourers could earn a minimum wage. Since there was no other useful work, a water reservoir alone was feasible, in the hope that when the rains came someday, it would get filled up.

'And when do you expect the rains?' KNZ asked me in a sarcastic tone. Often you have to bear the sarcasm of your boss with equanimity and a smile.

It was at this time that PM Indira Gandhi decided to visit Kutch. I was asked to show her one of our relief works. Since this tank was the largest relief work, employing over 15,000 people, I decided to take her there. She landed close by in a chopper and shifted to an open jeep. I took her around the periphery of the project under construction. She got down after every few yards to meet the labourers and enquire after their well-being. We named the lake after the PM—Indira Sagar. As luck would have it, there were heavy rains next year in the Rapar region, and the Indira Sagar got filled up. The water came in handy for many years, and the farmers of the surrounding villages were quite happy. Moosa's Folly did not prove to be such a folly after all.

Some years later, when I was commissioner of fisheries, I was returning in my old Fiat car with Husnara and my young children from Veraval on the coast to Ahmedabad. On the way, there was a road diversion sign that a stretch of the highway was under repair. Somewhere on that *kutcha* diversion, I lost my way. Since evening was falling and I was in the midst of nowhere, with a wife and four young kids, I started getting more and more anxious. Then to make matters worse, suddenly the car engine failed, the vehicle spluttered and came to a sudden halt. As the Persian saying goes: *ek na shud, do shud* (troubles don't come singly).

My ignorance of the mechanism of a car engine is encyclopedic. To impress my wife and children, I got down, raised the hood or whatever it is called and peered into the interior, pretending a knowledge I did not have. That was just to keep their morale up. I then announced to the family ponderously, 'Something is wrong with the engine,' a truism which my wife recognised immediately.

'Yes, I know that,' she said. 'But what is to be done?'

'I could walk to the nearest village and summon help. But since darkness has fallen, I dare not leave you all alone in this wilderness.' In any case, I had no idea how far the nearest village was or in which direction. Moreover, for all I knew, the denizens of the nearby villages would have had their dinners and gone to bed. Villagers in Gujarat dine at sunset.

Hafez Shirazi, the famous Persian poet, explained my predicament accurately:

Shabe tareek o beem-e-mauj-o gardabe-e chuneen hayal.
Kuja danand hal-e ma subaksaran-e saahil ha.

(The night is dark, the waves are rising, and I am being pulled towards the eddies.
How can those sleeping peacefully on the shore know my travails?)

Just as I was indulging in self-pity, I saw a light at a distance. A dhoti-clad villager was walking briskly towards the car, with a lantern and a staff. Having reassured myself that he was alone, I greeted him. I told him who I was, my predicament and whether he could go over to the nearest village and bring a mechanic. I offered him a reward of ₹20. The villager brushed aside my offer of the reward disdainfully. He said he would go back to his village, which was just a mile away, and inform the sarpanch of my predicament.

I waited by the car, hoping that succour would come soon. Just then a great hubbub was heard from afar. This time, I saw not one but several men advancing towards me with stout wooden staffs and lanterns. As soon as the large crowd of villagers reached me, the leader greeted me in the traditional way, bowing down and touching my feet.

'Sir, we are all sorry that you have been put to such trouble. But we are lucky, sir, that God has sent you to us. You may not remember, but in the drought of '72, you sent us two tankers of water daily, fodder for our dying cattle and provided us employment. This very track on which your car has broken down was built by the labour you provided us. We have come to take you to the village, and we are lucky to be given the opportunity to honour you. Don't worry about your car. It will be taken care of.'

So, they put me and my family in the bullock cart, which they had brought along, and we were taken to the village in a procession.

The ladies had already prepared an excellent dinner for us in anticipation of our arrival. While there was a *samuhik bhojan*, a common banquet, for all the villagers, the headman had dispatched motorcycle riders to fetch car mechanics. Before we finished dinner, the car had been repaired and brought to the house of the sarpanch.

We returned to Ahmedabad escorted by a posse of motorcycle riders to ensure we encountered no more problems on the way.

~

In the monsoon of 1973, there were good rains in Saurashtra and the drought was over. During the almost two years of the drought, we had provided jobs to more than a million-and-a-half labourers, fodder to 78 million cattle, dug more than 2,000 wells and used over 7,000 tankers to supply drinking water. We were able to do all this without the whiff of a scam, even a rumour of diversion of funds or the death of a single human being or brace of cattle. All this could be accomplished because of a deeply committed bureaucracy working dedicatedly for the welfare of the people, and an honest, understanding and non-interfering political leadership across the political spectrum.

Having successfully met the challenge of the drought, I was relaxing with my colleagues when I received a summons from the CM's office. Ghanshyambhai Oza was in a happy mood, chatting with his Cabinet colleagues. As I entered the room, Chimanbhai Patel said, 'Moosa, you have done an excellent job, and we all appreciate the efforts put in by you and your team in successfully overcoming the severe scarcity challenge. Our MLAs are all happy and relaxed. But we need your help to overcome a problem. The state assembly is meeting in a few days. The leader of the Opposition has given notice to introduce a resolution placing on record the assembly's appreciation of the work done during the drought.'

Ratubhai Adani intervened to explain where the rub lay. 'Coming from the Opposition, we would have appreciated the resolution and supported it wholeheartedly. But the problem lies in the wording of the resolution. It says: "This assembly places on record its appreciation of the excellent management of the drought in Gujarat by Mr Moosa Raza, director of famine relief, and his team of officials." Now we are advised that the assembly cannot pass a resolution naming a particular officer. If the leader of the Opposition was to change the wording, and instead of naming you, it says the government of Gujarat, we shall support it wholeheartedly.'

Chimanbhai said, 'I have tried to persuade the leader of the Opposition to that end. But he insists on the original wording. If the ruling party opposes this resolution, it means we did not do excellent work. We are placed in a dilemma.'

'So, what can I do, sir?' I asked.

'Since the leader of the Opposition has such high regard for you,' said the CM. 'We would like you to meet him and persuade him to change the wording of the resolution to enable us to support it.'

I met the leader of the Opposition that evening. 'Why should I appreciate the government? They did damn all except meet in the Cabinet room and indulge in crosstalk and accuse each other of diverting the relief supplies to their constituency. In real terms, you and your team of district officials did the good job. Sorry, I cannot comply with your request,' he said.

It took me over an hour of discussion, with an appeal that I would be personally embarrassed if he introduced the resolution and the Speaker ruled it out on some technical ground, to convince him.

In the event, rather than pay an 'underserved compliment' to the government (as the leader of Opposition called it), the resolution was withdrawn, and the government was saved from an embarrassing dilemma.

After I had pulled their chestnut out of the fire for them, the CM again summoned me. There were the ubiquitous trio of Ratubhai Adani, Chimanbhai Patel and Madhavsinh Solanki.

'Moosa, we appreciate the excellent work you have done for the state during the scarcity. We consulted the chief secretary on how best to reward you. We are advised that the All India Service rules preclude the option of giving you out-of-turn promotion and advance increments. Now that the scarcity is over, we have decided to offer you the choice of any post of your seniority in the government. Where would you like to go?'

I knew this was a tricky offer. If I named any prestigious post occupied by one of my colleagues, and the government posted me there, transferring the incumbent, all my colleagues would feel that I had taken advantage of my standing with the government to manoeuvre myself into a prestigious posting, throwing out the serving officer who might be doing an equally good job. This was not an acceptable option.

I thought over it for a few minutes while the ministers were chatting among themselves. Recently, one of our popular colleagues, Bhullar, who was the commissioner of fisheries, had died in a tragic car accident.

Gujarat was a predominantly non-fish-eating state, even though, because of its peninsular shape, it had the longest coastline among all the states of India. It landed a meagre catch, and the government, too, neglected the fisheries department as not of much account. It had a small budget of just ₹7 million per annum, so there were not many contenders for that post. Having manned the post of director of famine relief with a budget of ₹1200 million, and having travelled to almost 6,000 of the 12,000 drought-affected villages, I was feeling the need for some rest. I thought the commissioner of fisheries would be a post that would not put too much of a strain on me.

'Sir, I would be happy if you post me as commissioner of fisheries. That post is lying vacant since the death of Bhullar.'

They were surprised at my modest choice. They thought I would ask for some post with a large budget, paraphernalia of subordinates and opportunities for travel abroad. So, when I asked for a post that held no glamour, with a budget of less than ₹10 million, they could not digest my choice for a few moments.

I was transferred to the post of commissioner of fisheries, with its office in Shahibaug. However, I continued to live with my family in Gandhinagar, as my children were in school there.

OF FRENCHMEN, BOMBAY DUCKS AND CORAL ISLANDS

My stay in the fisheries department of Gujarat, though all too brief, was one of the pleasant interludes of my career.

I used to travel to Shahibaug in Ahmedabad, where my office was situated, by bus daily. Since Gandhinagar was located in the rural area, the bus was patronised by farmers carrying their field produce, poultry produce and milk cans. Sometimes a couple of bleating goats or a young calf would also be our companions. In summer, when the windows of the bus were closed against the hot desert winds, a variety of unpleasant smells would assail my nostrils. The villagers would be exchanging gossip and, as is the habit of rural folk acquainted with each other, their discussions often assumed a loud vociferous tenor. I, therefore, developed a technique to isolate myself mentally. I had read the Trachtenberg system of rapid mental calculation, I would start by multiplying a three-digit number by another three-digit number, and graduated to a six-digit by six-digit number. The result was that I would shut out all smells, sounds and discomforts, and reach Ahmedabad without any frayed nerves and with an intact mental balance.

The first thing I did on taking over charge was to get hold of Francis Day's two volumes on the fishes of India. One is compelled to pay tribute to the Renaissance spirit of a man like Francis Day. A doctor by training and profession in the service of the East India Company, Day was more interested in birds and fishes of India than in medicine. His monumental work, *Fishes of India*, in two volumes, was published in 1867 and was considered to be the bible of the department. Apart from detailed descriptions of both the marine and freshwater fishes of India, Burma and Ceylon, with their names in most languages of India, Day had painstakingly drawn and included sketches of all the fishes he described. During my travels as commissioner, I carried the book along with me to identify the fish caught by the fishermen, both in inland waterbodies and off the coast.

A few days of relaxation after my strenuous tenure as director of famine relief were enough to revive my exploration spirits, and I decided to visit the coastal cities of Veraval, Mangrol and Porbandar. Veraval, on the coast of peninsular Saurashtra, happens to be the headquarters of the marine fisherman community of Gujarat and is a part of the Junagadh district, famous for being the last refuge of the Asiatic lion. Veraval is also the town that prides itself on being the holy location of the Somnath Temple.

I visited Veraval, paid my respects to the rebuilt temple of Somnath and inspected the fishing harbour, which was nothing but a breakwater jutting into the sea. The fishermen complained that they did not have a protected harbour where they could tie up their boats, even a decent shed where they could transport and auction their catch, no ice factory where they could buy ice for preserving their surplus catch nor a decent diesel oil outlet for their engines. I was to hear similar complaints in the town of Mangrol.

The total annual budget of the fisheries department was a measly ₹7 million. In the government's view, the department was an unwanted legacy the state had inherited from the British Raj. The only reason the department was tolerated by a staunch vegetarian such as the chief secretary, Mr L.R. Dalal of the ICS, even with that nominal budget, was the fishermen's lobby, which helped in electing the member of the legislative assembly nominated by the ruling party. The fishermen were mostly left to their own devices, except when the elections were round the corner. They had established a very strong, well-managed internal governing body, a fishermen's panchayat, headed by an elected strongman. This panchayat made all the rules and laws that governed not only the fishing industry but extended its rule into civil disputes and matters of criminal law. The panchayat also regulated the relationship of the fishermen's community with outside agencies—district, state and central governments and other communities.

The panchayat chairman invited me to dinner in his house. That very morning, I had learnt that a fisherman who had murdered another member of the community had been executed under orders of the panchayat.

'Is this story true?' I asked the chief of the panchayat while enjoying the spicy crab claw that he had placed on my plate.

He smiled rather inscrutably. 'Ah!' he exclaimed, 'Such stories are set afloat to vilify our community.'

'But Navin Tandel did murder Karna, and the panchayat took evidence of eye witnesses before condemning Tandel,' interjected another dinner guest.

The panchayat chief frowned at this untimely intervention. 'You see, Commissioner Sahab,' he said. 'We have no patience with the government machinery. The community cannot wait until the police records an FIR, investigates the murder and then files a chargesheet. Witnesses have to travel to the district headquarters, spend their personal time and hard-earned money to give evidence. They lose the fishing season. At the end of a long-drawn hearing, the judge will acquit the murderer on grounds that there was insufficient evidence, there is benefit of doubt and so on. In the meantime, the widow of the victim and his orphaned children go hungry. The community has to support them financially. Sir, we *machhimar*s are a hard-working community. The community cannot afford the loss of time and expenditure in going to the court and giving evidence. So, we have evolved our own system of administering justice.'

'So, what do you do?' I asked.

'I do nothing, sir,' said the chief deprecatingly. 'It is the panchayat that decides.'

I understood the chief 's modesty and his reluctance to claim all responsibility. He was apprehensive that he would be called to account for the disappearance of the accused.

'We capture and confine the accused. Then we hold a meeting. The victim's widow or brother gives us names of all those who were present at the time of the murder. They are summoned. The accused can ask them questions if he wants. After hearing all the witnesses, if we come to the conclusion that the murder was committed, the panchayat collectively condemns the accused and confiscates his property to hand over to the victim's widow and children.'

'Do you record the evidence?' I asked rather naively. There was a burst of laughter among the diners, most of them being members of the panchayat.

'Sir, we are not literate or educated persons like the clerks of the court. We don't keep any records,' said one of the diners. Obviously, any written records would implicate all of them.

'Then what happens to the condemned man?' I persisted in knowing all facts.

'If there are extenuating circumstances (my language, not the fisherman's), the man is exiled permanently, excluded from the community in the state. If he comes back, he faces more serious consequences.'

'And if there are no extenuating circumstances?' I continued to press.

There was a long silence. The diners continued to munch on the roasted crabs, fried anchovies, white pomfrets and other dishes that were flowing in on tin platters from the kitchen.

I waited for an answer to my query for some time. When no reply came, I said, 'So, the story I heard this morning is true?'

'Tandel went to the sea with five other fishermen in a boat. The five men returned alone. What happened to Tandel?' I asked.

'They said he jumped into the sea and was drowned.'

Swift justice—not for them the law's delays, the contumely of the judicial office. They did not even need a bare bodkin; a ramshackle boat was good enough.

During dinner, the members complained to me that the government had stopped giving loans for diesel engines and nylon nets. A check revealed that most of the fishermen had not repaid the loans taken by them earlier for trawlers, engines, nets and other equipment. Millions of rupees were still outstanding.

'Why don't you have a recovery drive?' I asked the loan recovery officer of the revenue department.

'Sir, it is very dangerous. During daytime, they are out at sea. In the evening, they are all at the harbour, distilling hard liquor, drinking and making merry. Even the police are afraid to venture into that area after the sun sets. Neither the revenue offices nor the police are willing to cooperate with the department in the recovery drive.'

In my next meeting with the panchayat, I told them, 'Your members owe so many millions of rupees to the government. By not repaying these loans for years, you are doing injustice to your own community. The younger generation is not able to install Greaves Cotton or Yamaha engines on their boats nor buy nets and other equipment. The catch has not gone up for the last several years. Those who have boats and are landing good catches are wasting their money on booze!'

The panchayat members listened to my tirade patiently. 'Unless old loans are returned, no new loans can be given. You are the losers,' I continued.

'Will you give me a list of all those who have not repaid the loans?' asked the chief.

I instructed my recovery officer to provide the list to the chief. The next evening, the chief came to the guest house with a request, 'Will you please instruct the loan recovery officer to open his office tomorrow morning at 6 am?'

I did so. The loan recovery officer reported to me later that there was a queue of fishermen with cash, eager to repay their loans. Within the next week, we had recovered 80 per cent of the outstanding dues. And we started disbursement of fresh loans to new applicants.

Within a short time of my taking over as the commissioner of fisheries, in 1974, President's Rule was imposed in Gujarat. H.C. Sarin, ICS from Delhi, was appointed as one of the advisors to the governor. Mr Sarin, a very go-getting officer, brooked no nonsense, took over the room of the dismissed CM and functioned effectively from there, relegating both the governor and his own colleague, K.T. Satarawala, a mild Parsi gentleman belonging to the old school, to enforced leisure. He took a keen interest in the functioning of all the departments. Very meticulous in paying attention to all issues, he believed in extreme punctuality. He fixed appointments by the minutes—11:43 am, 2:32 pm, etc. He would ask me for weekly reports and would often ring me up early mornings and late evenings. Noting the frequency of his calls, Husnara once asked me whether the advisor was in charge of only the fisheries department or he had other responsibilities.

I learnt through the Delhi grapevine that a World Bank team was visiting India on a recce mission to select a maritime state for funding fisheries harbours, ice factories, boat-building yards, trawlers, processing factories and so on. Appasaheb Shinde, the minister in the central fisheries ministry, had selected Kerala, Tamil Nadu, West Bengal, Maharashtra and Andhra Pradesh, all major coastal states, for their visit. Even though Gujarat had the longest coastline—almost one-third of India's coastline—it was considered by the Government of India as a vegetarian state, with no marine or inland fisheries worth writing to the World Bank about. Both the Government of India and the state governments, for sentimental reasons influenced by cultural compulsions—that had been advanced by the powerful vegetarian clique that had created the myth that Gujarat was a vegetarian state—had throttled the development of fisheries in Gujarat. So, Appasaheb Shinde excluded Gujarat from the itinerary of the World Bank.

I took up the matter with Mr Sarin. 'This is a gross injustice to Gujarat, sir,' I pleaded. 'First, you do not allow the state to develop its infrastructure, and then call it a vegetarian state, and then you want to keep it permanently deprived of all resources.'

'Yes,' agreed Mr Sarin, 'Under the shadow of Mahatma Gandhi, they declared Gujarat a teetotaler state. Since coming here, I have received subtle invitations to parties. I am told liquor flowed freely in those parties, with the best of scotch and single malts.'

The upshot of all these discussions was that Mr Sarin spoke to Appasaheb Shinde, who then agreed to spare just two days out of the long itinerary of the World Bank team for Gujarat. However, Mr Sarin had no hope of Gujarat succeeding in overcoming its reputation within the short time allotted. 'I don't know what you will accomplish in those two days, in the last lap of the team's tour. They would have already made up their minds after visiting those four or five states. Shinde has spared these two days just to be politically correct,' Mr Sarin consoled me.

I decided to make the best use of those last two days of the team in India. I rang up each of my counterparts to check on the composition of the team, the nationality, background and character of its members, their responses to the presentations made and the kind of information they demanded. Some of my counterparts were quite contemptuous of my efforts. One of them told me that the leader of the team was French, who understood little English and spoke even less. He hardly ever opened his mouth during the visit, even to eat the best continental dishes served to him. I got apprehensive.

The team flew down from Bombay to Porbandar, and I was present with my full team at the airport to receive them. We got into the fleet of cars to proceed to Veraval, to the old Junagadh nawab's guest house.

The distance of about 125 kilometres, I knew, could be covered in about three hours. However, I had organised a couple of ten-minute halts en route for the visiting team to receive a traditional welcome and appeals from the fishermen to help them with harbour, boats, nets and ice factories—all organised by the fisheries department.

I could see that the chief of the visiting team—let us call him Capitaine Legrand—was quite impressed, though he never said a word nor showed any emotion through his expression. Once on the way, I opened the conversation.

'I believe you were in the French Navy during the Second World War, Captain,' I observed.

'Hmm,' said he, a non-committal response.

'I am sure you did not support the Vichy government.' This was a fairly reasoned conclusion, for if he had been a supporter of the Vichy government, the World Bank would not have employed him as a consultant later.

That provoked him. 'No, I was not a supporter of the Vichy government.'

After the fall of France, Marshall Petain formed a rump government at Vichy, which collaborated with the Germans. Admiral Darlan, who was the commander-in-chief of the French Navy was in constant contact with both Churchill and Roosevelt, and had managed to keep the bulk of the French Navy out of German hands. The fleet was stationed in the major port of Toulon when the Germans decided to take it over. Darlan ordered it to be scuttled. This was a major blow to the Germans.

'Were you in Toulon when Darlan ordered the fleet to be scuttled?' I asked the captain.

He became animated at that. 'Yes, I was there. My ship, too, had to be scuttled. I did so with a heavy heart. We were all loyal to Admiral Darlan.'

'Also sympathetic to the Free French,' I remarked. He nodded.

'Does this consultancy keep you very busy?' I asked, by way of changing the subject.

'Not very, I go wherever the World Bank requests me.'

'What do you do in between these consultancy assignments?' I asked him.

'I am doing some research,' he said.

'On fisheries or naval subjects?' I probed.

'On neither. I am researching on the foreign vocabulary in French language.'

'Are there many foreign words in French?' I asked.

'Yes, many—English, Latin, Greek, Swahili and some Chinese and Vietnamese too.'

'What about Persian and Arabic?' I probed.

'I don't think there are any Arabic or Persian words in French,' he said complacently.

'But you do have,' I said.

'For example?' he asked in a sceptical tone.

'Rose,' I said. 'Originally from old Persian "vrdhan", from Arabic "ward", it lost the initial "w" and added "ian" as a suffix,' I said. 'The French word "rue" for road, street, too, is from Persian "raft, raftan", so is the word "roue". I also mentioned amiral (admiral), alcohol, alchimie, café, caravelle, carat and chemise.

'I want the authority for that claim,' he said. So, I quoted a couple of etymological dictionaries for him. At his request, I promised to send photocopies of those books from my library to further his research. We got into an animated discussion on the subject of Grimm's Law, Verner's Law and other philological subjects. Once the ice was broken, we got along like a house on fire (the mixed metaphor is a coincidence). The taciturn captain turned out to be a pleasant and loquacious companion.

In the guest house, our team made a presentation on the fisheries of Gujarat—the quantum being landed, their species, the need to develop both Veraval and Mangrol as fisheries ports. The team asked relevant questions.

The captain met me for tea in the afternoon. He was a little curious about Bombay duck: how come a fish was called after a bird? I explained to him that the fish was named not after a bird but after a train. 'Curiouser and curiouser,' he exclaimed. 'The dried fish, smelling strongly, was transported to Bombay by the Bombay Mail. Mail in Gujarat is called *dak*, so Bombay *dak*, which, by association, became Bombay duck.'

'You say that Gujarat lands about 15,000 tonnes of this fish.'

'Yes, between the coast of Jafrabad and Nawanagar. But it has a potential of up to 30,000 to 35,000 tonnes of catch.'

'I tried to locate Bombay duck in my reference book. I could not find it,' said the captain, a subtle note of scepticism creeping into his query.

'You will find it under the name of *Nehereus harpodon*— its scientific name,' I enlightened him.

The visiting team gave us no respite. Immediately after lunch, the team decided to visit the Veraval and Mangrol harbour sites. Mangrol was a vassal state of the nawab of Junagadh, ruled by the sheikhs of Mangrol. A son of the last ruler of Mangrol, Major Muhammad Ali, died fighting for India in the 1965 war against Pakistan.

When the team returned to New York, the report they submitted to the World Bank recommended Gujarat for the award. That was just the first step, the recce. It was followed by a much larger team. They camped for about ten days in Veraval, holding meetings and enjoying our 'free hospitality', for which they insisted on getting bills.

Years later, after the ports had been built along with the ice factories and the fleet of trawlers had expanded manifold, a delegation of the fisherman's panchayat came to Gandhinagar with a recommendation that the Mangrol port be named 'Moosa Bandar'. I refused to entertain the proposal and dissuaded the panchayat from pursuing the idea. Today, the total fish landing of Gujarat has gone up to 8,00,000 tonnes from a meagre 1,50,000 tonnes before the World Bank project.

One day, as I was camping in Jamnagar with my family, I was visited by a group of fishermen from the Bedi area. Bedi was the port of Jamnagar in the Gulf of Kutch, and in the pre-Independence days, was known as a flourishing outlet for the products of the native state of Jamnagar. It had been reduced to a fishing port by the early seventies.

The delegation was led by a venerable looking Muslim fisherman of middle age, named Jusab. I learnt from him that many of the fishermen of Bedi area were Muslims, who eked out a living catching fish off the coast.

'What kind of fish do you catch?'

'Those of us who have boats with outboard motors venture out five or ten kilometres into the gulf. We get red snappers, mullets and eels. Sometimes we get catfish, ribbon fish, breams. If we are lucky, we also land pomfrets. Sometimes, once or twice a week, we venture out to the Pirotan Island. We get good-sized groupers, large-sized king fish, pomfret and halwa.'

This was the first time I had heard of Pirotan. I had no idea that off the coast of Jamnagar there were not one but several coral islands, of which Pirotan was the largest. My curiosity was aroused, and I agreed to visit the island.

Next day, Jusab along with a cohort of fishermen were waiting at the port when my family and I reached the jetty along with a couple of my departmental companions.

With some difficulty and much pushing and pulling, we all got into the country boat. Though it had an outboard motor, Jusab said that since we had to cross several intersecting lagoons, it was not advisable to operate the engine, whose propeller may get entangled in the weeds and mangrove roots. The lagoons, with mangroves on both banks, were not very deep, and two fishermen manoeuvred the boat with long bamboo poles and a couple of oarsmen propelled it forward. We saw many water fowls fluttering out of the mangroves at our approach, as well as teals, mallards, plovers and cormorants.

Then, suddenly, the channels ended, and we were in the open sea. The waves were much higher, and the boat responded to the motion. But Jusab reassured us all that this was a calm sea and there was no danger.

'We travel this route twice a week, Sahab,' he reassured me, 'Even in choppy seas. This is a gulf, sir, we don't meet much with stormy waters.'

Thus reassured, within the next two hours, we saw the shoreline of Pirotan. We had travelled for more than three hours to cover a mere nautical distance of slightly over twenty-two kilometres. Pirotan, I learnt, has an area of about three square kilometres at low tide. We reached the island as the tide was receding, and a large part of the exposed island was still covered in two to three feet of water. The boat could not reach the dry shore, as the draft was not enough. So, we had to get down into the water. Luckily, I was wearing rubber shoes, but Husnara was only in her rubber sandals. During the course of our explorations, Husnara sustained several cuts on her feet. The children rode piggy back on the fishermen. The water was so clear, we could see all the colourful corals that were strewn around on the seabed—red, green and blue, brain-shaped and flower-shaped.

After half a kilometre of wading through water, we reached dry land to discover that, though the fishermen claimed a much larger area for Pirotan, it was only about a square kilometre. Jusab informed us that there was a dargah of a legendary saint, Khwaja Khidar, on the island. Khidar is known as an immortal patron saint of all travellers and seafarers.

'Who looks after the shrine?' I asked.

'Oh, there is a *mujawar* (caretaker) who lives on the island.'

'But who takes care of the caretaker?' I asked, surprised. 'The fishermen who come to the island always visit the shrine to pay their respects to the saint before casting their nets. They make some offerings, enough to enable the *mujawar* to live on. Would you like to visit the shrine?'

The children and the rest were more interested in wading up to the periphery of the island, where the deep water started. We again formed into a procession and commenced wading into the water to go around the circumference. Just a few feet into the water, and we saw some large barges stationed at the edge of the shallows.

'What are those barges?' I asked Jusab.

'Sir, the Digvijay Cement Company in Jamnagar is dredging millions of tonnes of coral every year to make cement. They say, in a few years, there will be no Pirotan island left. It will all be converted into cement.'

I was shocked. Apart from the incalculable damage the cement company was doing to the environment and the ecology, the destruction of the flora and fauna and the rare corals that lived in the shallow seas off Pirotan, the livelihood of the poor fishermen, too, would be entirely destroyed.

'Did you bring this to the notice of the DM?' I asked Jusab. 'More than once, sir', he said. 'We have asked the MLA, the panchayat president and others. But the cement company is very rich and powerful. No one is willing to oppose the might of the Tatas and Birlas, sir,' he said.

Just then, one of the fishermen asked us to halt. He had spied something in the water.

'There is a big fish lurking in the crevice of that coral reef,' he said.

Jusab explained that as the tide receded, leaving just two feet of water, many fish were left behind. They got into the crevices of the coral reefs until the tide returned, either in search of prey or to escape human hands. The fisherman had a long thick nylon cord with a large hook attached to it. He got down into the knee-deep water, slowly inserted his hand into the crevice, attached the hook to fish lurking inside and gently pulled. Out came a large grouper, protesting its capture. The fish was about ten to fifteen kilograms, and the fisherman had no intention of carrying it around. So, he herded it along in the water. Since it had realised that it could not escape the hook and live, the fish lost its initial enthusiasm and followed us docilely like a tame dog drawn by the nylon cord. At several places, we halted, and the fishermen captured half a dozen large and a dozen medium-sized groupers. Once or twice the fishermen withdrew their hands hastily.

'Why?' I asked. 'No fish there?'

'There is a coral snake there, sir. They are most dangerous. Normally they do not bite. Once they bite, we die within minutes.'

As we waded along, followed by a 'herd' of coral fish on nylon cords, I asked the fishermen as to whether they had organised any protest against the fast erosion of their island, which will have vanished in a few years. I was told that there were several other smaller islands in the vicinity—Narara, Kalubhar, Dhani, Mundra, etc.—also under threat of vanishing through dredging for cement. I felt something had to be done to save them.

As soon as I returned to Ahmedabad, I wrote to the chief secretary, bringing all the facts to his notice.

'Unless there is a ban placed on the dredging, vested interests both in Jamnagar and at the state level would always favour the cement company in the name of industrial progress and will not protect the ecology.'

The minister in charge of industry was a highly educated politician, a postgraduate from MIT and a chemical engineer. When he saw my letter, he took umbrage at my use of the expression 'vested interest' and interpreted it as a slur on the government. Perhaps I was somewhat indiscreet in the use of that expression.

The upshot was that my letter was consigned to the morgue of unheeded files.

But I was too upset at the cavalier way both the cement industry and the government were turning a blind eye to this wanton destruction of an irreplaceable national heritage, and God knows how many others, in the name of industrial progress and development.

Luckily, the MP representing the Jamnagar constituency, Daulatsinh Jadeja, happened to be a very good friend and interested in ecology. As a third-time winner of the constituency, he was in the good books of PM Indira Gandhi, who was, like her father Jawaharlal Nehru, interested in conserving the heritage of India. When I briefed Daulatsinh about what was happening to Pirotan Island in his own constituency, he was deeply moved. I gave him a detailed note—an unofficial note, which he took to Delhi and briefed the PM. Though Indira Gandhi lost power at the end of 1975, the ball had been set rolling.

In 1980, the Government of India declared the entire area off the coast of Kutch, including Pirotan Island and several others like Narara, Kalubhar, Dhani and Mundra, a National Marine Park and banned all dredging and industrial activity in that area. Today, Pirotan Island is a centre of ecological studies and a limited tourist attraction. Though I cannot claim exclusive credit for saving that island, my deriving some satisfaction is not entirely misplaced since I am the one who initiated the process.

My work on the World Bank loan had earned me some esteem in the fisheries department of the Government of India. I was also the chairman of the Gujarat Fisheries Central Cooperative Association in my ex-officio capacity as commissioner of fisheries. So, I was included in a delegation to visit Japan at the invitation of the Government of Japan to attend an international conference of fisheries cooperatives.

One Mr Balakrishnan headed the delegation. He was the minister of fisheries of Kerala. When our plane halted in Rangoon on the way to Tokyo, his two brothers-in-law came to see him at the airport. Mr Balakrishnan had told us earlier that they were Burmese nationals—Mr Nan and Mr Than. I wondered how Mr Balakrishnan had ended up marrying a Burmese lady. When the two brothers-in-law turned up, we found them to be pure-bred Malayalis, named Ramakrishnan and Ramanathan. To merge with the local population, they had dropped the first part of their names. They were doing very well as businessmen in Rangoon, and Mr Balakrishnan was justly proud of his relatives by marriage. A rose by any other name would smell just as sweet, observed the Bard. A Malayali by any other name would remain just as enterprising, I observed to myself.

The Government of India decided that we should promote the sale of canned sardines, which was monopolised by the Portuguese and Moroccans. So, a delegation consisting of two private-sector canning-factory owners—Madhavraj of Malpe in Karnataka and Sadanand of Kerala—with myself as the leader of the delegation was mandated to visit Dubai, Bahrain, Kuwait, Egypt, Saudi Arabia, Syria and Iran, where we were to meet the importers of canned fish and establish a market for canned products, especially sardines, herring and shrimp. At first, I wondered why I was chosen to lead that delegation, since Gujarat had no sardine fishery nor a sardine factory. Later it dawned on me that since all the countries on the itinerary happened to be Muslim countries, and so by including me, the delegation, it was thought, would be given a sympathetic reception—an utterly false presumption.

In 1975, Dubai was still an underdeveloped part of the UAE. It was not so difficult to get appointments with both the government agencies and the private importers. The Trucial States had come together just two or three years before, and Sheikh Rashid bin Saeed Al Maktoum was still ruling Dubai. Sheikh Mohammed bin Rashid Al Maktoum, his son, the visionary, was still in his early youth. The Sheikh looked like one of the old Arab chieftains who must have ridden with Lawrence of Arabia, or going back further in history, with Khalid ibn al-Walid and Amr ibn al-As. He was very courteous and came up to the door to see us off. Both Madhavraj and Sadanand made some good deals and established long-term commercial relations—a bridgehead for other exporters to follow.

From Dubai, we proceeded to Kuwait, from where we were to proceed to Iran. On our last evening in Kuwait, I rang up our ambassador, who invited me to have breakfast with him the next morning. Since our departure to Tehran was scheduled at 2:30 pm, I accepted the invitation.

When we sat down to breakfast, the ambassador asked, 'I hope all your papers are in order?'

'What papers?' I asked.

'Your visas, your authorisation from the Government of India, your invitation from the Iranian Government, etc.,' he explained.

'Yes. But I was told in Delhi that if our stay in Iran is for less than seventy-two hours, we don't need a visa. We will be issued an entry permit at the airport. So, we don't have the visas for Iran.'

'You have been misinformed. Without a visa, you will not be allowed into Iran,' he informed me.

'Please rush to the Iranian Embassy and request them to issue you a temporary visa,' he advised, with a frown at our folly.

'Can you not help us with a letter to the Iranian ambassador to speed up the process,' I requested.

He looked at his watch. 'It is 9:30 am. Your flight leaves at 2:30. You have hardly any time. Please don't wait for all that rigmarole. Take your passports and rush to the Iranian Embassy.'

His advice appeared sensible. Luckily, his driver dropped me at the hotel, where I collected Madhavraj and Sadanand's passports, advised them to keep the morning's appointments without me, took a taxi and rushed to the Iranian Embassy. When I sent in my official card, I got immediate access to the first secretary, a venerable-looking, middle-aged gentleman with a kindly face, Agha Hussaini. He gave me several forms to be filled up and photographs to be attached.

I pasted the photographs at the right places and presented the completed applications to Agha Hussaini. He glanced through them, stamped them at various places, then he picked up the passports and stamped the visas. When he picked up my passport, red-coloured, he made a wry pause and turned to me.

'I cannot issue you a visa, Agha Raza,' he said. 'Why not?' I asked, shocked out of my wits.

'Because this is a diplomatic passport. Only the ambassador can issue a visa to a diplomatic passport holder!'

So much for the importance of a diplomatic passport holder, I said to myself.

'Then please send it to the ambassador to get it stamped, Agha.' I requested.

'That is not possible. The ambassador is away at Dubai to watch a tennis tournament. He will be back only after the weekend.'

'But we have to leave right away. Our flight is at 2:30 pm, and it is already noon. Can't you do something about it, Agha?' I pleaded.

'What can I do? Why did you not take care of all this before leaving Delhi?' he asked in exasperation.

The only reply I could give him was to quote a couplet from Hafez Shirazi, the national poet of Iran.

'Zin safar gar bi salamat bi watan baz rasam
Digar aanja ki ravam, aaqil o farzana ravam.'

(If I return home from this journey, safe and sound,
When I set out again, I shall stir out with wisdom and wit.)

Agha Hussaini looked up with a broad smile on his face. 'You have quoted Hafez, Agha. That is a very apt couplet, sir. One who can quote Hafez so aptly deserves an exceptional treatment.' Thus saying, he picked up my passport, stamped the visa and signed it. 'Look. I have broken the rules for the sake of Hafez!'

So, we were able to catch the flight in the nick of time, all because a medieval poet of Persia came to my rescue.

Our official meetings in Tehran went as all such meetings go. We discovered that the Iranians were not very fond of fish. They were basically a meat-eating race, fond of kebabs and pulao made with sheep and lamb meat. We were told that if we wanted to sell tinned sardines, we should visit the southern coastal districts of Iran, where they caught and ate marine varieties of fish.

Tehran, on my first visit, impressed me as a clean, beautiful city. Plain trees lining the long avenues, canals of cold water from the melting snows of Alburz mountains flowed through broad avenues, kiosks on the wide footpaths selling fresh pomegranate juice (just two tumans for a full beer mug), restaurants serving a plate of chelo kebab with a bottle of *aab-e-ali* (our buttermilk, cooled in the fridge), fruits of every kind, a special sweet (available only in Iran) called *gaz*, made from powdered poppy seeds, pistachios and a special kind of tree-sap with a mixture of pure honey—these were (and I am told, still are) the delights of Tehran.

From Tehran we proceeded to Baghdad, once the cultural, educational and intellectual capital of the world.

Baghdad was ruled by Saddam Hussain at that time, though President Qasim was in nominal charge. Women enjoyed full freedom and equality. In fact, the government team that negotiated trade issues with us was headed by a highly educated, intelligent and well-informed lady. The city was served by a well-functioning municipality, good public transport, honest administration and was corruption-free, unlike the contiguous Iran under the Shah. Iraq was benefitting from the oil boom, the support of the neighbours, and so did not need to make money through corruption. In fact, Baghdad gave us the impression that Iraq was a well-governed country (a few years later, the US bombed it into the stone age). And the administration was highly sympathetic to India, and therefore, we had good meetings and entered into mutually beneficial agreements.

Two things worried me about the fish processing technology on our coast. The unhygienic way the large quantity of Bombay duck was dried on the seashore, exposed to the flying sand and the ever-present flies that buzzed around and fed on the fish, and the large quantity of so-called 'trash fish' that had to be thrown away by the trawlers for want of space and ice. When they took out the trawlers to the sea for a three-day trip, the fishermen had to make an educated guess as to the quantity of high-quality fish—prawns, kingfish, pomfret, halwa and trevally—they were likely to catch. So, for every tonne of quality fish they would catch, they needed a tonne of ice. So, if they hoped to catch two tonnes of such quality fish, they carried two tonnes of ice. But if their estimates went awry and they landed only one tonne of quality fish, they retained the trash fish, weighing one tonne. But if they landed two tonnes of trash fish, they had to throw away the additional fish for the seagulls and the sharks! The so-called trash fetched only ₹2 per kilogram, which was bought by the cattle feed manufacturers! Protein for the milch cattle.

Actually, the trash fish consisted of a variety of smaller fish—anchovies, butter fish, lady fish, capony fish, herrings, sardines, lizard fish, blue surgeon and flounders. Such small fish were highly prized in Europe. I was once taken to an upmarket restaurant on the river Seine. For starters, they served six red-coloured fish—each about six inches long, called rouge. I discovered from the menu that they were costlier than the haddocks, hakes, cods and soles listed as 'entries'. The Middle Easterners prize the grouper fish called hamour, locally higher priced than pomfret, kingfish and halwa. In Chennai, I have seen the grouper fish being tossed aside by the fishermen as of low value. In the fish markets of South India, sole (priced as the costliest fish in the London upmarket restaurants under the name of 'Dover sole') is sold at trash value.

So, I decided to do something about these two problems. With the help of the Greaves Cotton Co., supplier of the trawler boat engines, I developed a 'freezer' hold in the existing trawlers, with some internal modifications. An auxiliary small engine had to be added. This eliminated the need to carry ice blocks onboard the trawler. Naturally, the price of the trawler increased. Though the fishermen received the 'pilot' trawler enthusiastically, they could not afford the cost. I recommended that the government subsidise the cost of the trawler—but the vegetarian government was not too enthusiastic. My project remained only on paper!

With the help of the Central Institute of Fisheries Technology (CIFT) in Cochin, I also developed a tunnel drier to dry the Bombay duck and installed it on the coast. This eliminated the smell to a large extent, made the fish into flakes, very tasty when fried. Since there were no takers in Gujarat for a dried-fish product, I exported some samples to the UK, where it found a receptive enthusiastic market in some pubs as a drink accompaniment. The problem of trash fish, too, was attempted to be solved. By steaming the trash fish in large boilers, removing the bones, scales, head and fins, and mixing the flaked-off meat with some mild spices, I created 'fish keema', wrapped in cellophane packets of 250–500 grams and frozen. They found a good market in Delhi, Bombay and Calcutta. In Delhi and Bombay, we sold it in our own outlets. In other cities, we tied up with some major shops (there were no supermarkets and malls in the mid-seventies in India). Value enhancement for the so-called trash fish was high, and the fisherman would have benefitted. But my stay in the department was too short for me to consolidate all the technological innovations.

L.R. Dalal, the then chief secretary (a staunch vegetarian, who disliked all non-vegetarians and who believed that he owned constructive responsibility for all the piscine lives I was destroying by increasing the fish catch), was unhappy with me.

'You have increased the fish landings three-folds, increased the export of frozen shrimps four-fold in your two-year tenure. The death of these fish and shrimp will be held against my karma!' he told me.

'I thought I was doing my duty as the commissioner of fisheries, sir!' I pleaded.

'But who told you to do it so enthusiastically? We thought you wanted to take it easy after your strenuous job as director of famine relief, but you have overdone it!'

Meanwhile, Indira Gandhi had declared Emergency in the country. Om Mehta, the state home minister, was in charge of the affairs of Gujarat. The fisheries department was not important enough to draw the attention of the Centre or even the state government. I was sailing along happily in my own unnoticed niche. As the Persian saying goes, '*hech aafat na rasad gosha-e tanhai ra* (No trouble reaches a secluded corner).'

OF EMERGENCY AND WEAVING LOOMS

I was not left to enjoy the safety of my seclusion for long. In 1975, the Centre decided to terminate President's Rule in Gujarat, revive the suspended assembly and appointed Madhavsinh Solanki as the CM.

One morning, I had just entered my Shahibaug office when my PA came rushing in to say that I was urgently needed by the chief secretary in Gandhinagar. Mr H.K.L. Kapoor had taken over as chief secretary after the retirement of Mr L.R. Dalal. I returned post-haste and reported to the chief secretary.

'The CM has desired that you should immediately take over as his principal secretary,' he said. 'He is ordering that you should be promoted to the secretary's rank.'

Though it was an unexpected and premature promotion, it was a bit awkward for me. Mr Solanki happened to be a friend of more than fifteen years. We shared many interests—poetry, books, films, mushairas, smoking and good food—which resulted in a deep bond of friendship between us. And this was known to many of my colleagues. There were six or seven officers senior to me in the cadre who would all feel that I had taken advantage of my proximity to Mr Solanki to land such an 'important post' with an out-of-turn promotion!

'Sir, there are several seniors of mine who would prove better principal secretaries than I. Many of them are hoping to be appointed to that post,' I said to Mr Kapoor.

Mr Kapoor reddened in the face. He was a stickler for rules and upholder of the principle of seniority in service.

'Are you questioning the wisdom of the CM's choice and my advice to him?' he asked in an acerbic tone.

I had not expected such a reaction from him. I fell silent, abashed at the rebuke.

'You had better go and report to him,' Mr Kapoor said.

The CM had already reached the office and was giving finishing touches to his proposed Cabinet, when I entered his room, occupied a couple of days earlier by H.C. Sarin, the advisor to the governor. He greeted me effusively, 'I was hoping you would come early. I wanted to pick your brains on some of the names I have included in the Cabinet.' I felt a little embarrassed at being called upon to indulge in political advice.

'Before that, sir, I have to say something to you,' I said, 'with your permission.'

'Yes, what is it?'

'Sir, you have done me great honour by appointing me as your principal secretary. I am just completing fifteen years in service and you have promoted me to the rank of secretary. I thank you for that. But, sir, there are two reasons that are likely to harm my long-term interests by this posting and the promotion.'

'And what are they?' he asked in a wondering tone. 'Firstly, sir, we have been very good friends for more than a decade. You have known me as a completely apolitical officer. But I have always been outspoken in my opinions on government action and never refrained from differing with senior officers and cabinet ministers, even openly, in the weekly Cabinet meetings during the drought relief operations. You were an observer of all that as a cabinet minister yourself. Now that you have become the chief minister, you may have to take decisions based on political considerations. I may not agree with them. I may offer unpalatable advice on such occasions, and you may not like it. That may affect our long-term friendship. I would rather retain that friendship and your regard for me than enjoy this temporary glory of post and promotion. Secondly, sir, there are certain able and competent seniors to me in the cadre. They would certainly resent their supersession. I would be making long-term enemies of them because they would sincerely believe that you chose me and promoted me over their heads because I manoeuvred it.'

He relaxed in his chair, remained silent for a few moments and replied, 'Your first reservation is hurting. Why do you assume that I would take decisions based on purely political considerations? Do you believe I am an unethical person who would go against the constitutional requirements, government's own well-established rules and regulations and ethical norms? I am a Gandhian and have actually worked with Gandhiji. I still believe in his principles and teachings. Your second reservation is easily overcome. Now that you are going to be the principal secretary, please get proposals from the chief secretary that all those seniors who were superseded be promoted in the next few weeks to the rank of secretary.'

Though my tenure as principal secretary with Mr Solanki was quite brief, as PM Indira Gandhi withdrew the Emergency in March 1977 and called for new elections, there are a few outstanding events in my memory from that period. My friendship with Mr Solanki continues even today on an even keel.

The Emergency imposed by Indira Gandhi is counted by many as a watershed in the polity of India—it laid down the grounds for absolutism, a committed bureaucracy, a docile judiciary, a subservient press and packing of most democratic institutions with committed and sympathetic individuals. Vinoba Bhave, a staunch Hindu, a famous Gandhian and the protagonist of the Bhoodan Movement, even went to the extent of supporting the Emergency by calling it '*anushasan parva*' (Era of Discipline). The central government, therefore, felt morally strengthened with the support of such leaders. I, however, felt differently. I saw the flip side of the Emergency—for creeping corruption, the political chicanery, the toadying to the powers that be, the moral and political excesses indulged in by even the petty dictators who took their cue from Delhi.

Within days of Mr Solanki's takeover as CM, I took up the issue of hundreds of political prisoners languishing in jails in the state for no fault but differing from the Emergency Law. Speaking out against the Emergency publicly attracted dire punishment—incarceration without legal recourse.

I got a list of those in jail from the home department and took it to the CM.

'Sir, look at this list,' I told the CM. 'Why are people like Babubhai Patel and Patwari in jail when their only fault is to have spoken out against the Emergency?'

He glanced over the names on the list, many of whom were personally known to him. Some of them had been fellow fighters with him in the independence movement.

'So, what do you want me to do?' he asked me.

He had been appointed by Indira Gandhi herself but was willing to listen to the other side.

'Except for a few, the rest are all non-violent protesters. Release them. They may hold protest meetings against the Emergency. That will take out some steam. Their imprisonment is making martyrs of them. This is counterproductive. Common people who are suffering from the *anushasan parva* are holding up these people as heroes.'

Mr Solanki looked thoughtful.

A few days later, Mr Solanki went to Delhi to call on the PM. This was his first visit to Delhi after taking over as CM. He asked me to accompany him. At the PMO, while the CM went into the inner chamber to meet the PM, I sat outside with R.K. Dhawan, the PM's private secretary who wielded more power than any cabinet minister. A dapper, well-dressed and alert Punjabi, exuding verve and nerve, I saw him in deep conversation with a tall gentleman clad in a dhoti with his torso bare. He had a full head of dark hair and there was not an ounce of extra fat on his well-muscled body. I learnt later that he was Dhirendra Brahmachari, godman and sadhu-adviser to the PM and many of the Congress leaders. Mr Dhawan did not deign to introduce us. (My next encounter with Dhirendra Brahmachari was in Delhi when we flew together to Jammu in the winter of 1988. Though in his sixties, he still sported a full head of dark hair and a dense black beard. He still wore a dhoti and kept his torso bare in the severe cold of Delhi winter. His ashram at Mantalai near Jammu, spread over 130 acres, was rumoured to be equipped with five-star facilities, an air-strip and a seven-storey guest house. He died in an accident in 1994 while flying his private aircraft.)

A few minutes later, Mr Dhawan, who received a buzzer on his phone, asked me to go into the inner chamber where the CM was talking to the PM. I went in, and the PM asked me to take a seat. Mr Solanki introduced me to her as his principal secretary. Indira Gandhi had already met me as the collector and DM of Surat in the aftermath of the notorious floods of 1968, as the DM of Bulsar when she had come campaigning in 1971 and as the director of famine relief in 1972, when I showed her around the arid regions of Kutch. She turned to me and said, 'I believe you have some observations about the people who are in jail in Gujarat?'

'Yes, Madam,' I replied hesitatingly. I could not guess how she would react to what I was going to say. 'I believe many people who are languishing in the jails have been freedom fighters in the past and do not believe in any violent action against the Emergency.'

The PM turned to Mr Solanki and said, 'I never ordered the arrest of any of these people. Om Mehta (the minster of state for home affairs), who has been visiting Gujarat off and on, must have taken these decisions based on local information. If you feel that no harm could be done if they are released, I have no objections. You can go ahead, Madhavsinhbhai, and release them if you wish.'

On our return to Gujarat Bhavan, I faxed the home secretary a list of those non-violent protesters against the Emergency and advised him to release them before evening. The advice was promptly carried out.

Mr Solanki was the one who introduced me to such books and authors as Milan Kundera, Tolkien (I still have the book *Lord of the Rings*, which Mr Solanki presented to me), the *Secret Diary of Adrian Mole*, etc. He is a real democrat and established a close rapport with the working classes of Gujarat, especially the Dalits, Adivasis, minorities and backward classes. Once he asked me whether during my travels in Gujarat, I had eaten roast chicken in Kaka's Dhaba, a roadside joint off the highway near Bharuch. When I showed my ignorance of that establishment, he advised me that next time I was in the vicinity I should try the excellent roast chicken at the dhaba. Years later, when Mr Solanki was in his second innings as the CM of Gujarat, once while travelling to Surat, I passed by Kaka's Dhaba, which was pointed out to me by the driver. I asked the driver to divert to the dhaba, recalling Mr Solanki's recommendations. The dhaba was nothing more than a medium-sized tin shack. There were many trucks parked in the open space around, and I hesitated to enter because I knew that it would be crowded by the drivers of parked trucks. However, having come thus far and recalling Mr Solanki's insistence, I decided to take a chance and succumbed to the temptation of roast chicken. As I anticipated, the interior was well-crowded by Sikh drivers from Punjab, Jat drivers from Haryana, Tamil drivers from Madras, etc. Right then, I saw Mr Solanki, the CM of Gujarat, ensconced in their midst, laughing and chatting with the truck drivers. He espied me from afar and called me over loudly. I enjoyed the roast chicken in the august company of the CM and the truck drivers. That showed the character of Mr Solanki. But I am jumping ahead.

As the principal secretary to the CM, I had to shoulder a heavy responsibility of getting the files from all departments cleared. Mr Solanki travelled extensively both in Gujarat as well as out of the state. As a result, files tended to accumulate on my table, awaiting his return. He had given me instructions to clear urgent files myself and get them ratified by him later. However, there were many files that required his personal attention and which I dared not clear without a discussion. We used to sit late into the night in his residential office and clear the files after a brief discussion. Once while clearing the files, Mr Solanki got up from his sofa walked all the way around the table to press the bell switch, which was located behind where I was sitting, to summon the peon.

'Sir,' I protested. 'You could have told me to press the bell switch without having taken all that trouble.'

'Moosa, for a simple task like that why should I trouble you? I could do it myself,' he said.

I was reminded of a Persian couplet from Iqbal's *Asrar-e-khudi*:

Khud farood aa az shutar misle Umar
Alhazar az minnate ghayr alhazar.

(Get down from the camel like Umar.
Beware of accepting another's obligation, Beware.)

I used to go to the CM's residence, which was close to my villa, on my bicycle. But Mr Solanki would not allow me to return in the middle of the night on the bicycle. He would call for the car, load the bicycle in the dicky and made me travel home in style.

Once, the CM asked me to request the revenue secretary, K.N. Zutshi (KNZ), to post a classmate of his to a vacant post in Surat as *mamlatdar*, a junior post. That man had studied in the village school with Mr Solanki. KNZ sent me a long-winded note explaining that according to the prevalent conventions, preference was given to officers who have requested for a post to the South on the eve of their retirement. This officer did not fall in that category.

I took the note to the CM and said, 'Sir, this is a very simple matter and it is not against the law or the policy to post somebody at the request of the CM to a particular vacant post. I will overrule this objection and ask KNZ to carry out the CM's desire.'

Mr Solanki said, 'Let it be, Moosa, if Mr Zutshi is quoting a practice, let him keep his conscience clear.'

Years later, when I was on tour of Gujarat from Delhi, I learnt that KNZ had been posted as the chairman of the Gujarat State Public Service Commission after retirement. Mr Solanki was still the CM. I asked him as to what prompted him to post an inflexible man like KNZ to that post. He replied, 'A man who refused to post a *mamlatdar* who was the classmate of the CM to a vacant post even at the request of the CM is not likely to succumb to any political pressures. That was the quality which I appreciated in Mr Zutshi, and hence, my selection.'

One of the events which remains vivid in my memory is the ferry disaster that took place in Godhra district where more than twenty people lost their lives. I got the news around 6 pm. Mr Solanki was in Delhi on an official visit. When I rang the Gujarat Bhavan, I learnt that he had gone out for dinner, followed by a visit to see a film. He was not expected back before midnight. Urgent action had to be taken, so I immediately passed an order in the name of the CM to release ₹2 lakh each for the next of kin of the victims and requested the chief secretary to release another ₹2 lakh from the government. I issued a press release condoling the survivors and next of kin, quoting Mr Solanki's deep sorrow and regret at the loss of life and the release of money from both the chief minister's fund and the government. I then rang up Jaideep Singh Baria, a minister in Solanki's Cabinet who hailed from Godhra district, and requested him to immediately proceed to Godhra to supervise the relief and rescue operations. This, too, went as a press release that the CM had instructed Mr Baria to proceed to Godhra to supervise and provide necessary relief to the affected. All this took me close to midnight, and I went home late. Next morning, I received an early call from Mr Solanki from Delhi.

'Moosa, it seems that I had been sleep-working last night. I saw from the newspaper this morning that I had taken several actions to mitigate the disaster-affected people in Godhra.' Mr Solanki has a gentle and subtle sense of humour.

Mr Solanki's Congress party government was in office with a very thin majority. Once the Emergency was terminated and new elections were held to the Parliament, the Congress party was defeated at the Centre. Indira Gandhi herself was arrested and jailed. Morarji Desai became the PM of India. The days of the Solanki government were numbered in Gujarat. The Janata Morcha led by Babubhai Patel, who had been in jail during the Emergency, was getting stronger even in the assembly.

One day when I was sitting with the CM, Sanat Mehta, labour minister and a very powerful politician of the state hailing from Baroda, came in with a petition that a suspended chairman of a Baroda cooperative should be released from jail and reinstated. This chairman had several cases against him for embezzlement of cooperative funds, cheating, fudging of accounts, forgeries and so on. There were many victims of his criminal activities in the Baroda district. Mr Mehta tried to persuade Mr Solanki to withdraw all the cases against the ex-chairman because there were several MLAs from Baroda who were supporting the ex-chairman. After Mr Mehta left, Mr Solanki asked me to call for the file and examine the proposal of Mr Mehta and give my recommendations to him. I discovered that there was overwhelming evidence against the ex-chairman, and if the cases were taken to their logical end, he would be imprisoned for several years. I simply returned the file to the home department without any comments. A few days later, Mr Mehta walked into my chamber.

'Moosa, what is happening to my representation to the chief minister about the Baroda cooperative case?'

'I am still examining the file,' I prevaricated.

'Mr Moosa Raza, you must understand that you are not only the principal secretary to the chief minister in administrative matters but you have to also advise him on political issues. This is a politically sensitive case and eleven MLAs are backing the cooperative chief. If we do not withdraw the pending cases, they may go over to the Janata Morcha.'

'Mr Sanat Mehta, I am the principal secretary to the chief minister, yes, and my advice to him will be to ensure that the government of this state is run on constitutional and ethical lines as laid down by the Constitution and the Cabinet in its various decisions. You are a member of the Cabinet and you have your finger on the pulse of the state. It is for you to advise the CM on whatever is in his political interest. For me, I have to advise him whatever is in the best interest of the state.'

Mr Mehta did not like my reply and walked out in a huff. A few minutes later, I was summoned by the CM.

'Mr Sanat Mehta was here, and he was quite upset. Have you examined his representation given some time ago?'

'Yes, sir,' I replied. 'I have seen the file and I have returned it to the department. The evidence against the ex-chairman of the cooperative is very strong and clear. Withdrawing the cases against him may be in the short-term interest of your government, which may last for a few more days. However, you will lose not only your reputation as an ethical chief minister but the government itself will continue to get blackmailed to take similar decisions. My advice to you, sir, is not to withdraw these cases and allow the law to take its own course.'

Mr Solanki did not withdraw the cases. A few days later, the MLAs defected to the Janata Morcha, and Mr Solanki tendered his resignation to the governor. I left my office after clearing my personal papers and went home.

Babubhai Patel, who now had a majority, albeit a thin one, became the CM of Gujarat. It was the convention that the new CM appointed his own principal secretary and gave a different posting to the one who had served the earlier CM. So, I decided to go home and wait for a new posting. I had just reached home when I heard the telephone ringing. The chief secretary was on the line.

'Where are you, Moosa? The chief minister is frantically looking for you.'

'I thought, sir, that the chief minister would appoint his own principal secretary. I am waiting for a new posting from you.'

'I have received orders from the CM that he wants you to continue as his principal secretary. He does not want to appoint a new principal secretary.'

I was taken aback. Two CMs belonging to two rival parties wanting to have the same principal secretary had no precedent. However, I went back to the office and reported to Babubhai Patel. Mr Patel was a very soft-spoken, nice man. He was a Gandhian to the core.

'Mr Moosa Raza, I have seen you working both as a collector and director of famine relief, and as the principal secretary to Mr Solanki. I have never heard a word that you allowed any hanky-panky to be done in the government. I see no reason to change your posting and appoint a new person as my principal secretary. Please continue.'

'Sir,' I said. 'I thank you for the confidence that you have reposed in me. However, I must point out that I have a long-standing friendship with your predecessor. I will continue to maintain that friendly relationship. I believe he has been allotted a bungalow adjacent to mine in the K sector. It is quite possible that some of your ministers may see me sitting and chatting with Mr Solanki on the lawns on a Sunday afternoon. Tales may be carried to you that I am sharing confidences with your rival. This will be embarrassing both to you and to me.'

'I have full faith and confidence in you and your rectitude, and I have no objection to your maintaining your friendship with Mr Solanki. I do not have a *kaccha kaan* (a gullible ear), and I would not believe any Tom, Dick and Harry carrying tales to me about my officers.'

I continued for a couple of months as the principal secretary to the new CM, but I was not very comfortable. At my request, the chief secretary managed to persuade the CM to post me as the health secretary, during which period I worked for a month or so with Makarand Desai, who was the then health minister.

In 1976, P.P. Singla, who was the managing director of the holding company of the National Textile Corporation (NTC) in Delhi, desired that I should join the Government of India and take over as the chairman and managing director (CMD) of NTC (Gujarat). I was very happy to leave the state government of Gujarat, and a few days later, I joined NTC (Gujarat), which was managing eleven textile mills nationalised by the Government of India. I remained as the CMD for a couple of years, during which period I made NTC (Gujarat) into a top profit-making subsidiary of the NTC. Two years later, I was promoted and went over to Delhi as the managing director of NTC (holding company) in place of Mr Singla. My tenure of five years in NTC was very challenging. I had to look after 111 textiles mills with nine subsidiaries all over India, with a work force of a 1,20,000, and officers numbering over 20,000. I had to deal with workers' unions of a wide variety of political hues—socialists, communists, rightists, etc.

As my tenure was getting over in the NTC, Shivraj Patil took over as the textile minister. By this time, Indira Gandhi was back in power. Mr Patil offered to extend my tenure by one more year. I was not happy to work for that one additional year in Delhi, and I requested to be repatriated to Gujarat, even though the education of my children would be disturbed.

In the meantime, Mr Solanki had put together a political combine known as KHAM (Kshatriya, Harijans, Adivasis and Muslims), which swept the polls, and he came back to power as CM with a majority of 140 out of 180 seats. I requested him to give me a posting in Gujarat.

'Why don't you come back as the principal secretary to the chief minister, the post you were holding earlier?'

'I think it will not be appropriate to go back to the same post,' I said. 'I shall be happy to get any post other than the principal secretary to chief minister.'

The CM was not very happy at my reply.

The tenure of the incumbent managing director (MD) of Gujarat State Fertilizers & Chemicals (GSFC) in Baroda was coming to an end. Mr Solanki posted me as the MD of GSFC.

I was happy to leave Delhi, lock, stock and barrel, and move over to Baroda to take over as the MD of GSFC. My tenure of over six years in GSFC was one of the most interesting, pleasant, fruitful and successful parts of my entire career.

OF STRIKES AND HANGING VESSELS

In May 1982, I joined as the MD of GSFC. H.K.L. Kapoor was the then chief secretary of Gujarat. When Madhavsinh Solanki consulted him regarding my posting, Mr Kapoor, it appears, had some reservations. Since I was being inducted into a totally new discipline of managing a fertiliser and chemical factory, the government in its wisdom thought that I should function as an understudy to the outgoing MD, Mr Gami, for about a month.

Mr Gami had a long tenure in GSFC, having started his career as a junior engineer there. Understandably, he was rather reluctant to move out of office. I noticed an initial coldness among the senior officials—an outsider muzzling in and throwing out a son of the soil.

Mr Gami was a technocrat, a chemical engineer. In my earlier stint as principal secretary to the CM, I was instrumental in getting him posted as the MD of GSFC, a post that the IAS fraternity believed should go only to an IAS officer. Subsequent events proved that I was wrong. Mr Gami proved to be a good chemical engineer but a poor manager. Hence the CM's mandate to have me take over GSFC and set it right.

I occupied a room on the first floor, which was generally used by the then part-time chairman of GSFC, Jaykrishna Harivallabhdas, whenever he visited Baroda. One day, as I sat in my chamber reading some files, I heard a great commotion outside in the lobby. Opening the door, I found a large number of workers beating on the door of Mr Gami's office. Mr Gami had locked himself in and was refusing to allow anyone to get into his room. I came out and was told that they were the workers' union leaders. It appeared that the issue pertained to a peon who had been promoted out of turn, as he was working at Mr Gami's residence, overlooking others senior to him.

'This is not the way to raise and agitate an issue. You are behaving in a very undisciplined manner by beating on the door of the managing director,' I told them.

'But, sir, the MD has behaved in a very unjust manner. He has promoted a junior peon, overlooking seniors. We cannot tolerate such injustice.'

'Normally, I would have taken severe action against you for this gross indiscipline, whatever be the cause. This time I am not proposing to take any action against you. There are ways of representing grievances. You could write a letter to me. I shall certainly look into the matter. But if you agitate the way you have done, I will be forced to take serious action against all of you.'

The union leaders, hearing my voice and my declamation, were quite subdued and went out quietly. There is a Persian saying: *roz-e awwal gurba kushtan* (kill the cat on the very first day). It is necessary to establish right on day one that you are the boss and will not tolerate indiscipline. When I took over full charge a month later, I issued a circular that no union leader should come up to the lobby of the MD's office without permission. During my six-year tenure, such an event was never repeated.

GSFC was established way back in 1962. Mr Harivallabhdas, who held a few shares, was appointed as the first part-time chairman, and K.R. Srivatsa, an IAS officer, was appointed as its first MD. Shortly after GSFC was established, I had visited the nascent GSFC as an officer on special duty (OSD) in the agriculture department when I was tasked with the responsibility of establishing the Gujarat Agro Industries Corporation

Limited (GAIC). All the fertiliser plants were in various stages of construction. I found Mr Srivatsa sitting in a tin shed and supervising the construction work. With his knowledge of the Japanese, Mr Srivatsa was able to establish a good working rapport with Japanese machinery suppliers, engineers and technologists. The ammonia and urea plants of GSFC were, therefore, based on Japanese technology and equipment, and its erection and commissioning were done under the supervision of Japanese engineers. To house the large number of these Japanese, Mr Srivatsa built a large appointed guest house and named it 'Shinatami'—new Atami—to make the Japanese feel at home.

Later in 1982, I found GSFC a flourishing company with over 5,000 workers and over twenty fertiliser and chemical plants and other supporting services. Unfortunately, however, while the technocrats were doing their work with due diligence, I found the management left much to be desired. Discipline was lax. Many of the senior officers were reportedly recruited based on caste considerations. Such personnel policies, with laxity in discipline, had brought down the productivity of the plants to below 70 per cent. The company was heading towards a red future. When I met Mr Gami, he portrayed a bleak picture of the prospects of the GSFC for the year 1982–83. The profits were dwindling, the old fertiliser plants were all functioning below capacity, there was unrest among the workforce and huge stocks of caprolactam, urea and DAP were lying unsold. Mr Gami assessed that for the first time in its history, GSFC was poised to make a loss. Stunned, I was reminded of an Urdu proverb which said: *sar mundat-e awley pade* (just shaved my head, and there was a hailstorm).

As soon as Mr Gami left and I took over full charge of the GSFC, I took a round of all the various fertiliser and chemical plants in the complex. To enhance my knowledge, I studied several books on the manufacture of ammonia, urea, phosphoric acid, cyclohexanone, cyclohexane, etc. Within a short period, I managed to dispose of all the accumulated stock of both fertilisers as well as caprolactam—by infusing motivational incentives among the staff and officers, rectifying their minor grievances, improving the infrastructure to make working conditions more comfortable, establishing an internal management committee consisting of all the senior officers, discussing all internal and marketing problems of the company in that committee every week, establishing rapport with both the fertiliser consumers as well as major nylon manufacturers in Bombay. Production in the fertiliser plants that year crossed the break-even point, and GSFC managed to make a profit of over ₹100 million instead of a loss, as apprehended by the outgoing MD.

The unrest amongst the workers and the senior supervisory staff was mainly due to the fact that under government regulations, only workers drawing remuneration within a prescribed ceiling were eligible for an annual bonus, that too not exceeding one month's salary. As a result, since GSFC was a good paymaster, many of the supervisory staff at the plant level and all the officers at the managerial level did not get any bonus even if they worked hard and the company made high profits. I felt this was an unfair dispensation and required to be rectified. Unless all the staff became stakeholders in the financial outcome, their commitment would remain peripheral. I, therefore, engaged a consultant and set up an internal committee to draft a scheme whereby all the staff up to the highest level (excluding the managing director) should be able to get a share in the financial prosperity of GSFC. I told the committee that I would like this new bonus scheme to be framed to be an integrated one so that the productivity and profitability of all the plants were interlinked. All the plants within the complex should be considered a single unit so that any failure, strike, absenteeism, low profit of any single plant should have an adverse impact on the overall bonus quantum. It took some time before such a scheme was drafted. I presented it and got it passed by the board of directors.

'Why have you excluded the MD from this scheme?' asked one of the directors.

'So that no one should accuse me of framing a self-serving scheme in which I, too, stood to benefit', I replied.

That silenced all questions.

However, the supervisory staff of the various plants and the middle-level officers of the company became too greedy and demanded that the proposed bonus should be doubled. They overlooked the fact that they were getting no bonus at all earlier. It is in human nature to 'catch hold of the hand if you offer them a finger,' as the saying goes in Hindi. In spite of my best efforts, neither the officers' union nor the workers' union agreed to the scheme that was going to benefit them immensely. Instead of getting only the ceiling of 8 per cent as per government regulations, restricted only to the lowest paid workers, they would have been eligible for more than 18 to 20 per cent under the new GSFC scheme. The workers resorted to agitation instigated by the officers' union both inside the plant and outside, work to rule, sabotaging the plant, etc. I was not willing to stand for such misbehaviour. I personally held several meetings with the presidents of both the unions and explained the implications of my bonus scheme and the immense benefits accruing to them if they accepted the new scheme.

The president of the officers' union said to me, 'Sir, I am a devotee of Goddess Durga. I have been advised by her that I should not compromise and I should continue to agitate until I force the management to accept our terms.'

I replied to him, 'Unfortunately, I have no access to the divine goddess. I, therefore, have to take what human measures are necessary to persuade you.'

Mr Dutta was the then commissioner of police in Baroda. He was a very sensible and reasonable officer but always inclined to support workers against the management. One day, I called him over to my office for a cup of tea, and I explained to him the prevailing situation and what I was offering to the entire workforce and officer-force in GSFC.

Mr Dutta saw my viewpoint, concurred with my approach, called the workers' and officers' unions to his office and tried to persuade them. They were adamant. He told me that since he had failed, I could go ahead and take whatever disciplinary action was necessary to bring around the unions, and that the police force would stand by the management. J.P. Shah, one of my very active and dynamic directors, in charge of marketing, was sent around to all the surrounding villages, who were shareholders of the company and who participated in the prosperity of the GSFC by getting schools, water works, medical benefits, internal roads and other facilities. Mr Shah apprised the sarpanches of the prevailing situation, and they all agreed to support the management. I then called on Makarand Desai, an ex-minister and an eminent BJP leader with whom I had worked briefly as health secretary, and apprised him of what I proposed to do. He was convinced of my stand and agreed to remain aloof and not to intervene politically. Since I learnt that the unions were approaching their sister unions of Indian Petrochemicals Corporation Limited (IPCL), Baroda Refinery, the Gujarat Alkalies and Chemicals Limited (GACL), etc., to solicit their support, I invited all those unions to come and have a meeting with me, where I and Mr Shah apprised them of the facts of the dispute. Some of the unions said that they would like to persuade their managements to adopt a similar scheme, which they appreciated highly. They, too, condemned the stand of their fellow unions of GSFC.

After having done this preparatory work, I met CM Madhavsinh Solanki and told him of what I proposed to do. He smiled and said, 'Moosa, I have appointed you as the managing director. You may go ahead and take whatever action is necessary. If you fail, it is your funeral.'

'Sir, I take full responsibility for my actions.'

'As a result of your proposed action, you anticipate all the workers and the middle-level officers to go on strike. How long do you think the strike will last? asked the CM.

'Not more than a month, sir. However, I propose to utilise that month for the regular annual turnaround and revamping of the fertiliser and chemical plants. As soon as the strike starts, I will close down all the plants safely, induct the turnaround companies waiting outside into the complex and start the revamping work.'

As soon as I returned that evening after meeting the CM, all the office-bearers of both the unions were served with suspension orders at midnight. I did not have time to follow due process of law, serving them notices, etc. It came as a shock to all of them, since it was not anticipated by them. Next morning, they all turned up at the plant gates to agitate. The commissioner had stationed sufficient police force to prevent their entry, and they were dispersed immediately. Thereafter, with the remaining officers and staff, all the plants were shut down smoothly and revamping companies were brought in to start their work on the same day.

The officers' union resorted to a hunger strike in the city of Baroda, sitting at the crossroads in the city. I printed pamphlets giving in detail the current salaries, allowances and other facilities of the various officers on hunger strike, what I proposed to give them as bonus and what they demanded. These pamphlets were distributed at the site of their hunger strike. By evening, people started gathering around them and pelting the officers on hunger strike with rotten eggs and tomatoes. Before nightfall, all the strikers had vanished from the site, leaving behind their tent, mats, pillows and tiffin carriers.

The strike lasted for nineteen days. By that time, all the plants had been revamped and were ready to restart work. The workers' union came to me and surrendered unconditionally. I allowed the workers to join but kept the union leaders under suspension. With the officers' union, too, I withdrew the recognition, sealed the premises allotted to them and debarred them from entering the Fertiliser Nagar complex. Subsequently, the officers' union went to the court. In the meantime, the plants worked very well. It was anticipated that GSFC would end that year with a profit of over ₹100 crore.

During the remaining part of my tenure, I faced absolutely no unrest, discontent or indiscipline from the workers or the unions. They worked hard and with full commitment. Many of my colleagues from IPCL, GACL, Baroda Refinery, etc., telephoned me to compliment me on the firm handling of the strike and told me that my example had induced discipline amongst their unions too.

One of the results of this clash and the new bonus scheme was that productivity in all the plants went up immensely. By the second year of my tenure, all urea, DAP and ammonia plants were working at 100 per cent capacity or more. GSFC was recognised as the best fertiliser company in the country, and award after award—for productivity, best human relations, worker satisfaction and participation, etc.—were received by us. By the third year, GSFC was winning all the awards of the Fertiliser Association of India (FAI). In fact, the trend continued right up to the end of my tenure. There was even talk in the FAI that a company which won all the awards continuously for more than three years should be excluded from competition. As a member of the FAI, I resisted this move very strongly.

~

Melamine, in the form of melamine formaldehyde, is an important industrial product, used in making crockery, laminates, currency notes, etc. GSFC was the only company in the country producing melamine (from urea). Its technology was based on an Austrian company, Voest

Alpine. Though the plant was small (only 5,000 tonnes capacity), it was plagued by several technical snags. The major one was that the coil, almost fifteen feet high, fixed inside a large boiler-like vessel, which would get detached every three months, necessitating a shutdown of three weeks.

This meant that the GSPC lost almost 25 per cent production of melamine, every year. When we referred the problem to the technology supplier, they told us that they, too, had the same problem in their Linz Plant. Several solutions were suggested by our technical advisers, but none appeared feasible. Since the huge vessel that housed the coil had to vibrate to ensure the uniform flow of the liquid chemicals, it was inevitable it would get detached after an interval.

Lashkar Singh, a general manager, suggested that instead of tethering the huge vessel to the ground, we should hang it from the roof.

'Lashkar Singh, how do you propose to hang a 50-tonne vessel from the roof?'

Everybody joined in the laughter. But the suggestion, though absurd on the face of it, germinated something in my mind. I summoned my top design people later and asked them, 'Instead of hanging the vessel from the roof, is it possible to detach the coil alone and hang it from the top of the vessel?'

Within a month, the idea was converted into a technical design, and at the next shutdown, it was implemented. There was no detachment thereafter. I think we patented the solution and sold it back to the parent company. Sometimes, even apparently absurd suggestions have a germ of sense in them.

Having settled the issue of productivity and human relations, I turned my attention to the issue of expansion. Polymer Corporation of Gujarat, an independent public-sector undertaking (PSU), was passing through a bad phase. It was the only company in India that manufactured acrylic sheets, which were in great industrial demand. At the behest of the government, I took over the polymer plant and applied our usual management practices. It turned the corner and started turning profits within a year. Since a lot of high-pressure steam generated in our ammonia plants was being wasted, I established several captive small power-generating units to reduce our dependence on the electricity board's supplies.

Later, I roped in the Petrofils, GACL, IPCL, etc., to establish a joint-venture power company, GSFC holding a major share of the equity. It has now expanded to almost a 1,000MW power producer, making its original equity holders almost independent of the state power supply.

Our caprolactam plant, with a modest capacity of 20,000 tonnes, was established with Swiss technology originally, supported by a company from Chur, Switzerland. But the parent company that supplied the technology had gone out of production. We were, therefore, deprived of any technical assistance from them to improve the productivity and quality of our caprolactam plant. The plant was producing substandard caprolactam with a PN number of less than 2,000, whereas the imported caprolactam ranged from 15,000 to 18,000. I, therefore, decided that since space was available, we should establish a large caprolactam plant with the best technology from international producers.

Sometime earlier, BASF (Baden Aniline and Soda Factory) of Germany had decided to establish a large caprolactam plant of their own in the state of Uttar Pradesh, with the encouragement of Narayan Dutt Tiwari, who was the industries minister in the Government of India.

I went to Delhi and engaged the three top legal luminaries of that time, including Nani Palkiwala, and filed a suit against BASF under the Monopolistic and Restrictive Trade Practice (MRTP) Act, 1969. MRTP issued a stay order on their proposal. Tiwari was furious with me, and I was summoned to Delhi by A.S. Gill, secretary of the industries department, under Tiwari. Mr Gill was a senior IAS officer of the Gujarat cadre, and we had known each other for many years. I have pleasant memories of having worked under him in Gujarat.

'Moosa, do you realise that as an officer of the IAS, you have taken a conflicting stand against the industries minister?' he asked me.

'Sir, I have not taken any stand either against the Government of India or against the minister. My case in the MRTP is against BASF wanting to establish a clandestine chemical plant with intermediate cyclohexanone rather than starting from ammonia and sulfuric acid. They plan to do value addition in Germany and reap the benefits of a high transfer price. I would withdraw the suit if they were to start from the basic raw materials in India as we do.'

'Moosa, you know very well that Mr Tiwari is interested in getting this plant established in his constituency in Uttar Pradesh. Therefore, you are directly coming into conflict with his desire to benefit his constituency.'

'I regret, sir. It is my duty to safeguard the interest of my company, the state of Gujarat and India. I cannot accept a high transfer price to benefit BASF. I cannot withdraw my case in the MRTP'.

The matter ended there.

Later, I was summoned by Mr Tiwari himself, who tried to persuade me to withdraw my objections and allow BASF to establish the caprolactam plant in Uttar Pradesh. Again, I had to regret my inability to do so. He even offered the part ownership and management of the Uttar Pradesh plant to GSFC. The board of GSFC rejected the idea.

Reluctantly, the BASF dropped their proposal to establish a caprolactam plant based on an intermediate raw material.

Much later, when I decided to establish a large caprolactam plant in GSFC, starting with the basic raw materials ammonia, sulfuric acid, etc., I found that there were only three or four companies in the world who owned the necessary technology. Amongst these four, BASF, Germany, was known to hold the best technology. I, therefore, approached them first with a request to start negotiations for helping me establish a 1,00,000-tonne caprolactam plant. BASF were naturally cut up with me for having blocked their efforts to establish a plant of their own in India, and flatly refused to even give me an appointment, when I approached them. The other holders of technology in America, Holland and Japan, too, refused flatly to help me with technology. In fact, the Japanese told me in confidence that BASF had threatened all the world technology holders not to have anything to do with GSFC on the issue of caprolactam technology. If they did so, their markets would be inundated with German caprolactam. I was faced with an international cartel determined to deny technology to India.

I called a meeting with my designers and technologists in GSFC to review the situation and find a solution.

'You have been running the caprolactam plant of GSFC for the last decade or more. Why is it not possible for you to do some reverse engineering and upgrade the Swiss technology? That should not be too difficult for you.'

'Sir, we can put in efforts and design a caprolactam plant based on the existing Swiss technology. But it will not have the latest developments in technology of BASF or others.'

I gave them three months' time to prepare a blueprint for a caprolactam plant based on the old Swiss technology, upgrading the equipment from 20,000 tonnes to 50,000 tonnes. They managed to prepare a detailed blueprint running into four or five volumes. I learnt a lesson that given encouragement and the opportunity, our own technologists and engineers could also compete with the best in the world. (Much later, I learnt that the Ammonia IV technology plant in Uhde of Germany was designed by an Indian technologist.) Mr Sridhar, my technical director, told me that if we set up a plant based on this blueprint, it would be very costly and with no guarantee that the final product would match international standards.

With the help of some friends in Germany, I managed to get an appointment with Dr Zeefelder, chairman of the BASF.

When we sat across the table in BASF headquarters in Ludwigshafen, the chairman said, 'Why should we give you our technology when you filed legal cases against us and blocked our entry into India?'

'Any managing director would have done the same,' I replied. 'If I had wanted to establish a caprolactam plant in Germany starting with an intermediate product with the right to fix the transfer price, wouldn't you have tried to block me from that?'

After some discussions, they saw the logic of my stand. However, they were still not willing to give me the technology. I then played my last card. From my bag I took out the five volumes of blueprints prepared by my technocrats and placed the bulk of volumes on the table and said, 'If you do not give me the technology, I can still go ahead and set up a 50,000-tonne plant based on the old Swiss technology, which I own now. I know that the product would be costlier than yours. And perhaps not as good as yours. However, I will ensure that the import duty of caprolactam from BASF into India is placed at such a high level against mine that my caprolactam would still be cheaper than yours.'

'How can you do that?' asked the MD.

'I am an IAS officer of Gujarat. I have the full backing of my state government. I have enough influence with the central government to accomplish what I claim.'

I knew this was a bluff. But the BASF had no way of calling it.

'Not only that,' I continued, 'but I would flood the markets of Europe with my product even if GSFC were to suffer some losses as a result. Don't you see that it is in your interest to collaborate with me rather than to enter into a conflict with me for all time to come?'

Ultimately, they agreed to supply the technology, and a 50,000-tonne caprolactam plant was set up in Baroda with BASF technology, which, I believe, has now been expanded to a 1,00,000-tonne plant.

My next target was to establish a large DAP plant with imported sulfuric acid and ammonia. This was done on the Saurashtra coast near Sikka in Jamnagar. The Gujarat Maritime Board said that constructing a jetty at Sikka, off the coast of Jamnagar, would take at least five years. Since the Government of India had announced withdrawal of accelerated depreciation benefits within the next two years, I had to complete the jetty and the pipelines within two years, and commission the DAP plant before the Income Tax Department withdrew the benefit, amounting to more than ₹25 crore.

The area through which the jetty had to pass was once heavily afforested by mangroves. But over a period of time, human habitations nearby had denuded the mangrove forest to use the wood as fuel in their homes. I engaged a team of forest department officers to replant the areas in and around with mangroves to restore the ecology.

I got into trouble with the Ministry of Environment of Government of India. I was summoned to Delhi by T.N. Seshan, then secretary of environment, and put on the mat. 'But I am merely restoring the original mangroves that have been destroyed by human intervention,' I pleaded.

'But you are doing the same thing that the denuders did. Who are you to intervene in regrowing the mangroves? Over a period, nature would have taken care of the matter,' said Seshan.

'But that may take decades and decades?' I protested.

'So what? You have no right to intervene.'

Though I came away chastened, I continued with my work. Today, on both sides of the jetty, one can see a forest of mangroves housing various varieties of flora and fauna.

In the event, the DAP plant and the jetty were both completed in a record time of two years. The plant was commissioned in the presence of the CM and the chief commissioner of income tax. I wanted to make sure that GSFC got the benefit of the accelerated depreciation before expiry of the date. The plant was commissioned just a day before that.

The GSFC mega complex, which housed both the chemical plants and residential complexes, was adjudged to be the most pollution-free than surrounding areas. With heavy afforestation and personal supervision by me, the temperature in Fertiliser Nagar was found to be four degrees lower than the surrounding areas even in summer. A deer park, an aviary, a firing range, etc., were all established within the complex for the benefit of the residents. The Honour's Club was revived and met every month to invite eminent personalities from all over India to come and give lectures both on technical subjects as well as subjects of general interest. I figured on the front pages of many national magazines, and GSFC continued to win awards in various fields.

I was sailing along happily with several projects lined up when I received a bombshell from Delhi. I was summoned to Delhi by the cabinet secretary, B.G. Deshmukh.

'Moosa, you have been selected to go over to Kashmir as chief secretary.'

In 1991, with the departure of Naresh Chandra to the US as Indian ambassador and before Mr Rajagopal took over the cabinet secretary, there was a brief gap during which Naresh had asked me to handle the job in his place. Every morning, when I reached the office, I would see my table and side tables loaded with hundreds of letters, confidential and top-secret letters from the governors of all the states of India, from the ambassadors, correspondence addressed to the PM and from the Army headquarters and defence chiefs, not to mention reports from the Intelligence Bureau (IB), from the Research and Analysis Wing (RAW), joint intelligence chief and hundreds of others. I attempted to read the correspondence and found that many of them demanded immediate response and substantial action from the Government of India. I was in a quandary. So, I called in Mr Nair, the additional secretary in the cabinet secretariat, an essentially secretarial man, and asked him what I was supposed to do with the hundreds of letters that landed on my table demanding instant action, with the implicit threat that unless such action was forthcoming, the writer would go ahead assuming that the Government of India concurs with the proposal of the writer.

Mr Nair laughed at my naivete.

'All you have to do is forward these letters to the concerned departments/ministries. The concerned ministry has to take the necessary action within the proposed timeframe. If they don't and a crisis happens, the concerned secretary/minister will be held responsible. The cabinet secretary and his secretariat are meant to service the Cabinet and its various committees.'

That relieved me from a severe mental tension.

'You mean, the cabinet secretariat is a mere post office?' I asked, a little amused at Mr Nair's explanation.

'No, sir,' replied Mr Nair, 'The Cabsec advises the PM and the Cabinet on all issues affecting the administration of the country.'

I realised that the Cabsec functions in the same way as the chief secretary does in the state. But the canvas is much larger and the issues far graver and more serious.

I was not very happy at the brief trappings of working in the cabinet secretariat at Rashtrapati Bhavan, and longed for a ministry where I could get my teeth into the real problems and issues that affected the progress of the country. My decades of experience both at the state and central level related to trade and industry, agriculture and fisheries—the real backbones of the country's economy.

It was during this interlude that the notorious Harshad Mehta Scam broke.

Harshad Mehta, a small-time, Gujarati operator rose to become the most famous stock broker of India in his time. He manipulated the chinks in the banking and share-broking processes, boosted the market at will, played bulls and bears and created havoc in the market.

A.N. Varma, secretary to PM Narasimha Rao, rang me up and requested me to hold a meeting with the finance secretary, Montek Singh Ahluwalia (who later rose to become the deputy chairman of the Planning Commission), and the banking secretary, Y.V. Reddy, and submit a report to the PM.

Both these gentlemen fidgeted a lot sitting in my office. Their nervousness in discussing how such a scam could have taken place right under their noses was understandable, though no blame could be attached to either of them. When I sent in the report to the PMO, Mr Varma summoned me and said, 'The PM has summoned a Cabinet meeting tomorrow morning. He desires to promulgate an ordinance to take over the assets of Harshad Mehta and all the companies he is running. Please get a draft prepared immediately and send it to PMO by today evening.'

That was a tall order. A draft of an ordinance to be considered by the Cabinet required to be prepared and vetted by the secretary of the legal department, Dr Rao, who also happened to be a friend of the PM, was away on holiday with his family at Dehradun. I managed to get him on the line and advised him to return to Delhi immediately for the emergency meeting of the Cabinet next morning. I had to make all necessary arrangements to send a special Border Security Force (BSF) plane to bring him to Delhi.

By late night, Dr Rao had drafted an ordinance and sent it to me. I was very unhappy, as it was not a well-drafted legislation and left many loopholes through which a clever operator like Harshad Mehta could escape and save his assets.

Though it was too late in the night, I still rang up Dr Rao and pointed out the various lacunae in the draft to him. However, he said, 'It is too late to do anything about it. Since I will be there in the meeting tomorrow morning, we would take care of your concerns.'

The ordinance was passed unanimously as drafted by Dr Rao.

In the event, it took several years before Harshad Mehta's conviction. In between, he claimed that he had delivered two suitcases of cash, amounting to over ₹1 crore to the PM. It was only a claim of a desperate man. There was no proof.

Under PM Narasimha Rao, ably advised by Dr Manmohan Singh as his finance minister, an air of liberalism and globalisation swept India. The previous Congress governments of India had focussed on building up the public sector to 'occupy the commanding heights of Indian economy'. The private sector in India, in any case, did not have the financial muscle to contribute to the development of large-scale industrial undertakings. As I have written in the previous chapter, it fell to my lot to nurse the outdated and junk machinery of 111 mills all over the country to continue to produce a variety of cloths and keep our shops stocked.

The steel industry of India, mostly in the public sector, too, had created behemoths in Bhilai, Bokaro, Rourkela, Durgapur, Salem, etc. The only private-sector steel plant in Jamshedpur, belonging to the Tatas, was doing well. But the others, because of excess manpower and costs of running cities like Bokaro, Bhilai and Rourkela, were running into losses.

This posed a grave challenge to the Steel Authority of India Limited (SAIL), the holding company. Steel had become a scarce commodity and was being rationed out. Corruption is a natural consequence when any commodity is rationed out!

To dole out the meagre supply of steel, the government established what was known as a Joint Plant Committee (JPC). Actually, there was no committee but an executive officer who functioned under a joint secretary in the ministry. But there were numerous complaints against this so-called JPC, and rumours were rampant that a lot of money was made.

In 1991, When I received the orders appointing me as steel secretary, the cabinet secretary, Mr Rajagopal called me and said, 'The post is vacant. Don't lose time. Go and take over immediately before the minister changes his mind.'

Perhaps Mr Rajagopal was keen to get rid of me. My earlier interaction, as chief secretary of Jammu and Kashmir, with Mr Rajagopal as power secretary was not very pleasant. This was not my fault. Mr Seshan, who was then the cabinet secretary, being a hard task master, would not hesitate to humiliate even secretaries to the government in an open meeting.

As steel secretary, I would want to establish a good working relationship with Santosh Mohan Dev, steel minister. I did not want to take over without first meeting the minister.

In my very first meeting with him, I told him, 'Sir, I am here to carry out laid down policies of the Government of India under your guidance and directions. It is my duty and responsibility to bring to your notice the legality, the practicability or the deviation from the law, which will occur if I carry out all your behests without looking into all aspects. As a civil servant, I do not want to be either a hero or a martyr. Neither you nor I would like our internal differences, if any, aired in the media. If you do not like my continuance with the ministry as a secretary, all you have to do is to tell me to my face. In that case, I shall apply for a long leave, enabling you to find a suitable replacement. Even before taking charge, I would like to have your assurance that you have no reservations about my joining.'

Santosh Mohan Dev appreciated my candour.

'In fact, Mr Moosa Raza,' he said, 'I never ask for any specific officer nor do I reject anyone offhand. That allows me to independently assess the performance of the officer posted with me by the PM. That also enables me to approach the PM in case I need to change him. He cannot then say: "You asked for him or her."'

That established an excellent working relationship between me and the minister. During my stint as steel secretary, there were many occasions of difference of opinion; however, that never led to any breach of understanding between us until I retired from government.

At the farewell party given to me at my departure, Santosh Mohan Dev had said, 'I have worked with nine secretaries during my tenure as a minister. I have no hesitation in saying that Mr Moosa Raza was the best secretary I ever worked with. He was not a secretary with the ministry only but he was also my personal friend, philosopher and guide.'

On the eve of my taking over as steel secretary, a friend from Calcutta had dropped in to pay me a left-handed compliment.

'So, you are joining the bandwagon of pen-pushers.' he said. 'Why do you say that?' I asked him, a little piqued at that remark.

'So far, you dealt with concrete issues on the ground. They were all down-to-earth departments with concrete results and measurable outcomes! What does a secretary do? He receives the files his under-secretaries, joint secretaries put up to him. Most of the times, he simply signs. Rarely he differs. He attends some meetings. Come 5 pm, he goes to the club, plays rummy or bridge. I call them the Bridge Brigade. I meet them all in the club. You will now do the same. I feel sorry for you. Waste of a good executive.'

I took his lament in good spirit. I decided that I shall not end up fulfilling his (Cassandric) predictions.

When I took over as steel secretary, the total output of iron and steel in the country was a mere 25 MT. Most of the mini steel plants were lying closed. By delicensing the industry, abolishing the unnecessary controls on sale and distribution, India is today producing close to a 100 MT of iron and steel with a dozen integrated steel plants and over 600 functioning mini-steel plants.

Though I cannot claim the credit for all the progress, I certainly contributed to removing most of the chains that were holding back the industry from moving forward.

THE DESECRATION OF A MOSQUE

Historians claim that an edifice called the Babri Masjid was erected in Ayodhya by a general of Babur, the Mughal conqueror of India, in 1528. It is also claimed by some historians that the general Mir Baqi erected the 'mosque' on the orders of Babur. Reportedly, there is an inscription testifying to this claim. Babur had just won the battle in Panipat and had to conquer and occupy Delhi. He had to subdue the opposing Afghan nobles, the defeated army commanders of Ibrahim Lodi, who had dispersed over Delhi and its environment.

However, the actual history around the Babri Masjid is shrouded in the mists of history, clouded by legends, old people's tales, motivated comments of European travellers and hagiographic histories written mostly by Muslim court historians, praising Babur and his dynasty as great upholders of Islam, demolishers of temples, destroyers of deities worshipped by Hindus and so on.

I had no opportunity to see the Babri Masjid before it was demolished. I only saw it on TV when the destroyers, perched on its old weather-beaten domes, were chipping away at the bricks and mortars. I visited Ayodhya on the evening of the 8 December, 1992, more than twenty-four hours after the demolition and after the makeshift Ram temple had been erected on the rubble of the mosque. I only saw the listless security force officials standing idly by as though waiting for another catastrophe to happen. I learnt later that more than seventy companies of the state police had been posted to Faizabad—a classic case of safeguarding the stables after the horses had fled.

On the morning of 6 December, 1992, however, I sat before the TV in Delhi watching the unruly, milling crowds, with their saffron headbands and robes, gathering in the open ground before the Babri Masjid. Though the meeting was taking place under the sun, the volunteers, the *karsevaks*, had come well prepared to brave the weather. The top leaders of the Ram Janmabhoomi movement were already in Ayodhya. The commentator on the TV was waxing eloquent about the anticipated arrival of L.K. Advani, Murli Manohar Joshi, Uma Bharti, Kalyan Singh, Rithambra Devi and others at the site. Even Atal Bihari Vajpayee was expected to 'grace the dais' and address the large mass gathering of *karsevaks* who had gathered from all parts of India, fired with religious zeal.

That day, I wondered how Kalyan Singh, the BJP CM of Uttar Pradesh who had given a solemn undertaking to the Supreme Court of India that the mosque would not be demolished, was planning to keep these *karsevaks* in check. When I noticed the *karsevaks* on top of the first dome of the mosque, with their pick-axes, mattocks and large steel chisels, digging away at the dome as though their lives depended on bringing down the dome, I knew that a new chapter was being written in the history of India.

I was still hoping that the central government would intervene at this blatant breach of the Supreme Court orders. I should have known that court orders and solemn undertakings given even to the highest court in the land are meant to be broken with impunity. After all, the very Supreme Court, which tried Kalyan Singh for defying the court orders after giving a solemn assurance, punished him with a mere token punishment of one day in jail (till the sitting of the court) and a trifling fine of ₹20,000. Such is the punishment for a defiance that led to the demolition of a mosque and thousands of deaths in subsequent riots.

So, as I watched, nothing happened to prevent the demolition. The second dome was under attack. It would take the whole day for all the three domes to fall, along with their supporting walls and pillars. Though the mosque was close to 500 years old, made of mere brick and mortar, weather-beaten, never maintained or protected against the heavy rains, squalls and Sarayu floods, its plaster and paint already peeled off, it still resisted the combined destructive might of hundreds of *karsevaks* with all their chisels, mattocks and pick-axes. *Muqabila toh dile natawaan ne khoob kiya* (The frail heart still gave a tough fight).

Earlier in 1988, the late Mr Shahabuddin, former MP and firebrand political leader, attempting to safeguard the interests of the Muslims of India, had occasion to call on me when I was chief secretary of the state of Jammu and Kashmir. A mob, agitating for adequate power supply and control of meat prices, was attempting to set fire to a critically important bridge over the river Jhelum in Srinagar. When persuasion, tear gas and lathicharge by the state police failed to stop their advance, the police opened fire. There were some casualties. The national press had highlighted the incident. Mr Shahabuddin had come to Srinagar perhaps at the invitation of the locals to get a first-hand account of the so-called 'high-handed' behaviour of the police. And considerable criticism was aimed at the state administration for having 'mishandled' the mob.

I had known Mr Shahabuddin, a former Indian Foreign Service officer and a diplomat who had represented India abroad several times. Being a fair-minded man, he was satisfied when he heard our explanation. Thereafter, the conversation veered towards the conflict between Hindus and Muslims over the status of the Babri Masjid. Mr Shahabuddin was then the leading light in that conflict in the late eighties. As a student of the geopolitical trends in the country, the zeal and organisational capabilities of the Hindutva forces and the consequences of the march of psycho-history, I was apprehensive of the impact on the minds of the

Hindus and the status of Muslims of India as a whole, if the conflict led to a more widespread involvement of the larger Hindu community of India. I was apprehensive that the agitation would only lead to strengthening the radicals and the defeat of secular forces.

'I think, as one of the important leaders of the community, it might be advisable to work out a compromise with the RSS [Rashtriya Swayamsevak Sangh] leadership and remove the issue from the national narrative,' I suggested to Mr Shahabuddin.

'What kind of compromise do you have in mind?' he asked.

'After all, the ruined mosque has not been in use for several decades. It is already being used as a temple. There is hardly any Muslim population in the vicinity that uses it even for Friday prayers. Part of the premises has already been in use as a temple. Would it not be advisable to let the Hindus have it, in exchange for withdrawing all claims on all other mosques in India? There are more than thirty mosques in Ayodhya. You could ask for their support to pass suitable legislations to be incorporated as a part of the Constitution to safeguard status quo of all mosques as on 15 August, 1947,' I suggested.

'The RSS is not ready for any compromise on those lines. The moment you talk of surrendering Babri Masjid, they immediately follow up with a demand for Varanasi and Mathura. Their other affiliates, like Vishwa Hindu Parishad [VHP] and akharas, talk of other mosques in the rest of India.'

At that time, I had no idea that the Babri Masjid was being used as an emotional symbol of the Hindutva ideology. Any compromise on removing Babri Masjid from the national narrative would remove a powerful Hindutva symbol in the drive for establishing the Hindu Rashtra in India.

As I watched the demolition on TV, little did I anticipate that I would be landing into the maelstrom the very next day. In the aftermath of the demolition, the Kalyan Singh government was dismissed and President's Rule imposed in the state of Uttar Pradesh. At that time, Satya Narayan Reddy from Andhra Pradesh was the governor of the state. Two senior IAS officers, Ashok Chandra and B.K. Goswami, were immediately despatched to Lucknow to take over as advisors to the governor. Before they were in place, under the shadow of the President's Rule and under the governor's direct control of the director general of police, a makeshift temple had already come up on the debris of the mosque without any hindrance. A situation was allowed to be created where through an illegal fait accompli, the Hindus could claim possession, being nine points of law.

On the evening of 7 December, a day later, I was ordered to proceed to Lucknow and take over as the third advisor to the governor. Obviously, since rioting had already started in Uttar Pradesh and other parts of India, and most of the victims happened to be Muslims, the government thought a Muslim advisor in place would divert criticism from the government of acting in a partisan manner. I was supposed to represent the secular face of the central government. By the time I reached Lucknow and was in position in the capital on 8 December, Mr Chandra in consultation with Mr Goswami had distributed the portfolios among the three advisors.

Mr Goswami was allotted the crucial home portfolio and Mr Chandra kept the general administration and finance with himself. Most of the other portfolios, like revenue, agriculture, irrigation, animal husbandry, health, public works, higher education, medical education, power, urban affairs, irrigation, textiles and miscellaneous other departments, were allotted and put under my charge. Home, personnel and finance were considered to be glamorous departments. None of these were allotted to me. All three of us occupied adjacent rooms in the circuit house in Lucknow. We met frequently and took all important decisions jointly. Since we were going to be there for six months during the President's Rule, we could not occupy temporary quarters in the circuit house for long, and I, therefore, requested Mr Chandra, who was in charge, to allot bungalows to all of us. He ran into some difficulty as most of the bungalows were still occupied by the former ministers of the Kalyan Singh government, and they were not in a hurry to vacate. Subsequently, when some bungalows did fall vacant, Mr Chandra and Mr Goswami occupied them.

The issue of accommodation was the least of my worries, what was of more concern was the total collapse of law and order in the state. Many of the urban areas of the then large state of Uttar Pradesh, which had more than 20 per cent Muslim population, were facing serious communal riots after the demolition of Babri Masjid. *Karsevaks* from Uttar Pradesh, Maharashtra, Haryana, Rajasthan and other states of India, who had influxed into the state, were roaming around in groups in the state. They were now targeting the Gyanvapi mosque in Varanasi, adjacent to the Vishwanath temple, and the mosque in Mathura. Reports of more than twenty deaths were already there on my table, and I had noted these figures for the 9–10 December. Kanpur, which was always a hotbed of communal politics, was facing serious agitation against the Muslims. As an industrial city, it had a fairly large population of workers, a permanently disgruntled segment of the population. Lucknow, Gonda, Deoband (where the most important Muslim religious seminary Darul Uloom was located) and Muzaffarnagar had already suffered casualties. Saharanpur had seen several deaths in the wake of the demolition of the mosque, with the active connivance of the local police. Faizabad, close to Ayodhya, suffered many casualties. Allahabad, Agra, Noida, Kanpur and Varanasi, too, were badly affected. Barabanki, Unnao and Tanda were in the grip of marauding *karsevaks*, both local and imported.

The VHP and the bodies affiliated to the RSS had been demanding the surrender of three mosques, Babri Masjid of Ayodhya, Gyanvapi of Varanasi and the mosque of Mathura. After the demolition of the Babri

Masjid, a wave of jubilation ran through the radical elements of the country, thoroughly indoctrinated by the hopes of a Hindu Rashtra. A call had been given out that people should not remain satisfied with the *karseva* in Ayodhya. If they want to earn *punya* (salvation), they should conduct *karseva* in their localities—meaning demolish all the mosques wherever found.

Reports indicated that many *karsevak*s were assembling in Varanasi to give that *dhakka* (push). On Friday, which was three days after we joined, a large number of Muslims would be gathering in the Gyanvapi mosque for congregational Friday prayers. As curfew was in force, the administration would not permit them to join a large congregation in the mosque. Unlike Babri Masjid, Gyanvapi mosque was fully in the possession of Muslims and in active use, as it was surrounded by a large Muslim-populated area. Serious trouble was anticipated on that day.

An atmosphere of Muslim phobia prevailed in the entire state. The media, too, could not remain unaffected by this phobia. Many of them, especially the Hindi newspapers and magazines, were quite vociferous in their hostility towards Muslims. Many complaints were received that the local papers were even publishing the daily programmes put out by the *karsevak*s and the right-wing parties to incite the people.

Since the three advisors were jointly responsible for the administration of the state as a whole, I decided, in consultation with Mr Goswami, to fly down to Kanpur and assess the situation. After reaching there, I called a meeting of the peace committee comprising Hindu and Muslim leaders. Though they assembled at the behest of the advisor, it was obvious that they were reluctant participants. Neither group saw eye to eye on the various issues that were at that time agitating the emotions of the two communities.

Sensing the hostility, I advised the then DM to take special care of the vulnerable areas, post strong non-communal inspectors, sub-inspectors and the Provincial Army Constabulary (PAC) officials to control potential trouble spots, round up all elements on both sides, who would take advantage of the preoccupation of police in looting and rioting for their own benefit. I also urged the district administration to requisition the army's help once any trouble started. The police forces were too thinly scattered to control the whole city. Moreover, the PAC did not enjoy the reputation of an impartial force. Memories of the Hashimpura massacre were quoted, in which forty-two Muslim youths had been taken by the PAC to a canal near Meerut and shot down in cold blood. Hence, induction of the army would be crucial in case of any large-scale rioting.

My long experience as DM of several districts in Gujarat had afforded me a lot of expertise in handling such situations. There were many useful suggestions offered during the meeting. The DM and SP, who were present, noted them all. I noted a few in my diary. Had these suggestions, even half of them, been put into action, many of the over 150 subsequent deaths in Kanpur could have been prevented.

I returned to Lucknow after taking all these steps, reasonably assured of compliance. On 9 December, receiving disquieting reports of impending trouble from Varanasi, I decided to take the single-seater state plane to Varanasi to review the situation.

When I reached the city, I first went to the Viswanath temple adjoining the mosque, and I could see groups of people standing at corners (perhaps *karsevaks*) glaring with great hostility at our cavalcade.

The Kashi Viswanath Temple itself was under police protection, so was the adjacent Gyanvapi mosque. Among the twelve most holy temples of the Hindus, the Kashi Vishwanath Temple is considered holier than others, as it is located in the holy city of Varanasi on the banks of the holy river Ganga.

The responsible leaders of both the Hindu and Muslim communities who had gathered to meet me in the vicinity of the temple-mosque complex told me that complete amity had prevailed between the two communities earlier. The city was well-known for its silk sarees, and since the Muslims were weavers and the Hindus were the financiers and marketeers, the two communities were interdependent and integrated. Haji Abdur Rab, a prominent Muslim leader, expressed his lack of confidence in the police, especially the PAC, to control the situation, if it developed.

Pragyanand Sharma of the Congress party complained that no meeting of the peace committee was called by the local administration nor did the DM or SSP keep in touch with the prominent people's representative in view of the developing situation. Saleh Ansari, the mayor of Varanasi, complained that the *karsevak*s did not allow even ambulances to move in the city to help the injured. Because of curfew, even the groceries needed for daily living were not available. He demanded that the curfew be relaxed to allow Muslims to offer prayers in the Gyanvapi mosque. Mufti Abdul Wasi apprehended that any relaxation in curfew may lead to a conflict. He advised that only a select few should be given passes to come to the mosque. Mr Bagga asked, 'What is the use of a peace march after peace has been restored. It should be during the riot itself.' Harichandra Upadhyaya of the BJP said, 'Expression of sorrow (by Muslims) and happiness (by Hindus) have been done sufficiently. It is time to stop this and for the administration to take strong steps to arrest the rioters. However, the police are entering houses to arrest suspects. This should not be done.' Mr Pande of the local Bar Association agreed with this and added, 'Police is arresting even innocents, just for breaking the curfew.'

Apart from these suggestions, no leader affirmed that the rioting would stop. So, while I advised the DM/SSP to take note of the suggestions and implement them, I was not reassured of the safety of the temple and the mosque on Friday.

The situation in Varanasi was touch-and-go after the influx of the aggressive *karsevak*s from other parts of the country. I gathered the impression that the local civil administration could not be relied upon to control the militant *karsevaks*, who were bent upon earning more *punya* by demolishing a second mosque. There was every possibility of Babri Masjid being repeated here. Gyanvapi mosque would be defended vigorously, leading to a pitched battle between Hindus and Muslims. The reports were so grave that I summoned the local army commander, a colonel, and requested him to post some army companies on site to protect both the temple and the mosque. The colonel demurred.

'Sir, the army is a mobile force, they cannot be utilised for static duties. For that you should rely on PAC or CRPF [Central Reserve Police Force]. We can do flag marches but cannot stand and guard buildings. The safeguarding of the temple and mosque should be the responsibility of the CRPF, PAC and the local police.'

From the Varanasi guest house, I contacted the home minister, S.B. Chavan, apprised him of the grave situation in Varanasi and my apprehensions for the safety of the Gyanvapi mosque and also, perhaps, the temple. I also apprised him of my assessment of the capacity of the local law and order forces. I requested that unless the objections of the army were overruled and the army was posted in sufficient strength to protect these monuments, the safety of the mosque and the temple could not be ensured, especially when both Hindus and Muslims were expected to come for prayers in large numbers. Perhaps the home minister contacted the defence minister, who in turn contacted the army chief. The result was that the local army commander received instructions from Delhi to comply with my request and post sufficient army personnel at the two places for the ensuing Friday.

After seeing the army deployed, I called a meeting of the peace committee, exhorted them to utilise their good offices to ensure peace in the city. Unlike Kanpur, many of the leaders told me that while the local citizens would perhaps be persuaded, the *karsevaks* who had come from all over the country were an unruly lot. They were drunk on their success at the Babri Masjid and were feeling that one more push would demolish the Gyanvapi mosque. Willy-nilly, I had to place some faith in the local police and summoned them separately in the circuit house and conveyed to them in no uncertain terms that in case of a riot and casualties in the city, they would be held responsible. Having taken all these measures, I returned to Lucknow late in the evening.

After I reached, before I could return from the washroom, I received messages that severe rioting had broken out in Kanpur.

Mrs Subhashini Ali, MP and a Communist Party of India stalwart, rang me up from Kanpur (which was her hometown) and informed me that already more than sixty to seventy Muslims had been killed in Kanpur by communal elements (Mrs Ali is the daughter of the famous Captain Lakshmi Sahgal of the Indian National Army). Mrs Ali's reports were corroborated by Mr Sulaiman, a local Muslim leader. Groups of marauders were rampaging in the streets of the city, shouting provocative slogans and bent upon killing and looting in the various mohallas where they could find vulnerable households. They had not been arrested as I had advised. The district administration, rather than controlling the situation, was allegedly turning a blind eye and allowing the riots to go on. There was an implication that they were in collusion with the leaders of the rioters. I rang up Mr Goswami and Mr Chandra, and told them that unless we take immediate action, the casualties in Kanpur may exceed 200–300. That was the assessment of the local intelligence. It was obvious that the district administration had utterly failed. But in spite of clear advice, they had not even requisitioned help from the army, which was on standby in the vicinity. The three of us met and decided that both DM and the SP should be immediately removed and replaced by more efficient, secular and impartial officials. After some deliberations, we found out a very good officer, Mr Kapil Dev, who was at that time posted in Lucknow. (Subhash Joshi was identified for the post of SP.) He was summoned in the middle of the night and was advised to proceed to Kanpur immediately and take over as DM. He drove down to Kanpur, and by four in the morning, he had taken over as DM.

General Lakhera was the chief of staff for the Central Command Army Headquarters in Lucknow at that time.

General Lakhera had worked with me as corps commander in Srinagar during my stint as the chief secretary. He was an excellent officer, a competent and suave gentleman and deeply committed to the best traditions of the Indian Army. On receiving the dire reports of the massacres in Kanpur from Mrs Ali and the IB, I had rung him up and asked him about the deployment of the army. I told him that in certain cases, the army may not get a formal requisition from the DM in time or at all, as happened in the case of Kanpur. He was good enough to tell me that if I apprehended serious trouble in any area and I sent him a requisition in writing, he could give necessary instructions to deploy the army immediately without a formal requisition from the DM. I utilised his kind concession on several occasions during my stint in Uttar Pradesh. Later, I wrote to the defence minister placing on record my appreciation of the excellent services of General Lakhera.

The toll in Kanpur reached a hundred before the new DM and the army could be inducted.

The deployment of the army on guard duties in Varanasi had a salutary effect, and no attack took place on the Gyanvapi mosque. But Saharanpur saw the killing of almost ten Muslims at the hands of a local police inspector. They were shot dead in cold blood. It was brought to my notice by Rasheed Masood, a local Muslim political leader who had been a cabinet minister in Delhi. On enquiry, I learnt that the local police inspector, who perhaps had a personal agenda of his own, took the law into his own hands and shot down these innocent Muslims on the concocted accusation that they were rioters. My independent enquiry revealed that the inspector had acted in a very high-handed manner, as he was affiliated to a local radical outfit, and deserved to be at least shifted from there. He did not even allow the dead bodies to be removed for the last rites—shades of Major Hodson at the Khooni Darwaza. Mr Goswami was kind enough to pass instructions to the DGP to transfer that inspector from Saharanpur. Though the orders were passed, the governor overruled the DGP and stayed the transfer. Later, I learnt that he did so under instructions from Delhi. The inspector or the outfit he was affiliated to had close access to the powers that be.

While all this was going on, I summoned the IB chief for Uttar Pradesh, Mr Sharma, on 12 December, to get an assessment of the unfolding situation. Sharma, too, had worked with me in Kashmir. I found him also to be an intelligent man and fully au fait with the local developments. 'I had been waiting for the last three months to be summoned by the local administration so that I could give them the information I had from various parts of the state and also the likely repercussions of the situation that was building up. I received no summons. I had, of course, kept the headquarters fully briefed. This is the first time that I have been asked to give my assessment.'

Mr Sharma told me that he apprehended close to 5,000 casualties all over the state if proper timely action was not taken to control the situation. He gave me a city-by-city estimate and his assessment of the possible casualties of both communities. Since he was the local IB chief and had his informants in every city of the state, his assessment was not too far off the mark. Having gained this information, Mr Goswami and I together decided to use the available units of the army to the largest extent possible. The governor, too, was informed of the situation in the weekly meeting.

Immediately after the demolition of the mosque, Saxena, the then chief secretary of Uttar Pradesh, was also transferred. Saxena happened to have been my batchmate in the IAS. He, too, became a casualty of the demolition, though he appeared to be more sinned against than sinning. With a mild, non-assertive and accommodating personality, what could he have done under a forceful BJP CM like Kalyan Singh, who was actively engaged, even defying the Supreme Court?

T.S.R. Subramanian of the 1961 batch was brought in as the chief secretary, replacing Saxena. He was the opposite of Saxena, not merely assertive in his approach. He regularly attended the meetings of the governor's council, where the advisors briefed the governor on crucial issues.

There were existing rules of the Uttar Pradesh government to compensate the survivors of the dead victims in the riots. It was brought to my notice by the families of the victims that they were getting a sum of ₹50,000 for the loss of life of the head of the family. This niggardly amount was supposed to sustain the victimised family who had lost the earning member for the rest of their lives. Even this amount was not paid in time by unsympathetic local officials, who demanded all kinds of proofs that the victim had really died in the riots, the doctor's certificate and so on. It was often impossible to offer such proof where whole families had been confined and burnt alive. I summarised the plight of the survivors in a couplet:

Woh khoon baha ke bhi na sazawar ho sake
Lashon ki jo daleel mayassar na kar sake

(They could not become eligible even for the blood money,
As they could not produce the dead bodies for proof.)

In the governor's council, I pleaded that this compensation should be raised to ₹2 lakh, as was the case in states like Gujarat and Maharashtra.

Mr Subramanian did not favour this suggestion. He felt that the state would go bankrupt if the compensation was increased.

'Do you expect such large numbers of deaths?' I asked him. 'I am recommending a compensation of ₹2 lakh for the so-far-assessed casualty of 200. The total compensation at this rate would amount to only ₹4 crore. That certainly would not bankrupt a state like Uttaar Pradesh.'

Mr Subramanian argued, 'You are advocating such a high compensation for the victims because they happen to be Muslims.'

The victims included some Hindus too. In the case of widespread riots, it is my experience that a majority of the victims belong to the slum-dwellers, the daily wagers and the poor categories. Hence, I felt they deserved a larger compensation. Mr Subramanian was hitting below the belt, accusing me of adopting a communal approach, not a humanitarian approach.

I told Mr Subramanian, 'Mr Chief Secretary, there are more than sixty secretaries to the Government of India in Delhi. Many of them are more competent than me and with longer experience. I was chosen to be posted as an advisor in Uttar Pradesh after the demolition of the Babri Masjid because the Government of India obviously felt that a Muslim face is needed in Lucknow, on the basis of their information that riots would take a heavy toll on the Muslims of the state. As advisors and as chief secretary, our responsibility is to support the victims and rehabilitate them fast, rather than protect the aggressors. In the communal situation in Uttar Pradesh, it happens that the majority of victims are Muslims. If the majority victims had happened to be Hindus, I would have advocated the same compensation as prevails in other states for victims of fire, earthquake, floods and riots. Therefore, I would advise you to withdraw your accusation of bias against me.'

The governor intervened to assuage my feelings, but I remained upset for a long time. My relationship with Mr Subramanian remained strained for the rest of his life. He was known as an honest, efficient and upright officer, and rose to become the cabinet secretary. Honesty and efficiency need not necessarily fall with secularism and a socialist approach.

The raised compensation was not approved in that meeting. Later, I obtained the orders governing the quantum of compensation from Gujarat and Maharashtra and wrote to Home Minister Chavan. He advised the governor accordingly.

Immediately after the demolition, a general atmosphere of hostility to Muslims prevailed not only in the state of Uttar Pradesh but as far as Maharashtra, Gujarat, Haryana, Madhya Pradesh, Bihar and elsewhere. Many of the local papers talked of the 'Muslim problem' of India (like the 'Jewish Problem' in Nazi Germany) and possible solutions. There were articles advocating a 'permanent' solution to the 'Muslim problem'. Some of the local papers even published extracts from the draft new constitution framed by the RSS and VHP to be enacted once they came to power, disenfranchising Muslims and making them second-class citizens without any protection as a minority. Talk of a National Register of Citizens (NRC) was already in the air, way back in 1992—a full two decades ago. Some even strongly advocated that the mosques in Varanasi and Mathura should be acquired by the Government of India and handed over to the Hindus for demolition. The Voice of India, a publishing house of the RSS, brought out two books wherein it was stated that 3,000 temples all over India had been demolished and mosques constructed on their ruins during the reign of the Muslim rulers. The implication was that all these mosques/temples should be 'liberated' and converted. Arun Shourie, an otherwise intelligent scholar, lent his name to the front page of these books. All this was highly provocative, and an atmosphere of Islamophobia was being built up, especially in North India. The local press and even some of the national English newspapers did not remain immune.

While living alone in the circuit house of Lucknow in the winter of January 1993, I found that the old water heater in the bathroom had broken down. I requested the state PWD to repair or replace it. There were some in the PWD who resented my posting as an advisor, and so promptly took the opportunity to inform the press of my extravagant request for a functioning water heater—a luxury which the state could ill-afford. The next day's front-page headlines of some local papers proclaimed that the advisor, Moosa Raza, was frittering away state funds lavishly to install a luxurious bathroom. There were similar loaded 'news items' about my official and personal life. Every noting I made on the files (specially in favour of a Muslim aggrieved party) was leaked out and highlighted prominently in the local press with adverse comments. There were no other comments on the other two advisors. Since I had done nothing to earn these special mentions, the only provocation was obviously my religion. I should have taken such reporting in my stride. However, being human, I reacted a little strongly. I was apprehensive that it would affect my administrative ability. I was anxious that such continuous sniping and adverse reporting should not affect the actions of my subordinates while carrying out my decisions. I summoned my staff officer, Chambers, a very good dedicated officer who himself suffered from discrimination because he had committed the crime of being born in a lower caste. I dictated a draft note to him more or less as follows: 'It appears that many of the local Hindi papers are averse to my posting as advisor to the governor of Uttar Pradesh and take a very hostile stand without any justification against every action I take to give even-handed justice to everyone in the state. My religion, apparently, is the only provocation for these papers. Obviously, this is due to their bias. I am not able to accept such hostile prejudicial reporting, which is adversely impacting the just administration of the state and the discipline of the employees. This will also aggravate the communal situation in the state. I am enclosing cuttings of the various reports that have appeared in many of the newspapers along with this note. They speak for themselves. They are all false, prejudiced and needlessly hostile. I have, therefore, to advise that all these newspapers named, who are contributing to the aggravating communal divide, should publish an apology prominently acknowledging their mistakes and for their prejudicial communal reporting in their newspapers by tomorrow morning and promise to desist from such unfair, prejudicial, biased and communal reporting. If they fail to do so, I will be constrained to instruct all the departments under my charge to stop releasing advertisements to these newspapers forthwith.'

Chambers thought this action was too aggressive, 'It will only make them more hostile.' But I was convinced that bullies rarely fight back and should be dealt with strongly.

I called a meeting of all the editors of those newspapers in my chamber. I gave them this note and requested them to publish an apology on the front page of their newspapers for the hostile reporting about my actions.

They argued that they were not communal nor were they hostile. They were merely performing their duty. However, since there was no evidence of bias on my part and no such reporting was being done about the other two advisors, and I alone was being targeted by them, they could not escape the conclusion that they were being communal and bigoted. My staff officer tried to persuade them outside my chamber and told them that I never made a false promise nor ever held out an empty threat, and they were likely to lose substantial revenues if the advertisements were stopped. Those newspapers that relied most heavily on the government for advertisements did publish an apology of some sort next day. From that day onwards, hostile reporting stopped and positive slants were given to my legitimate actions. Some of them swung to the other extreme and started to publish encomia!

Since General Lakhera had become a good friend, and I asked him, when he formally called on me, as to why the army took no action to save the Babri Masjid. He laughed sardonically. 'I invite you, sir, to visit the army headquarters, and I will explain to you with maps and plans as to what were the reasons for the inaction of the army.'

In the governor's council, the next day, I mentioned that I proposed to visit the army headquarters in Lucknow for a briefing. I invited the other advisors and the chief secretary to join me. Mr Subramanian was opposed to the idea for reasons best known to him, but he advanced a specious rationale for his opposition—he said that the advisor was a senior functionary of the state in the place of the cabinet minister, and therefore, he should not visit the army headquarters, as it would be a breach of protocol.

Next day, I visited the army headquarters. On a big map pinned to the wall in the operations room, General Lakhera showed me the various army units located at strategic places in the state, especially in the vicinity of Ayodhya.

'We had located a helicopter squadron close to Ayodhya. We had also alerted various army units in the vicinity of Faizabad, fully equipped with armoured cars and ready to move at a very short notice. When a large rally was announced for 6 December, we apprehended trouble and alerted all our units to be in readiness. Army intelligence kept informing us of the developing situation and the imminent destruction of Babri Masjid. It was apprehended by us that the demolition would also lead to large-scale rioting in the state. We were, therefore, ready to move at a moment's notice to assist the civil administration, both in helping prevent the destruction of the mosque and in preserving the law and order. We kept watching the gathering of *karsevak*s, the arrival of the various strident leaders on site, and we listened and monitored the fiery speeches. Once the *karsevak*s got on to the roof of the domes of the mosque, all it required was a flight of three helicopters over the domes, and the *karsevaks* would all have fallen off the domes with only minor injuries. The sound and propeller blasts were enough. A couple of more passes would have cleared the crowd of *karsevaks* in and around the mosque. This was the most effective and safe option. We waited for orders from the administration, central or state. But we never received any such summons for the whole day as the demolition proceeded. We can act only at the behest of the civil administration. The army has its own discipline and, without legal protection, it does not act on its own. I waited for some intimation about the need for action by us. No such orders came, and the mosque fell.' There was deep regret in his voice as he made the last statement.

I was quite taken aback. There were, of course, some intellectuals, like Mulk Raj Anand, Kuldip Nayar, Khushwant Singh and others, who took up cudgels on behalf of the secular and pluralistic polity of India, and condemned the demolition of the mosque and the silent complicity of the powers. Silence many times amounts to consent, especially silence of the persons in authority who wield power and yet do nothing to stop an iniquity happening right before their very eyes, or provocative speeches, writings and actions taking place before them.

~

During my time as advisor to the governor in Uttar Pradesh, I had set up two systems to address the people's grievances, one was by allotting time in the forenoon to meet the MLAs and MPs and the other VIPs with prior appointment and listen to their advice, suggestions and recommendations. I used to receive written applications from the petitioners, go through the grievances, ascertain the basic facts and make a marginal note for redressal. Chambers computerised all these petitions with my instructions and the time limit fixed, and passed them on to the concerned departments. Every day, he put up to me how many of these grievances had been resolved, how many were still pending after the time limit, and he would remind the concerned departmental secretaries and commissioners, if delayed. As a result, most of the petitions received by me got attended to in a very systematic manner within reasonable time limits.

Once, an old lady from a village in Azamgarh came to me with a petition. She had severe arthritis and walked half-bent with a walking stick. Her sparse white hair, her wrinkled face and shrivelled hands spoke of her penury and poor health. I learnt that she had retired as a teacher in a far-off primary school ten years ago. She had not still received her pension and had been shunted from pillar to post to get her dues. No one came to her help. Unfortunately, the department of primary education was not with me. It was with another advisor. So, I told the old lady to go and meet the other advisor, who was sitting three rooms away. With tears in her eyes, she said, 'Beta, I have come all the way from the village with my grievance. I have been shunted too often from place to place. I was told that you are the only one who can help me get my pension. I do not want to go to anybody else.' I empathised with her helpless misery.

I called my staff officer and told him to look into the business rules and to find out how I could help this old lady. He showed me that under the Rules of Business, I could call any file from any department, irrespective of whether the department was under me or under any other advisor, and pass such orders as I deemed appropriate. That rule came in very handy in this case. I, therefore, instructed on her petition that her pension should be released within twenty-four hours on pain of action against the concerned secretary. I was meticulous in fulfilling promises I made and carrying out all threats. That was the best way of establishing credibility and ensuring compliance. The staff officer, perhaps, did some tail-twisting. The papers were processed very fast, and she got her pension released the very next day. She came back to me and walked across to my chair round the table to put her hand on my head, 'God bless you, beta. For ten years, nobody bothered about me. You got my pension released within twenty-four hours.'

I also established another system to address issues that affected whole villages and regions. I selected several districts in the state and held a big darbar in that district headquarters with the commissioner, DM, the SP and all departmental heads sitting on one side under a *shamiana* and all those who had any complaint and recommendations to make and the leaders of the community sitting on the right. I would throw open the meeting for general representation of the district issues to be aired by the leaders and others who were interested. I informed them that this occasion was meant to locate and resolve common grievances relating to the civil administration as a whole. Individual grievances were to be written out and handed over to my staff officer. Once the grievance was aired, I requested the concerned departmental head to respond and explain. If the response was reasonable and the reason for non-redressal genuine, I would advise the petitioner accordingly. Else I would openly fix a timeline for redressal in consultation with the departmental head. This established transparency. This was government in the open, not functioning in cloisters behind the closed doors of the secretariat.

The public loved this method, though it had its drawbacks.

The officials were unhappy, as it put great pressure on them to show results within specified timelines. This became a very popular system and attracted the attention of the common man in the state, and the media supported it wholeheartedly.

I received letters from other districts requesting that I hold similar darbars in their districts. But I had my own priorities and limitations.

There were many hospitals in the state, where doctors, for some reason or the other, had been suspended and issued chargesheets. But no enquiries were conducted thereafter, and the doctors remained under long suspensions, with hospitals remaining understaffed. This did not affect the doctors, as they got their suspension allowance, in some cases 75 per cent of their salary, with plenty of leisure time on their hands to attend to their private practice. It was the poor general public that suffered. When I got the statistics from the director of medical health and services (DMHS), I found that there were more than 200 such doctors from various hospitals and health centres in the state under suspension for months and, in some cases, for years at a time. No enquiries had been conducted. The doctors also did not follow up the matter vigorously, as they were getting a substantial suspension allowance and set up their private practice.

I called in the DMHS and asked him how long he would take to get these enquiries completed and the cases settled. He asked me to give him a month's time. 'You have been sleeping over these enquiries for more than two to three years in some cases, which was a criminal act because those rural areas had no benefit of medical services in the absence of the qualified doctors. It was the general public who suffered. However, I shall give you one month to complete the job and report to me. If you do not complete this job within the promised one month, I promise you that I shall suspend you and appoint somebody else in your place,' I told him.

The staff officer followed up the matter on a regular basis. However, at the end of the month, reports indicated that only thirty enquiries had been completed. Apparently, the director did not take me seriously. He was confident that no advisor would have the gumption to suspend such a senior head of department. I passed an order suspending the DMHS and appointing his next in line to that post. There was consternation all around. Such action against such a senior official had never been taken before. Next day, I was called by the governor, who asked the details of suspension from me. When I gave him the reasons, the governor concurred with my decision. However, he advised that I give some more time to the DMHS to complete enquiries, as he had not taken me seriously when I held out the threat of suspension. I gave another fifteen days' time to the DMHS, and somehow or other, he managed to complete 90 per cent of the enquiries and reinstated the doctors in those cases.

As these lines are being written, the Babri Masjid remains demolished.

In 1949, in connivance with the DM, some miscreants smuggled idols of Ram and Sita and installed them on the mimbar and mihrab of the mosque. In its 9 November, 2019, judgment, a five-member constitutional bench of the Supreme Court called this clandestine illegal act of installing idols in the sanctum sanctorum of a mosque a 'desecration'. Desecration means defilement, sacrilege, act of profanity or impiety, according to the dictionary. The DM, the upholder of the law, who actively helped in this act of sacrilege and defilement got away with no punishment and joined the Hindu radical outfit whom he had helped. The civil court, too, took a lenient view of this illegal sacrilege and put the mosque under a court-appointed receiver. It permitted the mahant of the Nirmohi Akhara to enter the mosque twice daily to perform the morning and evening *aarti*s for the deities now illegally ensconced in the mosque. The keys of the side entrance were in the custody of the mahant. While the idols received the homage of a puja twice daily, Muslims were prohibited from offering prayers. The police guard would not permit the entry of any Muslim, much less permit him to offer prayers!

The Supreme Court of India held the demolition of the mosque an illegal act. The Supreme Court also found no evidence that the mosque had been built after demolishing a Hindu temple. It also agreed that the Muslims could not prove continuous occupation of the premises.

Having said all that, the Supreme Court awarded possession of the 2.77 acres where the mosque once stood to the Hindus. This in spite of holding the placement of idols as illegal and the desecration and the demolition itself illegal, in defiance of the orders of the very Supreme Court itself. So much for fairness and justice.

During this period, I had to travel extensively and remain in office for long hours after sundown. Moreover, the cook in the bungalow-kitchen perhaps did not maintain proper hygiene in the absence of family supervision. I ran into some gastric health problems, later diagnosed appropriately. My wife was away at Madras, and I was deprived of home-cooked food. I could not get a decent cook to man my kitchen. All this continued to affect my health severely. Lucknow did not have decent medical facilities. I was advised by the local medical faculty to get a colonoscopy. I thought I should get such tests and treatment done in Madras, which was familiar territory with better medical facilities. So, I took leave from the governor and went to Madras. After the tests, I had to be hospitalised for surgery.

I was getting telephone calls to report back to duty. The governor came to Madras on an official visit, and perhaps wanted to check up whether I was really ill or was I malingering. He rang up the hospital and was satisfied that my illness was genuine. In the meantime, the governor himself demitted office and Motilal Vora was appointed. He chose his own advisors. I was spared a return to Lucknow and got reposted to the Ministry of Steel.

EPILOGUE

Do not go gentle into that good night,
Old age should burn and rave at close of day;
Rage, Rage against the dying of the light …
Blind eyes could blaze like meteors and be gay, …
Do not go gentle into that good night.

—Dylan Thomas

I never believed in the concept of retirement. One retires from work, one retires for the night, but one never retires from life. Long ago, I translated a Persian couplet:

I am a wave, engaged in an eternal quest.
I will die if I retire and rest.

On the morning of the day I retired from government, I received a call from Mr Mandelia, the right-hand man of Aditya Birla, who said that Mr Birla would like to come and see me.

'Mr Mandelia, you know I am retiring this evening. If Mr Birla has any problem that he wants to discuss with me, I don't think I will be able to help him,' I told him.

'No, sir. It is only a courtesy call,' replied Mr Mandelia.

Mr Birla met me in the afternoon, before I had signed the retirement papers. He told me that he had been watching my career for many years and that he would like me to join his group of companies in whatever position I deemed proper. He also said he would offer me a blank cheque to write my own emoluments. I politely thanked Mr Birla for his kind offer and told him that having served the nation for thirty-five years, I would not be able to bring myself around to serve any private organisation. We had a cup of tea together, though disappointment was writ large on his face.

A couple of days later, the Department of Steel and Mines gave me a send-off with the mandatory tea and biscuits.

For some time after leaving Udyog Bhavan, I had no intention of joining any private-sector organisation. However, as the poet Akbar Allahbadi said on his retirement:

Uttha tha ek valvala yeh dil mein
Ke sirf yaad'e khuda karenge
Ma'an magar ye khayal aaya
Mili na roti toh kya karenge

(Akbar on retirement enthused that he would sit in a corner and indulge in prayers to God. However, immediately the thought occurred to him, if you do not get bread, what will you eat.)

Within a short period of my retirement, I was offered the post of the chairman of the Union Public Service Commission, membership of the Election Commission of India, vice chancellorship of Aligarh Muslim University and Jamia Millia Islamia and, above all, chairmanship of the Central Minorities Commission, a cabinet minister rank position—

all of which I declined for varying reasons. One of the main reasons was that the meagre pension of ₹4,000 that I received after retirement would not have sufficed me and my family to sustain even our moderate lifestyle.

During my tenure in the government, in the early days of my service, my wife Husnara used to stitch clothes for my daughters. When I was posted in Baroda as CMD of GSFC, my daughters used to go to school in a public transport bus. As commissioner of fisheries, I used to travel from Gandhinagar to Ahmedabad in a rural public transport.

Considering this, I realised that joining a government organization would mean that I would continue to live a hand-to-mouth existence. Luckily for me, it appeared that I had earned a reputation as a manager and administrator. Although I received many offers from the private sector, I was not inclined to join any of them. However, I indicated to them that I would be happy to provide my knowledge and advice to them whenever they required. Because of the regard that many of the private-sector companies had for me, I was offered consultancy assignments in many of these companies. Getting clearance from the government of India, I joined some of them as an advisor so that I could be renumerated appropriately without committing any breach of service rules. That helped me and my family over the years in sustaining my standard of living and creating some assets.

Within a short period of leaving the government, I vacated my official residence and shifted to my own house in Noida. It was during that period that Mulayam Singh Yadav, who had developed a high regard for me during my tenure as advisor to the Uttar Pradesh governor after the demolition of the Babri Masjid and who, at the time, was serving as defence minister in the Union Cabinet proposed my name for the vice presidentship of India. However, nothing came of it. Mr Singh later told me that a senior political leader of the then J&K state, who I had believed was my friend, and his colleagues in the Cabinet had opposed this proposal vehemently.

Most major steel-producing companies viz. SAIL, Tata Steel Limited, JSW Steel Ltd, etc., all joined to form the Indian Steel Association (ISA). Mr Irani, then MD of Tata Steel, persuaded me to accept the position of president of ISA. For five years, I remained its president at a reasonable remuneration. Then IDBI, HDFC, SBI, etc., asked me to chair Iridium India, a telecom company. For twenty years, I have also chaired Nirlon Ltd. and helped to turn its fortunes from a BIFR (Board of Industrial and Financial Reconstruction) to a high net-worth company.

It was during this period, too, that I decided to give back to the nation what the nation had given me during my tenure. I established a technical institute for training people in the upcoming science of Information Technology. I believe it is still functioning in Delhi.

It was in 1996 that I became the director general of the India Islamic Cultural Centre (IISC). The then prime minister of India, Indira Gandhi, had allotted land for building a centre on Lodhi Road, New Delhi, and in 1984, had herself laid the foundation stone. Unfortunately, there was no progress on the building for the next twelve years, and the centre continued to languish in a makeshift dilapidated colonial bungalow at the site. Once I took over, I charted an aggressive fund-collection drive for getting donations for constructing the centre. Using my connections and friendships I had built over the course of my career, I travelled across India and to the UAE, Kuwait, Libya, Saudi Arabia, Iran and the UK, managing to collect over ₹10 crore. I persuaded the then foreign minister of Iran, Ali Akbar Vilayati, and the then president, Ayatollah Rafsanjani, to donate Kashikari ceramic tiles, which today adorn both the façade and the inside of the prominent dome of the IISC. One of the major donors who happened to have been a personal friend of mine, BS Abdur Rahman, helped me collect over ₹4 crore and also helped me set up the electric generators and air-conditioning plants, which are, perhaps even today, serving the entire complex. The auditorium of the IISC is named after Mr Rahman. My name does not figure anywhere on the walls and boards of the IISC. There are many around to claim credit. That does not matter. As a Persian poet once remarked: 'Look not for monuments of brick and mortar. Look for our monuments in the hearts of men.'

By 2005, my son, Jafar, had got employment in Dubai and left with his family for the UAE; my eldest daughter, Shahla, had shifted to Bombay with her family; my second daughter, Gazala, moved to Dubai (and then to Canada having acquired Canadian citizenship); and my youngest daughter, Maliha, had married and moved to the US. Since Husnara and I were on our own in Noida, we were persuaded by the family to move to our native city of Chennai, then called Madras.

It was at this time that I was persuaded to take over as chairman of the South India Education Trust, which runs a ladies' college, schools and other institutes in Chennai, with close to 10,000 students, including 1,000 boys, and with around 600 staff members. The college has emerged as one of the top educational institutions of Tamil Nadu with 'Star College' and 'Potential for Excellence' status. The National Assessment and Accreditation Council recently accredited the college with A++ status, the highest accolade. I continue to serve the community through my services to the trust as its executive chairman.

My writing has kept me busy all throughout. I have published eight books in English, two translations in Tamil, and a book of poetry in Persian and Urdu. I am now engaged in completing two more books and that gives me immense satisfaction.